Sylvia
Browne's
BOOK
OF DREAMS

Sylvia Browne's
BOOK
OF DREAMS

WRITTEN WITH LINDSAY HARRISON

PIATKUS

Copyright © 2002 by Sylvia Browne

First published in 2002 by
Judy Piatkus (Publishers) Limited
5 Windmill Street
London W1T 2JA
e-mail: info@piatkus.co.uk

First published in the USA in 2002 by Dutton,
a member of Penguin Putnam, Inc

The moral right of the author has been asserted

*A catalogue record for this book is
available from the British Library*

ISBN 0 7499 2321 0

This book has been printed on paper manufactured
with respect for the environment using wood from
managed sustainable resources

Printed and bound in Great Britain by
The Bath Press, Bath

DEDICATIONS

From Sylvia:

To my friends, family, staff and ministers,
and especially
to Montel Williams,
a friend
and a wonderful, giving person,
not only to me
but also to millions of others.

From Lindsay:

To Mom, always,
and, from the heart,
thanks, Bernie, for being our "dreamcatcher."

CONTENTS

The Dreamer

Come through my door,
>   O weaver of schemes,
And you, ol' dear,
>   With many lost dreams.

Come into my room,
>   Where stories are read,
And let yesterday's sorrows
>   Lay long and dead.

Come in, young lad,
>   With the world in your eyes.
Come in, young maid,
>   And please don't cry.

The people come through,
>   Young, middle, and old,
And each life a tale
>   That has to be told

To the ear that is bent,
>   And the heart that is full,
And hopeful help is given
>   To destiny's pull.

Come into my world,
>   O dreamer of dreams.
Come into my world,
>   O schemer of schemes.

There is no one too small,
    Nor one too tall,
That there isn't some grace
    From God for all.

Come take the adventure,
    And hold bravely my hand,
And we'll reach
    That talked of promised land.

Of life now with its struggles,
    And with all of its glee,
Let me help you through it,
    And in time we'll be free.

The only thing you'll hear
    Is perceptive truth.
What I perceive for you
    Will be living proof.

You cannot have cherries
    Without some sour cream,
So come into my room,
    O dreamer of dreams.
                    —Sylvia C. Browne

INTRODUCTION

*D*reams, and all the other rich journeys our spirits take while we sleep, have been a passion of mine for more than thirty years. I've studied countless volumes of research about dreams. I've explored dreams with literally thousands of clients. I've read about the importance of dreams in the world's many great spiritual works, with 121 references to dreams in the Bible alone. I've lectured on the subject of dreams. I've taught courses on dream interpretation. And I've promised myself for years that someday I'd write a book about dreams that would make them simpler, less confusing, more accessible, and above all, more comforting, to the point where we'd understand that even our nightmares are blessings.

On September 11, 2001, our lives changed forever, in more ways than we've begun to realize yet. When our lives changed, our dreams changed, too, as we tried to process the tragedy, the fear, the loss, the sorrow, the courage, the pride, the unity, and the palpable, exquisite faith in God and in each other that was there when we needed it and always, always will be. Through it all, our dreams were and are there for us too, helping us escape, helping us hope again, helping us relive and release the worst of it to spare us some of the pain during the day, taking us to the past and the future and even The Other Side for much-needed comfort from loved ones, silently helping us heal and go on. More and more clients, more and more letters, more and more phone calls, and more and more audience members wanted and needed to talk about their newly intensified dreams, and I finally realized it was time to keep that promise to myself and write the book I'd been preparing for almost half of my life.

Wanting this book to embrace some of these newly intensified dreams without its becoming a book about 9/11, I put out a call at lectures and on my website, asking you to send me your dreams, to add to the files of them I've kept through all these years. You responded with your usual openness and generosity, and I'll always be grateful. You'll find many but not all of them throughout this book, with precautions taken to protect your anonymity so that you won't have to claim them as yours unless you want to. That so many of you were willing to confide in me, knowing up front that I intended to publish the dreams, is an honor I don't take lightly and will never abuse. To those of you whose letters don't appear, please be assured that I read every single one of them, with witnesses who'll attest to that, and if my dear but strict editor Brian Tart would have let me get away with it, I would happily have included them all.

This book, then, has been compiled from literally mounds of research, file cabinets full of material from dream classes I've taught and dreams sent in by the hundreds. It's a tribute to this fascinating, uncharted territory of which we're still just scratching the surface, this amazing phenomenon called dreaming that we all have in common. It will give you insights into why we dream, how we release negativity while we sleep, how we gather information, and even why monsters and demons sometimes intrude. It will guide you toward long-awaited reunions with loved ones you thought you'd lost, and with your own extraordinary history. It will help you understand that dreams are a world within themselves, a world we live in for about six years in an average lifetime—and all time converges into God's eternal "now"—a world full of past life memories, current problems and solutions, and precognitive insight into what our tomorrows may bring, a world in which messages, warnings, hope, help, Spirit Guides, and even a cure for our universal Homesickness wait patiently for us to find them.

Dreams, I'm convinced, are just one more dimension of our minds, a dimension that, when put into perspective, gives access to a whole new wealth of knowledge. The subconscious mind that takes charge while we sleep is where our passive memories are held and where the key lies to the records of all of our lives, every life we've ever lived on earth and on The Other Side. Dreams form our path to that key. That key unlocks the door to an eternity of wisdom. And the more wisdom we acquire, the more understandable, useful, and affirming our dreams become.

Thanks again to your hundreds and hundreds of letters, this isn't just my work, it's a collaboration. So welcome to *our* "Book Of Dreams."

Sylvia Browne's BOOK OF DREAMS

Chapter One

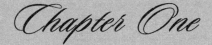

THE MIRACULOUS JOURNEYS OF SLEEP

There is nothing more fascinating, more intensely personal, and more uniquely ours than the voyages our minds and spirits take while we sleep. These dreams and other adventures confuse us, alarm us, preoccupy us, relieve us, amuse us, comfort us, inform us, enlighten us, and above all, keep us more sane and whole than we could ever hope to be without them. Our sleep journeys, even the nightmares, are gifts, our allies, to embrace rather than dread, and worth every effort it takes to unravel their mysteries and cherish every valuable lesson they have to offer.

I've been studying the worlds of sleep and dreams for more than thirty years. In the course of those studies I've read a lot of the same dream interpretation material you have, and often come away feeling more confused when I finished than I was when I started. Some "experts" swear that there's great cosmic significance in every dream, if we were only bright enough to figure it out. Others are convinced that dreams are nothing but meaningless little vaudeville shows to keep us entertained while we sleep. Still others strain to find sexual symbolism in each tiny detail of our dreams (I'd love to have met Sigmund Freud just once, just long enough to say, "What's *wrong* with you?"), while a few geniuses even insist that the minute we doze off, we disintegrate into any number of vapor blobs and go darting around the universe for reasons I can't figure out for the life of me.

I might have thrown up my hands and dismissed the whole subject of dreams as being too confusing to conquer if it hadn't been for some basic realities I wasn't confused about at all:

First and foremost, I grew up with my grandmother Ada, a brilliant psychic and teacher, who shared her passion for dreams, especially prophetic ones, with her adoring granddaughter and taught me that the subconscious mind understands their meaning whether the conscious mind can make sense of them or not.

Then there was my own passion for world religions, which led me to read and reread every great sacred work and to appreciate how prominently dreams are woven into the exquisite fabric of every one of them. If the Bible included those 121 references, how could I ignore them?

In addition, maybe because I was born psychic, I devoured the books of all the great psychics, from Edgar Cayce to Arthur Ford to Ruth Montgomery, in the hope of not feeling quite so out of place. At the same time, endlessly curious about exactly how the human mind operates (thinking I could *learn* to be "normal," I guess), I read and studied every book and course I could find on the subjects of psychiatry, psychology, and hypnosis, even becoming a master hypnotist in the process and forming lifelong friendships with some of the finest psychiatrists and psychologists in the country. I'm sure there are some members of the psychiatric community who won't appreciate hearing this, but the truth is, the psychic world and the psychiatric world have a lot in common, including a deep interest in uncovering and understanding the secrets hidden in dreams.

Once my career as a psychic was under way, more and more clients were asking for my help with interpreting their dreams. In most situations, I don't mind a bit saying the words "I don't know." But when a client wants and needs something from me, I owe them better than a shrug and a simple "Beats me." So it was for my clients' benefit as well as my own insatiable curiosity that I made it my business to unravel the mysteries of dreams as best I could, to the point where for many years I had the pleasure of teaching very successful dream interpretation classes to the growing number of clients who were as fascinated as I was.

And then one day I found myself so shaken by a dream that I went to one of my professors for help, and the value of decoding a message received in dreams hit home like it never had before. It was during a period of huge personal upheaval in my life, which, by the way, is when our sleep adventures tend to be more vivid, intense, and meaningful than ever. I was juggling my two full-time careers, as both a psychic and a schoolteacher, taking an advanced hypnosis class, and most of all, in the midst of a nasty divorce from my first husband Gary (technically my second, but that's another story for another book). There was no dispute over money or property, since neither Gary nor I had any money or property to fight over. But there was a huge, ugly dispute over the custody of our two precious little sons, Paul and Chris, and our beautiful foster daughter, Mary, and I wasn't about to let anyone on this earth separate me from my children, *period*. It was a painful, terrifying time that I can still feel in the pit of my stomach as I write about it now, thirty years later.

In my dream, at the height of my fear, I was standing in a classroom, tightly holding my three children Paul, Chris, and Mary, who were huddled beside me, the four of us in the center of a protective circle I'd drawn on the floor. Several androgynous, nonthreatening figures wearing faceless green masks were walking single file around the outside of the circle, chanting, "Beware of the three, beware of the three," over and over again. The figures themselves didn't frighten me, but their repeated warning did, and I woke feeling helpless and more afraid than I'd ever felt in my life.

I was awake and almost frantic the rest of that night trying to make sense of what "beware of the three" could possibly mean. What "three" was I supposed to beware of? Surely it wasn't the three innocent children I was trying so fiercely to protect. Was it an upcoming date for a custody hearing that wasn't going to go well for us, maybe the "third" of the month, or "three" months later? Had my estranged husband somehow manufactured "three" charges against me to try to convince the judge that I was an unfit mother? Most unthinkable of all, was I getting a premonition to emotionally brace myself because I was going to lose these "three" children, which I'm not at all sure I could have survived? I must have come up with a thousand possibilities that night while I paced around the house like a lunatic, but none of them felt quite right, let alone offered the kind of help a warning like that should give. I've always said, I'll vigilantly beware of an enemy, I'll bravely square off with an enemy, but I can't do a thing unless I know what or who the enemy is.

Luckily, I was studying advanced hypnosis at the time, and my professor was a genius about the workings of the subconscious mind, including the messages it sends through dreams, and I still count him among my most trusted and insightful colleagues. I was waiting outside his office when he arrived that morning. I was so frantic by then that I hope I didn't grab him by the lapels, but I can't swear I didn't. He patiently led me to the chair beside his desk and simply said, "Tell me what's wrong."

I filled him in on the fierce custody battle that was consuming my life and then described my dream, in all its disturbing detail. I don't cry often, especially in front of other people. I cried that morning.

"You wouldn't think a psychic of all people would feel this helpless," I told him, "but as you know, I'm not one bit psychic about myself. If that dream was trying to tell me something and I blow this custody case because I didn't understand the message, I'll never forgive myself. What am I missing, John? What could 'beware of the three' possibly mean?"

His smile was patient and compassionate. "Tell me," he said, "who's fighting against you for custody? Who's trying to take your children away from you?"

That was easy. "My husband, his mother, and believe it or not, *my* mother."

Instead of pointing out the obvious, he let me catch on all by myself. It took me a few seconds, but finally I added, "In other words, three people. Three people I need to beware of." I was hit with that wave of relief that comes when you know something right and true has just been uncovered. The dream wasn't some dire prediction. It wasn't teasing me with mysterious new information in a kind of infuriating guessing game. It was simply clarifying and reminding me to stay focused on the three people who were conspiring to use my children to hurt me.

I felt as if the weight of the world had been lifted off my shoulders as I left John's office that morning. The fear that had kept me awake and pacing most of the night was replaced by a sense of resolved power, like when you turn on a bright light and discover that the terrifying, shadowy monster in the corner of your bedroom is nothing but a pile of clothes on a chair. My lawyer and I paid even closer attention to "the three" from that day on and, because we did, we won. I was awarded full custody of my children. Thank God.

If any one event sealed my commitment to explore the world of sleep and make its magic more available and understandable to my clients and to myself, it was that dream, its aftermath and everything I learned from the experience.

I learned that there's valuable clarity to be found while we sleep if we can just master the vocabulary to translate it.

I learned firsthand how lost, confused, and often frightened my clients felt when they came to me for help with their dreams, and I promised God and myself I would do everything in my power not to let them down.

I learned how important objectivity is when trying to figure out the purpose of a dream, and how easy it is for the conscious mind to overcomplicate a dream's meaning when very often the simplest answer is the right one.

I learned, above all, that the sleep world is richer, more varied, and far more vast than I ever imagined and that, as we'll explore in the course of this book, dreams are only the beginning of that world.

The Basics of Sleep

We all know how to sleep, and we all know that sleep is a biological and psychological necessity. But in the 1950s, researchers began doing formal, well-documented, and exhaustive studies of the whole process of sleeping, and more than fifty years later the studies continue, proving how infinitely complex the world of sleep really is.

I've read the published results of most of these studies. Some

of them are fascinating, and frankly, some are so boring, techni-
cal, and just plain badly written that I could barely get through
them. Much of this research provides valuable information about
sleep, though, and about when and how we dream, that can help us
take maximum advantage of those luxurious hours when our conscious minds step back and let our subconscious minds and our
spirits take center stage.

It's fairly common knowledge by now that there are two basic
stages of sleep: REM, which stands for "rapid eye movement" and
is the lightest stage of sleep, and Non-REM, which is the deeper
sleep when eye movements and our other muscle responses become almost nonexistent. It's during REM sleep that we dream,
and it's when we're awakened during or immediately after REM
sleep that we're most likely to remember our dreams.

The Non-REM stage accounts for about 75 percent of our
sleep, leaving 25 percent for REM sleep. Thanks to a lot of brilliant
minds, tirelessly curious researchers, and great advancements in
the world of medical technology, we also know that our brain
waves fluctuate in approximately ninety-minute cycles while we
sleep. Brain waves, measured by the EEG, or electroencephalo-
graph, have been charted into distinct levels for those ninety-
minute cycles:

Beta Level: We're wide awake, active, and alert.
Alpha Level: We're awake but relaxed, and our eyes are closed.
Theta Level: We're very sleepy or in the process of falling
    asleep, and usually in the REM stage.
Delta Level: We're very deeply asleep and in the Non-REM
    stage.

Once we reach the Delta level of the cycle, the order simply re-
verses, and our sleep becomes progressively lighter again. When

we wake up feeling rested and refreshed, it's very likely that these ninety-minute cycles have been allowed to progress on their own without interference or interruption.

Scientists have become so specific in their studies of sleep cycles, and of REM sleep in particular, that they've discovered our eyes actually move horizontally while we're dreaming about viewing something from side to side and move vertically while we're looking up and down at something in a dream. Fortunately, this business of our bodies acting out the movements in our dreams pretty much stops with the eyes. The same parts of the brain that control our sleep cycles also inhibit our other motor activities. That explains why, in the relatively light sleep of REM, when we're still asleep but vaguely aware of our surroundings, we'll occasionally have dreams in which we desperately want to run but our legs refuse to move—it's a blend of the situation in the dream and the normal, temporary, sleep-induced inhibition of body motions. As frustrating as those dreams can be, the alternative, in which biology doesn't stop us and our bodies actually take off running while we're asleep, would be worse, not to mention potentially embarrassing, don't you think? In fact, there's a rare brain malfunction called "REM sleep behavior disorder" that causes those who suffer from it to physically act out their dreams without being consciously aware of it and end up injuring themselves and anyone around who might happen to get in their way.

Because successful sleep depends on the natural balance and flow of the REM and Non-REM cycles, and the various levels of brain wave activity, I can't stress enough how I hope that, unless it's prescribed by a qualified doctor, you'll resist the temptation to medicate yourself with drugs or alcohol to help yourself sleep. Chances are, self-medicating will make you fall asleep more quickly. But it's a guarantee, proven by countless experts and researchers, that it will also disrupt the balance of your sleep cycles. You'll either spend too much time in the Theta level, hit by a barrage of dreams that will make you wake up feeling as if you've spent the night in some sort of bizarre, relentless house of mirrors, or you'll stay too long in the Delta level, sleeping so deeply and dreamlessly that you'll wake up feeling hungover and emotionally flat.

And believe me, in spite of some ongoing debates among a handful of researchers who I think have buried their humanity under too many piles of data, there's not a doubt in my mind that dreaming is as essential to us as breathing. Whether we remember our dreams or not, whether we can even begin to understand what they mean, they're a release valve, an absolute survival mechanism, our minds' way of protecting and preserving some sense of balance in a waking world that often seems to offer very little balance at all. Sleep researcher William C. Dement once said, "Dreaming permits each and every one of us to be quietly and safely insane every night of our lives." I couldn't agree more. Dreams are so necessary that in clinical studies it's been found that after several nights of REM deprivation, the first thing the mind and body will do when allowed to sleep uninterrupted is indulge in a dramatic increase in the length and frequency of REM cycles to make up for lost time. They're so necessary that without them, we can experience everything in the cold light of day from disorientation to an inability to concentrate or be logical to anxiety to depression to hallucinations— in other words, those often disquieting indulgences we can freely express in private while we sleep.

So before we start this exploration together into the extraordinary, indispensable world of dreams, all I ask is that no matter what we uncover, no matter how dark or light or bizarre or joyful or scary or upsetting it might be, you remember to celebrate the fact that you do have dreams, and make a promise to yourself to dream bravely and without apology, starting tonight and for the rest of your happy, healthy, spiritual, inquisitive, God-given life.

✳

Chapter Two

INSIDE THE
DREAM WORLD

As I said earlier, I've read the same dream interpretation books you've read, and often come away just as mystified as you have. The books that get on my nerves the most are the ones that start by marveling over how easy it really is to interpret our dreams and then proceed to offer such complicated, convoluted explanations of dream symbols that we come away feeling either hopeless or just plain too stupid to bother trying. So let's get a couple of things straight right up front.

For one thing, interpreting our dreams isn't always easy at all. Like so many other worthwhile skills, it takes practice, time, accurate information, and a willingness to keep an open, self-honest mind. It's usually harder to interpret our own dreams than it is someone else's, since we're often so close to a situation that we "can't see the forest for the trees." So the more objectivity we can bring to the process, the more successful we're likely to be.

For another thing, there's rarely only one "right" answer to what a dream means. A few different possibilities can make all the sense in the world. And frankly, as long as we come away understanding the overall message of the dream, I don't think the literal meaning of the details matters all that much.

A perfect example is a client who came to me several months ago, just as I was starting this book. (It's amazing how often life brings me relevant situations at the exact time I need them.) We were in the middle of a reading that had nothing to do with dreams at all when suddenly she felt compelled to tell me about a recurring nightmare she'd been struggling with for months:

"I'm trapped in this small room with gray walls and no windows," she told me. "I'm holding a baby, and I love babies, but this one isn't bringing me any joy at all, it's just making me anxious and frustrated because it has an insatiable appetite. No matter how many bottles I give it, it keeps wanting more and more and more, like it's desperately needy but I'll never be able to satisfy it. I feel hopeless and stuck, because I know I'm responsible for this baby, but all I really want to do is escape from it and let it be someone else's problem."

The baby? Her husband. The bottle? His severe alcoholism, which he refused to address, let alone deal with. Or, just as legitimately, the baby was her, feeling as helpless and defenseless as an infant in the face of her husband's drinking problem. Whether the baby represented him or her isn't nearly as important as the repeated snapshot she was being given while she slept of the truth she couldn't face in her waking hours: she felt trapped in a deeply troubled marriage that had long since stopped giving her any joy. She wanted to run away, but her sense of responsibility wouldn't allow it.

I didn't pick up that information about her husband's alcoholism psychically. I didn't need to. She'd told me about it earlier in the reading. She'd also told me how much she loved him and how it wasn't really that bad, certainly not bad enough to threaten her marriage. It was as good an example as I've seen of being too close to a situation to see the obvious message of a dream, and of how much more honest the spirit mind in the subconscious can be while the conscious mind is busy making excuses and flexing its defense mechanisms.

By the way, I got a letter from her eight months later, telling me that after repeated refusals by her husband to admit to, let alone deal with, his alcoholism, and after a lot of therapy on her part, she'd left him. It wasn't easy, but she knew it was the right, healthy thing to do. I especially loved one comment in particular: "Frankly, if you'd been the one to tell me how lost I was, I'm sure I would have refused to believe you. But since *I* was the one who was telling me, I couldn't exactly deny it."

Which illustrates another wonderful point I want to make about dreams before we get started: our dreams and the spirit minds behind them are usually a whole lot smarter about us than we are, so what a waste not to master their language and then *listen*.

The Eternal Pursuit of Dreams

It should inspire, not discourage us that people have probably been trying to solve the mysteries of dreams for as long as there have been people. Written interpretations of dreams date back to around 4000 B.C., but even before that, "primitive" societies (sometimes much wiser than we "civilized" societies, let's face it) thought of the world of dreams as nothing less than a more powerful version of the real world in which they spent their waking hours, so that those two worlds were inseparable, interdependent, and of equal importance.

Ancient Romans, who believed that dreams were messages from their gods, routinely relied on the Senate to interpret dreams that seemed significant, while the Greeks often assigned dream interpreters to be aides to their military leaders. In Africa, healers and shamans looked to their dreams for clues about diagnosing and curing illnesses. The Chinese and Mexicans thought of the dream world as a whole separate dimension that the soul travels to every night, a dimension where their ancestors waited to share comfort and wisdom. The Egyptians believed dreams to be sacred, and honored priests with the responsibility of interpreting them. Almost five hundred years before the birth of Christ, a northern Indian queen named Maya had a dream one night in which she was playing with a pure, perfect white baby elephant. At the end of the dream the elephant entered her womb, and when Maya woke she knew she'd been given a sign that she would someday give birth to an equally pure, perfect child. That child was Siddhartha, who became the brilliant Buddha, and another great world religion was born, like Christianity would be, in the divine promise of a heeded dream.

The gorgeous spirituality of Native Americans has also been reflected since ancient times in its deep reverence for the dream world where its ancestors lived. It was the Ojibwa nation, in fact, that created dream catchers, beautiful woven webs of willow hoops and plant cords with a single feather hanging from them. According to their legend, when dream catchers were placed on the headboard of a sleeping child, all dreams would be attracted and come to them. But the bad dreams would get stuck in the weaving, unable to find their way through, while the good dreams knew their way through to the center so that they could slide down the feather and into the child's spirit mind. And in the first light of morning, the sun would shine on the bad dreams trapped inside the dream catcher and melt them away forever.

I share these anecdotes not only because I love them but also because they illustrate so beautifully the infinite depth of the relationship between humankind and our dreams. Our curiosity about them is ageless. Our efforts at understanding them are limitless. Our emotional need for them is undeniable. And as we'll discover in upcoming chapters, the psychic outlets they provide give us access to our own extraordinary power, our great wealth of spiritual talents, an eternity of knowledge and memories and reunions and Homecomings, and nightly affirmation of our blessed, God-given immortality.

It's estimated that we dream for a minimum of two hours every night. If our lifespan in this incarnation is seventy years, that means we'll spend 51,100 hours of our lives dreaming. 51,100 hours in God's presence, exploring, learning, getting glimpses of the future, glimpses of the past, glimpses of loved ones both here and on The Other Side, sometimes doing nothing more than just letting off steam or solving some mundane problem, sometimes doing nothing less than saving a life, soaring with Angels, or receiving divine inspiration that could benefit all of humankind. 51,100 hours' worth of answers, ours and ours alone, just waiting for us to understand.

The Five Categories of Dreams

As I said, I've been avidly studying and researching dreams for thirty years, developing and revising my own approach to interpreting them as I continued to learn more and more about what makes sense to me and what doesn't. And let's face it, if something doesn't make sense, I don't care how wise or clever or fashionable it might look on paper, or how glibly it's delivered in lectures or on tape, it's useless as far as I'm concerned. I love logic, the simpler and more plainspoken the better, and logic is an essential element in my method of dream interpretation.

I also unapologetically underscore my views on the dream world with two other basics that propel and inspire every moment of every day of my life: my absolute devotion to God and spirituality, and the psychic gifts God has given me. That's not to say that in order to benefit from this book you have to completely agree with my belief system. It's simply to let you know my point of view right up front and ask you to respect my commitment to it, just as I will always respect your commitment to yours. I'll never say that my approach to interpreting dreams is *the* approach. I only offer it as *my* approach, with God, spirituality, and logic at its core, through the eyes of a psychic, which are the only eyes I can offer. I believe with all my heart that somewhere in these pages you'll find some answers you've been searching for about the intimate relationship between you and your dreams, or at the very least, enjoy trying.

And so, with all that in mind, I'll start, logically, with the first step I take in understanding every dream: answering the key question *What kind of dream was it?*

It's pleasantly surprising how easily the answer to that question comes, once you know to simply ask it. And it's amazing how much easier it is to interpret a dream, and the emotions it might leave you with, once you've put it in its proper context.

Every dream experience is one of five kinds:

The Prophetic Dream
The Release Dream
The Wish Dream

The Information or Problem-Solving Dream
Astral Visits

Here's a quick personal story about the value of categorizing a dream. Since my early twenties I've had a very sporadic recurring nightmare. I'm standing in an open field, and an endless herd of strong white horses is trampling me. Oddly, they're not hurting me, and they don't seem menacing, they're just overwhelming me, and I'm always aware that I'm in that field, in the path of these horses, by my own choice. I'm not as afraid as I am helpless and powerless.

Before I understood that there are five different kinds of dreams, I couldn't figure out that dream for the life of me. But once I learned to ask myself what kind of dream it was, and what kind of dream it wasn't, it became much easier. A wish dream? Hardly. A prophetic dream? Not likely. An information dream? Not when I didn't come away with any new information. A problem-solving dream? Probably not, since I wasn't doing anything to try to stop the horses or escape from them. Definitely not an astral visit, I felt safe in saying. But as a release dream, it made perfect sense. This supposed nightmare was really just my spirit mind waving a red flag about the fact that I was overdoing things. It's true, I'm blessed with a life devoted to God, spirituality, and the use of my psychic gifts in whatever ways I can to try to leave this world a little better than I found it. At the same time, I'm as involved and impassioned a mother and grandmother as you'll ever, ever meet. I'd be either lying or crazy if I claimed that I never, ever get overwhelmed by it all. Doesn't it make the most perfect sense that what overwhelms me in this dream is not a flood of dark, vicious, hurtful monsters, but a herd of beautiful horses as strong, pure, powerful, and magnificent as the forces that drive me? So thanks to learning to categorize dreams before I try to figure out their meaning, I finally understood that my recurring "nightmare" was a blessing, my spirit mind letting out a tired sigh to say, "I'd slow down if I were you."

Again, knowing what *kind* of dream I'm trying to interpret is always my first step in unlocking its mysteries, and it's easier than you might think, since each of the five categories of dreams has its own distinctive characteristics, starting with a category so many of you are blessed with, even when it feels like a curse, the fascinating Prophetic Dream.

Chapter Three

✳

PROPHETIC DREAMS: WITNESSING THE FUTURE DURING SLEEP

"I was in a place that was dimly lit but not scary. It was like an auditorium, and Sylvia was speaking there. Or, more specifically, her guide Francine was speaking through her. There was an audience, all of whom seemed to be in a trance. And there was a little old lady ahead of me. She was asking silly questions, and I was getting impatient. My wristwatch and the clock on the wall read one minute till twelve. There was no time left for me to ask anything, and Sylvia got up to leave. Then she looked directly into my eyes and said, 'You don't want to be in New Jersey on 7/10. Pray for New Jersey on 7/10.' I was concerned about this and went over to my mom, who was in the audience. I put my arms around her and said, 'Don't worry, Mom, we won't be in New Jersey on 7/10.' Mom put her arms around me and I kissed her forehead. She began to cry. Then a lady in back of her woke up and looked into my eyes. I repeated the message: 'You don't want to be in New Jersey on 7/10. Pray for New Jersey on 7/10.' The lady got hysterical and began to cry. Then the words and the emotion swept back through the audience and they were all hysterical and crying."

That dream was sent to my office by a woman named Kathryn. It's a classic example of a prophetic dream. It's also a classic example of how careful the dreamer and the rest of us have to be not to jump to conclusions and overreact when prophetic dreams present themselves.

Every prophetic dream has two qualities in common. First, even though Kathryn didn't mention it, they're always in color, never in black and white. And second, the action in the dream takes place in sequence, with one event leading to another, which leads to another, in some kind of logical order. Unlike other kinds of dreams that can be hilariously random and incoherent, the prophetic ones unfold in the form of step-by-step stories and, because of that, can usually be tracked more easily by the conscious mind later, when the dreamer is awake. As we'll discover in later chapters, not every sequential dream, or every dream that appears in color, is a prophetic dream. But every prophetic dream is sequential and in color.

But there's also a common problem with prophetic dreams, including this one, and it's exactly why I'd strongly recommend against evacuating the state of New Jersey on 7/10: they're often too unspecific to be of any real help. There's no question that Kathryn's dream sounds like a warning. But who is it intended for? Is there danger waiting for Kathryn, or her mother, or both of them in New Jersey on 7/10 that she'll avert by avoiding the whole state on that date? Or, if there's more general danger waiting for New Jersey residents on 7/10, what is it, where is it centered, and what if anything can be done to prepare for it or prevent it? Sadly, odds are that something awful is probably going to happen to someone in New Jersey on 7/10. When it does, it would be too big a stretch for all of us who know about this dream to leap up and say, "Aha! You see? That dream was right!" Again, when a dream, or any prediction, is that general, it's too likely to apply to some situation, somehow, somewhere. For that matter, assuming 7/10 means July 10, wouldn't it be helpful to know which year? Or who's to say that 7/10 isn't a reference to July of 2010? And let's not even start with a possible reference to 7:10, either A.M. or P.M., instead of a date. See what I mean? The closer you look, the less "obvious" and more confusing the dream becomes. No wonder Kathryn was upset by it. She was only given part of a glimpse into some dark future warning, without nearly enough information to act on it. I applaud her for having the courage and the humanitarian impulse to pass along the details that did present themselves, just in case.

A woman I'll simply call Ellen had a similarly upsetting prophetic dream, with more startling ramifications: "In June of 2001 I had a dream that now haunts me daily. It began with my husband and me in a car, with him driving, which was a shock, since my husband is physically challenged and has never driven. The skies were darkening, as if a summer storm were approaching. I suggested we turn around and go back home. Along the way home we encountered dark, blackening skies, with strong winds. In the distance was a city skyline with tall buildings, like the Emerald City scene from *The Wizard Of Oz*. As we approached this city, I saw two tall 'columns' which I assumed at the time were tornadoes. The sky was now black, yet these two towers were ablaze with fire at the top. We continued to drive toward them and encountered a family (man, woman, and child) along the side of the road in a bright yellow Ryder rental truck. We asked if we could shelter them in our car. They thanked us and climbed into the back of the truck for their safety.

During this, I told my husband I needed to use the rest room, yet there were no businesses anywhere to stop. I spotted a house ahead and told him to stop there and I would ask them if I could use their facilities (something I would *never* do in real life). In the house I saw a woman in a rocking chair reading a book. I asked her if I might use her rest room and she warmly invited me in. She was extremely calm and unbothered by the 'storm' going on outside her house. After I used her bathroom, I thanked her and asked if she would be all right. I remember telling her I had never seen anything like this before, asked if it was more than a storm and then asked if she was afraid. Her reply was, 'Why, certainly not. And why are you?' I asked her if this was the end of the world, and at that point she looked up at me for the first time and said, 'Yes, as we know it.' I awoke to the alarm and was shivering and trying to put the pieces together. One evening last week, while watching the scenes of devastation to the World Trade Center, the dream came back to me, tenfold. I began to tremble. I can't understand why I would have been the one to have this dream. If I have some latent ability to see into the future, I'd like to know how I can use it to be of some assistance."

Ellen is only one of many, many of my clients who had some sort of prophetic dream about the unspeakable tragedy of September 11. Yes, that is the bottom line of this dream—Ellen definitely foresaw the attack, and her feeling while watching television was exactly right, those two blazing "columns" she saw were absolutely the towers of the World Trade Center. Ellen, and anyone who has had a prophetic dream about September 11, needs to take a lot of heart in knowing that she certainly wasn't given enough information to have done anything to prevent a single moment of the tragedy, and in noticing that throughout the dream she was so kind, caring, and concerned about other people. In fact, with very few exceptions, all of my clients who have shared their prophetic dreams with me over these many years are invariably most interested in knowing how to use those dreams to help others, and God bless every one of them for their beautiful, compassionate humanity.

Let me make several important points:

For one thing, for the sake of total honesty, I've already said this on national television, but I should say it in print, too, since the subject is so much on all of our minds. As psychic as I am, not for one moment did I see the terrorist attacks of September 11 coming. In the week before, I kept dreaming about fire, but I kept thinking maybe it was at one of my sons' houses and just warned them both to be extra careful. I've done my share of agonizing over September 11, wishing that maybe somehow I could have kept even one of those people from going to work that day, or staying off of an airplane. But that didn't happen, and I do have my own ideas of why that might be, which I'll go into momentarily. None of those ideas, though, completely takes away the searing heartbreak I know we've all felt since that unspeakable morning, and my prayers for the victims' loved ones, for our countless heroes, and for all of us who worship a kind, loving God are constant and soaring among the millions.

For another thing, don't ever get the mistaken impression that you can't have prophetic dreams just because you've never shown signs of being able to predict the future when you're awake. I spend most of my waking hours being prophetic, but I've never once had a prophetic dream. My Spirit Guide Francine keeps reminding me that if there were no difference between our waking minds and our sleeping minds, we'd all be insane. I have to admit, she's got a point. I've learned to bless my psychic gifts and be grateful for them, but believe me, I'm just as grateful for the nightly break from them. Gifts are gifts, whether they manifest themselves when we're awake or asleep, so learn to embrace them whenever they appear.

For still another thing, take it from someone whose daily waking life is very much involved in the future, those of you who have prophetic dreams need to protect yourselves from the frustrating anxiety that particular gift can create. As I've said in lectures and in writing many times, if you want to make me certifiably nuts, start showing me plane crashes and car wrecks and murders and natural disasters all day, every day, but don't give me the flight number, or a description of the car, or the identity of the intended victim, or the location of the natural disaster, and I'll just run up and down the streets waving my arms like a madwoman screaming, "Look out, everybody!" That would do all of us a real world of good, wouldn't it?

I start every day with the same prayer, and I can't recommend it strongly enough to all of you who experience prophetic dreams, to save yourselves a lot of frantic tears:

"Dear God, if you choose to give me a message about the future that I'm meant to use for someone's benefit, please give me enough accurate details to be of help. If those details are to be hidden from me, please spare me the message to begin with. But if there's more You want me to know, or something You want me to do about it, please give me the dream again, in whatever form You choose, so that I can understand for Thy service."

Offer that prayer every night before you go to sleep. It helps eliminate a lot of clutter, and it can also help important details of prophetic dreams to come into a sharp enough focus that you can work with them. In the case of Kathryn, for example, whose dream we discussed earlier, she may not have the same specific dream again as a result of that prayer. But she might have others in which the numbers 7/10 will appear, in the form of a phone number, a street address, a credit card bill, or something similar, and the details she's prayed for will start revealing themselves, *if she's meant to receive and act on them.*

It should help clarify why we're not always given as much information as we feel we need during glimpses into the future if I explain how those glimpses are possible in the first place. Believe me, they're not nearly as random and haphazard as you might think.

Where Prophetic Dreams Come From

I've written at length in other books about this, particularly in *The Other Side and Back*, so I'll be as brief as possible about it in this one. Before each of us chooses to come to earth from The Other Side for another incarnation, we write an incredibly detailed chart for this lifetime to assure that we'll accomplish the goals we've set for ourselves. In that chart we include everything, from our parents and siblings and friends and spouses to our joys and tragedies, our illnesses, our challenges, our likes and dislikes, the good and bad choices we'll make along the way, and even our "exit points," or the precise times and ways when we'll leave here and go Home again. We each arrive having chosen five designated Exit Points, and we can use any one of the five we want as we go along, depending on whether or not we feel we've accomplished enough of what we wanted from this lifetime to begin with.

When, either awake or asleep, we see some future event, such as someone's death, what it means is that we've telepathically tuned in to a chart or charts, and/or to someone's Exit Point, or sometimes even our own. Monika, for example, wrote, "My friend Stefan is very ill. He's started having a recurring dream in which he's at his fifty-fifth birthday party, and all the other guests are departed loved ones." It's not often that we're allowed to read our own charts (I've never met a psychic who's psychic about his or herself, including me), but Stefan knows that he chose an Exit Point on or very near his fifty-fifth birthday, and he's being given this recurring prophetic dream to help prepare and comfort him for the happy reunions that are waiting for him when he arrives back Home.

But please understand, from the heart of someone who's really wrestled with this issue, that not every prophetic message is meant to be delivered, precisely because *those of us who do receive those messages are not meant to intervene in every chart or Exit Point*. It's that simple, and sometimes that devastating. So by all means, pay close attention to your prophetic dreams. Get as many details as you can, and keep praying for as many of those details as you need to be useful if you sense some importance or urgency to what you're being shown. But if, in the end, you find that you weren't able to stop some disaster, or warn someone away, or protect someone from harm, because you couldn't be specific enough, don't spend one moment blaming yourself. It only means that whoever it was you might have warned or protected was determined to stick with the outcome they charted for themselves long before they came here.

Another problem faced by a handful of you who have prophetic dreams is a tendency to empathize with someone else's chart or Exit Point so much that you're unable to remain separate and objective. An excellent example came from a client I'll call Karen: "In one very vivid dream, I was a middle-aged, slightly overweight man working in an office that had glass walls facing the rest of the office. I got up from my desk, walked around it, and shut the blinds. I then walked back to my desk, retrieved the gun that was lying on it, stood beside my desk, and shot myself in the stomach. I could feel the entry of the bullet, and I clenched my stomach and fell to the floor. I then felt myself drift off as I bled to death. I woke up as soon as I lost consciousness. The next day a girl I work with received a call that her brother had shot and killed himself the night before, under disturbingly similar circumstances."

Karen, and anyone else who's found themselves over-personalizing someone else's future event, needs to ask God to help her maintain a healthy separation from her dreams, and never, ever go to sleep without first surrounding herself with the white light of the Holy Spirit, as all of us should do several times a day anyway as a matter of habit to protect ourselves.

I can't leave the subject of charts and Exit Points without addressing a question I've been asked a thousand times since September 11, 2001: "Are you saying that all those innocent victims of the terrorist attacks *chose* to die that way?" The answer is yes. That's exactly what I'm saying. It may take the rest of our lifetimes and the lifetimes of our children and grandchildren, but the day will come when we begin to understand the enormity of our growth in spirituality, humanitarianism, decency, courage, integrity, kindness, compassion, and sense of unity that the events of that awful morning inspired. And we can thank those thousands of enlightened, highly advanced spirits who agreed, long before they were born, to make that sacrifice for a greater good we can only begin to imagine now. Please don't spend a moment wondering how God could "let" such a horrible tragedy happen. He couldn't. He didn't. As with all evil events, that one was strictly human-made and defines the word "Godless." God is in the aftermath, and in welcoming every one of those magnificent souls into His eternal love back Home.

God and Prophesies

Jane recently wrote, "I've had many prophetic dreams. But through what I've been told as a child, and because of my own beliefs, I sometimes become confused about how to get past my concerns about whether these dreams are evil and move toward what God wants from me."

A more detailed letter from Tammy reads, "For as long as I can remember, I've seen future deaths, medical problems, and even the dead themselves while I'm sleeping. I saw my father-in-law's death in my sleep before it happened. I was in Maine a few weeks ago and saw a woman I knew was dead standing in a doorway. I've dreamed about loved ones' illnesses before they were even diagnosed. My problem is, I don't understand if these dreams are truly from God, or if this is the work of the devil. I was brought up in a Christian household, but I can't talk to the church about this without being judged or made to feel as if I'm crazy. Can you help me? If dreams about the future really are from God instead of the devil, what proof is there to back that up?"

For starters, please understand that I don't happen to believe for one minute that there *is* such a thing as "the devil." As I was just saying earlier, I passionately believe that the most evil entities in existence are in human, not spirit, form, and they're most definitely not powerful enough to bestow anyone with the gift of prophetic dreams. A chapter called "The Dark Side" in my book *The Other Side and Back* explains my views on evil, so I won't belabor it here. But since Jane and Tammy and so many other clients who wonder about this exact thing are Christian, and since I'm a Gnostic Christian myself and an avid student of the Bible, I understand how many seemingly conflicting points of view there are from one book of the Bible to another on the relationship between God and those to whom He's given the gift of prophesy. Take Leviticus 19:31, which reads, "Do not turn to mediums or wizards; do not seek them out to be defiled by them." Or Jeremiah 27:9, which says, "Harken not to your prophets, nor to your diviners, nor to your dreamers . . ."

On the other hand, look at the cherished, devout servants of

God whose dreams lie at the core of our faith. Jacob, in Genesis 28:12, "dreamed that there was a ladder set up on the earth, and the top of it reached to heaven; and behold, the angels of God were ascending and descending on it." Genesis 37 begins the story of Joseph, son of Israel, whose ability to interpret dreams elevated him from prisoner to the second in command to Egypt's pharaoh, and according to Genesis 39:21, "the Lord was with Joseph and showed him steadfast love . . ." It was through such great prophets as Moses, Samuel, and Elijah that God spoke to His people. And as a Christian, I can hardly find anything but the most divine prophesy in Matthew 1:18–24: "When Jesus' mother Mary had been betrothed to Joseph, before they came together she was found to be with child of the Holy Spirit; and her husband Joseph, being a just man and unwilling to put her to shame, resolved to divorce her quietly. But as he considered this, behold, an angel of the Lord appeared to him in a dream, saying, 'Joseph, son of David, do not fear to take Mary for your wife, for that which is conceived in her is of the Holy Spirit; she will bear a son, and you shall call his name Jesus, for he will save his people from their sins' . . . When Joseph woke from sleep, he did as the angel of the Lord commanded him . . ."

In other words, to suggest that prophets, and prophetic dreams, come from something evil is to suggest that it was "the devil," not God, who sent an angel to Joseph while he slept to announce the approaching birth of Christ, and that, in fact, most of the world's great religions, with prophets at their core, are all some inexplicable plot of Satan's. Does that make one bit of sense to you? Me neither. Please trust me when I tell you that it's God who gives us *all* our gifts, including the gift of prophesy. It's how we use those gifts that determines whether they're "good" or "evil." I promise you, if I didn't know with absolute certainty that my life as a psychic is God-given and God-centered, I would give it up in the blink of an eye and find a way to repay every dime I've ever made. So dream your prophetic dreams without apology or embarrassment or fear of displeasing God. Instead, thank Him for giving you that gift by devoting it to Him for His divine, loving purpose.

When Prophetic Dreams Are "Wrong"

I put "wrong" in quotation marks because there really is no "right" or "wrong" in the world of dreams. There can be confusion, misread messages, converging images, and any number of logical but misunderstood conclusions. All of those things occur for any number of reasons, from our conscious minds inadvertently combining two or more dreams into one, to our natural tendency to project our own fears onto the interpretation of our dreams, to the simple fact that we often remember much less of our dreams than we think we do. Sleep researchers estimate that we lose half the substance of a dream five minutes after it's ended, and that after ten minutes almost 90 percent of it is gone. No wonder so many of our dreams look like jumbled messes in the cold light of day.

A dream from a woman named Wendy illustrates my point beautifully. "I dreamed that my husband was driving down a certain road and his car broke down. (I think it was a flat tire.) He pulled over to fix it, and someone in a clown mask stopped to help him and hurt him very badly. I mentioned the dream to him the next morning. A few days later, he was on that exact road with his good friend. His friend pulled up his pant leg to show my husband his new tattoo, and it was of the same scary clown that I'd seen in mask form in my dream. His car didn't break down, and his friend never has and never would hurt him. Why are my dreams so often half prophetic and half wrong?"

See what I mean? There's nothing "wrong" in that dream. The imagery is very clear and precise, it's just transposed. She saw the road where her husband would be, she saw another person with him, and she saw the image of a scary clown attached to that other person. As a dream interpreter, I can promise Wendy she is just experiencing the prophetic dream version of a mixed metaphor. As a psychic, I can promise that her instinct is exactly right: her husband is in no danger at all from his friend. I would simply make sure that he starts being more diligent about getting his tires checked.

Kara wrote, "I had several dreams that my husband had died, but I was never sure how. About a month after the last dream he was diagnosed with a dramatically enlarged heart, and his doctors immediately put him on the heart transplant list. Is he going to be okay?"

A similar theme came in a letter from a woman named Stacy: "I have a recurring dream that my boyfriend and I are riding in an airplane. It's his first time flying, so I'm comforting him and reassuring him about what noises are normal on a plane and what to expect. Just after takeoff, we end up crashing, but everyone survives. I have this dream a couple of times a year, and it's making me worried about any future trips we might take together. We want to go to England in the next couple of years, but I'm afraid to fly with him in case these dreams are warnings."

These are two classic examples of the dreamer's own fears being projected onto what could easily be mistaken for prophetic dreams. In the first, Kara's repeated dreams of her husband dying without her knowing why are expressions of her fear of being alone. I can assure Kara psychically that the dream is prophetic in its informing her that she will outlive her husband, but he'll survive this current crisis, and they have many years left together.

Stacy's recurring dream about her and her boyfriend surviving a plane crash expresses a fear that a lot of us associate with flying, the fear of being in situations in which we have no control. But even her own subconscious is reassuring her that she has nothing to fear from flying with her boyfriend, because even when the worst happens in her dream and her plane crashes, *everyone survives.* This is actually a "release dream," which I'll cover in the next chapter, that feels prophetic because of Stacy's anticipation about the trip to England she's hoping to take. I say Stacy should go to England and have a good time.

Incomplete, imprecise, or combined prophetic dreams are not uncommon, and they can cause a lot of unnecessary fear and anxiety. Asking God for clearer messages, and only messages that you can do something about, will help sort things out. But just as with any other gift God gives us, the gift of prophetic dreams can always use sharpening. It's an easy, interesting procedure, one that countless clients have found useful in becoming more precise in their ability to "read ahead," so to speak, in those lifetime charts we compose in such detail on The Other Side.

I don't ever want you to fall asleep from now on without first surrounding yourself with the white light of the Holy Spirit. That goes for all of us, including me. It's cleansing, it's purifying, it's comforting, and it provides conscious awareness of being in the divine safety of God's arms.

Then, once you've protected yourself with a cloak of white light, before you fall asleep, for at least a week or two I want you to ask yourself a question about some simple event that's coming up in the near future. Let me really emphasize the word "simple." Who will win an upcoming football, baseball, or basketball game? What will a certain coworker be wearing at the office tomorrow? What song will you hear on your car radio the next day? What unexpected friend or relative will you be hearing from before the end of the week? Again, something simple, and nothing you have any particular stake in one way or the other, so that your

conscious mind isn't tempted to try to interfere with whatever answer you might get while you sleep. It's entirely possible that no
answers at all will present themselves for the first several nights. In
fact, it's probable. Having the gift of prophesy and getting answers
on demand are two different things, after all, just as being a gifted
athlete or musician doesn't mean you never have to practice. So stay
at it, varying the questions as often as you like, and write down any
responses you wake up with, whether they seem relevant or not.
Remember, this part of the process is just to help you focus and to
start developing a skill, it has little or nothing to do with accuracy.

Once that week or two has passed, escalate your question
slightly to something still simple and minor but a little more personally involving. "I'm hoping to play golf on Sunday. Will it rain?"
"I'm expecting a call from an old friend on Friday. What time
should I make a point of being home so that I won't miss the call?"
"What piece of mail will arrive on Monday?" "Who will I run into
at the grocery store tomorrow?" Again, no high-stakes questions,
nothing urgent or earth-shattering that will put unnecessary pressure on you, just focus on the question as you ask it, write it down
if you want, and then relax and go to sleep.

The minute you wake up, write down any and all of the dreams
you remember, or even fragments of them. Don't strain to apply
them to your question. Simply write them down and set them aside.
Sooner or later, with patience and an open mind, you'll start seeing a connection between your dreams or fragments and the answer you were hoping for. This is no time to be literal. It doesn't
matter if you don't have a dream about playing golf. If all you have
is a flash of a dream in which you're outside, or even looking out a
window, notice what the weather was like in that flash, jot it down,
and then see if the weather on Sunday matches your dream. You
want to know what time to be home on Friday for a phone call?
Pay attention to any moment when you might glance at a clock in

your dreams, no matter how incidental it might seem. And watch for anything in a dream that could be translated into hours and minutes, like an apartment number or a street address or an area code, make a note of it, and then check out your accuracy when Friday rolls around. You get the idea. This is simply a way of strengthening and helping define this unique "muscle" you've been given, to learn how your dreams speak to you and to get a sense of how reliably you can ask and answer prophetic questions through your dreams. The more you practice, the better you'll get, and the more you can begin expanding the questions into more important issues, for yourself *and for others*. Believe me when I tell you, the gift of prophesy, either awake or asleep, is meant to be shared, generously, gladly, and responsibly. Let selfishness or greed enter the picture and you'll wake up some morning with one less gift than you had the night before.

As for accuracy, keep your expectations realistic. Only God is perfect. For the rest of us, 100 percent accuracy is laughably impossible, and any psychic who tells you they're right 100 percent of the time is a liar. I don't want you to get too hung up on grading yourself, especially as you're working on building your skills, but an eventual goal of 60 to 80 percent would certainly be better than average when it comes to prophetic dreams.

Personal Notes

I don't want to leave the subject of prophetic dreams without addressing a couple of letters that struck a particularly strong psychic chord with me.

The first, from M., reads, "My son's father and I have been split up for two years. It took me about eighteen months to fully get over him. I still adore him, he's a splendid father to our son and he was a good man in the relationship. I was very ill with Grave's disease (hyperthyroidism) throughout most of the relationship. But I have a recurring dream, every two months or so, that we're back together. In the dream, we always end up having sex and then I wake up. I'm really puzzled. Can you help?"

Nine times out of ten I would say that a dream like this is a wish dream, which I'll go into a few chapters from now. And I'm a firm believer that false hope is ultimately unfair and destructive. But I have to give M. the information I'm given psychically, without judgment or editing, and that information is that this actually is a prophetic dream. M. should be patient, be the generous, loving soul that she is, and whatever she does, she shouldn't push or try to hurry things along. She and her son's father are going to find their way back to each other. All she has to do is stay out of her own way and simply let it happen.

A young woman I'll call A.K. wrote, "I have a recurring dream that I'm pregnant, or I have a little child, and that I'm by myself, that somehow the baby's father ends up leaving me alone. And basically, that's the story of my real life. I'm a single mother with a young son, and his father is long gone. Is my recurring dream as accurate a prediction as I think it is? Is everyone I let into my life really going to leave me?"

I understand how prophetic A.K.'s recurring dream seems to her, but in her case, it's something else—she's programming herself, both awake and asleep, to feel that she's not worthy of giving or receiving lasting, committed love. A.K.'s dream isn't prophetic, it's a reflection of the self-fulfilling prophesy she's created for herself, a sense of "Sooner or later he's going to figure out that I'm a loser and take off, so why put any real effort into this relationship in the first place?" Remember, if A.K. can program herself into low self-esteem, she can program herself into self-confidence, too. In fact, for A.K.'s son's sake as much as her own, I insist on it. In the next chapter I'll address positive dream programming techniques in far more detail. But for now, every single night from this moment on, before A.K. goes to sleep, after surrounding herself and her son with the white light of the Holy Spirit, I want her to ask God for dreams that will assure her that, as His child, she is not just worthy and capable of enduring love, she is treasured, treasuring, and divine. If A.K. can reinforce that confidence-building habit with some counseling, so much the better. I happen to be a big believer in the value of skilled professional therapists who are trained to guide us step by step through the learning process of leading a fulfilling, productive, emotionally healthy life. The more A.K. learns about being a self-confident child of God, the more she can teach her child, which will make her a wonderful parent, and that's as worthy and divine a pursuit as there is on this earth.

And finally, a prophetic dream from Mrs. L.: "I dreamed that my mother had terminal cancer. I told my husband about it the next morning, but no one else, and I cried myself sick for several days because somehow I knew this was one dream that was going to come true. Six months later my mother died from ovarian cancer."

As sad as this dream is, it's also an inspiration in so many ways. Mrs. L. knew in her soul that this dream was prophetic, and she acted on it beautifully and very appropriately. For one thing, she didn't give in to her grief and hysteria by terrifying the rest of her family, and especially her mother, with this dream. For another, she used that dream positively, by seeing to it that the six months she had left with her mother on this earth were loving, close, and deeply spiritual. I'm proud of Mrs. L., for giving her mother such a peaceful send-off, and for giving herself memories with her that she'll always treasure. She made it to The Other Side easily, and in the midst of her very happy life there, she is with Mrs. L. and visits her often.

* * *

If you're one of God's children to whom He's given the gift of prophetic dreams, enjoy them, but take them seriously, too. I can personally assure you that with this gift comes the responsibility of using it with kindness, compassion, and discretion, in His service or not at all. And don't ever let your prophetic dreams frighten you. You wouldn't have been blessed with them if you hadn't also been blessed with the courage to make a difference, and with God's help and guidance, you can. He believes in you, and so do I.

Chapter Four

✴

THE RELEASE DREAM

Release dreams are usually the most confusing, chaotic, preposterous, and disturbing
dreams we experience. They're also among the
most necessary, because it's through our release
dreams that we dispose of the everyday mental and
emotional garbage we collect. Some release dreams
are silly and worth only a good, brief chuckle when
we wake up. Many more of them are nightmares
that can stay with us for a very long time, since fear
is such a strong emotion and hard to shake off. But
without release dreams, including the nightmares,
we'd all be either chronically stressed out or completely psychotic, so they're more than worth the
discomfort they often put us through.

Here are three classic release dreams/recurring
nightmares, typical of so many I received, to give
you an idea of the pattern they often follow:

"I have three children," Lyn wrote. "On separate

occasions I've had dreams that each of them has died. Why would I dream about the death of the most precious people in my life?"

Similarly, J.'s letter read, "I dreamed my eight-year-old son was shot. Both awake and asleep, the very thought of such a horrifying thing happening makes me sick to my stomach. Please tell me I'm not foreseeing a tragedy I couldn't possibly bear!"

And then there was L.B.'s: "I've had a recurring dream since shortly after I got married that never fails to haunt me for days. In the dream, my husband has left me and won't even speak to me, and I have no idea why. I seem to know where he is, but I can't reach him, and almost invariably I'm aware that there's another woman involved. I wake up extremely angry and frightened. During my waking hours I have no reason at all to be suspicious of him. We have a very strong friendship and marriage, so where on earth are these dreams coming from?"

Dreams, or nightmares, like these are very upsetting, obviously, and they're also very, very common. You've probably had your share of similar ones. I know I have. They're not prophetic dreams, and they're certainly not expressions of some terribly disturbed subconscious wishes. What they are—*all* they are—is a subconscious release of our "worst case scenario," the most awful thing we can possibly imagine, so awful we refuse to let our conscious minds fantasize such a thing for more than a second or two before we force our focus onto something, anything, more manageable. What our conscious minds push away as quickly as they can, our subconscious minds keep track of and act out, not to be perverse and see how much they can frighten us but to reassure us that even if our version of "the worst" happens, we'll somehow manage to survive it, emotionally devastating as it might be. Notice that none of the three dreams I quoted, and none of these particular "worst case scenario" release dreams you and I have, end with "And I was so distraught from what happened that I died." It's normal and human that, awake or asleep, no matter what the circumstance, we need to believe that somehow, in the long run, we'll be okay. One of the purposes of release dreams is to give our wise, eternal subconscious minds the opportunity to show us that, ultimately, we really will be.

Release dreams in general, then, can give us an infinitely expansive view of ourselves, of what's going on in our lives and of how we really feel about things, feelings that, just like those "worst case scenarios," our conscious minds are often too busy, confused, or afraid to let us confront. A couple of dreams from a woman named Aurelia demonstrate that point very nicely. In the first, "I keep dreaming that the door of our house is not closed at night and that it should be fixed, that anyone could push it open. Sometimes I even dream of closing it at night and finding it open in the morning. I keep thinking of leaning a chair against it, or putting a brick there, but I know I need something heavier to keep someone out, and I don't know what to do." In the second, "I find out that my mother has thrown away my black pocketbook and a lot of my clothes. It makes me angry, and I tell her she has no right to dispose of my things and interfere in my business."

Again, these aren't prophetic dreams. And they're not signals from Aurelia's subconscious or spirit mind that she's afraid of being burglarized. Let's face it, who in their right mind isn't afraid of being burglarized? No, if she were to stand farther back from her current situation and look at it objectively, I'm betting she'd find that she's feeling used these days, that those around her have become accustomed to "invading her space" at their convenience rather than hers, and that even something as personal as Aurelia's privacy (What is more personal to a woman than her purse and her clothes?) isn't being respected as *hers*. She doesn't know how to

deal with it during her waking hours because she doesn't want
to offend anyone, but her subconscious mind will speak up and
defend her rights as she would so love to do. If she were in a reading with me, I would tell her to start setting up some reasonable
boundaries for those people in her life who are taking advantage of
her. Once she sets up those boundaries and enforces them dili-
gently, those dreams will disappear.

The Symbolism of Dreams

The discussion of release dreams is a perfect opportunity to
explore the symbolism that our subconscious minds use to communicate with us, symbolism that runs through all of our dreams
but is often at its most evident and most confusing in release
dreams. Like me, you probably wish that sometimes your subconscious would knock off the guessing games and just spell out whatever it's trying to say. But there are reasons why it doesn't, and
won't.

Never forget, or doubt, that our subconscious minds, where
our spirit minds live, are infinitely more sophisticated than our
conscious minds can ever hope to be. They've been alive and wide
awake for an eternity, as they'll continue to be for the rest of eternity. They've experienced and retained every moment, from incarnations on earth to brilliantly active lives on The Other Side, and
they've constructed a deep, eloquent language of symbols that they
understand perfectly, even when our conscious minds are standing
there, dumb as shovels, staring at those symbols with nothing but a
big "duh!"

In addition to eternal lives, our spirit minds have eternal patience. They understand our human limitations, so when there's an
important message they want our conscious minds to really get,

they'll keep sending it over and over, in different forms with different symbols, until we finally catch on. It's not our subconscious minds that are being dense and cloudy when they send us symbolic dreams we can't make sense of, it's our conscious minds that are having a translation problem. And we can always rest assured that our subconscious minds get the point whether our conscious minds do or not, and even whether we consciously remember our dreams or not.

Our subconscious minds are also ultimately kind, gentle, loving, and very aware of what our conscious minds can and cannot handle. The symbolism in even our most shocking dreams is guaranteed to be a more graceful form of storytelling than a cold, hard, literal depiction would be. We face all the up-close-and-personal reality we need while we're awake. Being hit with more of it while we sleep would be a disastrous overload—easier to interpret, maybe, but ultimately no relief or break from reality at all. So, confusing and frustrating as it sometimes is, dream symbolism is a blessing, and essential to our sanity, and thank God for it.

After thirty years of exhaustive research and reading on the subject of dreams, and studying more theories than I can count, I finally found that the most helpful approach for me is a combination of gestalt psychology and the works of the Swiss psychologist Carl Jung.

Gestalt psychology was founded in the early 1900s by a German psychologist named Max Wertheimer. *Gestalt* is a German word meaning "pattern, form, or shape." To oversimplify it dramatically, gestalt psychology basically takes the position that the whole of an experience is more important than any of its individual parts. In other words, as it applies to dreams, if you understand the overall meaning of a dream, the interpretations of the details within the dream are pretty much beside the point.

So in Aurelia's dreams, for example, as far as I'm concerned, we could drive ourselves crazy picking them apart, trying to figure out what the chair she referred to and the brick she mentioned really mean, or why she specified a *black* pocketbook. Maybe it's the way my mind works (or occasionally doesn't), but I find that examining something too closely makes it too easy to lose my perspective about the "something" I'm interested in. And I think it's more worthwhile to Aurelia's life for her to get a message about the importance of establishing boundaries than it is to obsess over what color purse she's been dreaming about.

The fascinating Carl Jung, who was one of the greatest psychologists of the twentieth century, devoted a great deal of his life to dreams, their symbolism and their overall importance in our lives. In his book *On the Nature of Dreams*, published in 1945, Jung described an approach he called "taking up the context." That means that in order to fully decipher the meaning of the symbols in our dreams, we have to take our own "context," or personal associations with those symbols, into account. Let's say that birds frequently appear in your dreams. Nine "dream dictionaries" out of ten say that birds mean a yearning for freedom, and/or an indication that good news is coming. But you happen to have been terrified of birds all your life. So your dream about birds might easily be a nightmare about feeling threatened or under attack, while for me that same dream might be happy and liberating. And furthermore, we'd both be right, *for ourselves.* My favorite quote from Carl Jung on this subject, in fact, is "Learn as much as you can about symbolism; then forget it all when you are analyzing a dream."

Many dream interpreters take the gestalt approach at its most literal and believe that everything in every dream—each person, each inanimate object, each animal, each and every symbol—is really *you*. In order to put that to use in the simplest possible way, think of your dream as a movie in which you're playing all the parts, and see if that answers any questions you have about the dream. If it works for you, that's great. Never let anyone, including me, tell you that there's only one "right" way to unravel the mysteries of dreams. "Understanding" is the goal. As with any other destination, you should always take the route that gets you there most effectively and minimizes your chances of wandering off in the wrong direction.

Like Jung, I feel that the most effective route is the approach that everything in a dream that you have any kind of emotional reaction to is *about* you, and about your own personal association with the people, places, and things in that dream. And I really want to stress everything in a dream *that you have any kind of emotional reaction to.* It doesn't matter what or who evokes the feeling. Insight and understanding can come from surprising places.

Later in this book we'll discuss archetypes, which are simply common dream symbols and the meanings they tend to have most often among people whose associations with those symbols are fairly impartial. These archetypes, or those you might read in any other dream book or "dream dictionary," can be helpful. But the important thing for you to remember about the meaning of any dream symbol is that it's only valid if it's valid for *you*. No published list of archetypes will ever be as useful as the list of dream symbols and their meanings that I urge you to make for yourself. Don't get impatient, or expect to come up with your list quickly and easily. Just start jotting down, in list form, the people and things that appear with some regularity in your dreams, and then, slowly but surely, as memories and insights start occurring to you, fill in the blanks in a list of meanings right next to the first list. Don't edit or judge your list, and don't feel compelled to share it with anyone else unless you want to. Remember, it's *your* list of archetypes, like no one else's on earth but every bit as accurate as anyone else's, and it will be an invaluable map as your exploration of your dreams continues to deepen.

I've never forgotten a client named Elise, who a little sheepishly asked me to help her figure out why she kept waking up in a near panic every time she had one of her recurring dreams about peaches. Not spiders. Not monsters, or car accidents, or losing her job, or her husband leaving her. Peaches. In bowls, on a tree, on the floor of her closet, in her purse, sometimes prominent, sometimes just part of the background, but always, always upsetting her for some reason she couldn't imagine. I asked her several questions trying to get to the bottom of it, but we were both mystified until I took her through a meditation. Elise had already told me during her reading that when she was twelve years old, her mother had died suddenly from rare pregnancy complications. But relaxed through meditation, with her mind quiet and open, Elise also unearthed a long-forgotten memory: in the weeks before her death, Elise's mother had an insatiable craving for peaches. So in all these dreams of peaches, Elise was trying to make peace with the suddenness, the trauma, and the grief of her mother's death, and her list of dream symbols and their meanings would include "peaches = loss; death; tragedy." Probably not very applicable for the rest of us, but absolutely valid for her, and a perfect example of why our own list of archetypes will always be much more accurate *for us* than any general list in any dream book, including this one. Again, the list you'll find in Chapter 9 is only a guideline, not to be taken literally unless certain symbols and their most common interpretations resonate within you as the truth.

Rewriting Your Release Dreams

There's good news and bad news when it comes to release dreams. The bad news is that they're rarely enjoyable. The reason is obvious: we rarely feel the need to release the things in our lives that we're happy or content about. When is the last time you came home from a great day or a great evening thinking, If I don't let off some steam soon, I'm going to explode? And of course, that's exactly what release dreams are for, to bring unresolved or unexpressed issues into a spotlight and subconsciously act out whatever frustrations, anger, regret, guilt, resentment, betrayal, embarrassment, or shame we've been lugging around. That makes for a very busy, emotional night's sleep, and we're likely to find it hard to shake off right away when we wake up, whether we consciously remember the dream or not.

The good news is that with practice, patience, and determination, we can actually program ourselves to rewrite the endings of those recurring release dreams we have that leave us feeling anxious and upset, giving us the opportunity to let off that healthy steam but also get out of bed with a gratifying sense of having ultimately won.

A dream from C.C. will help me show you exactly what I mean: "I was widowed five years ago, while my husband and I were estranged and living apart. Since that time I've had a recurring dream of a dark figure that fills my bedroom doorway. Of course, it frightens me greatly, and I pray to God to keep me safe. After this dream I always dream that my husband has come back from the dead and I have to be with him, even though I don't want to be. I cry and cry and pray that this is really not happening. I thought these dreams would dissipate as time went by, but they still happen."

First of all, please trust me when I tell you that, like most of our dream "monsters," the dark figure filling C.C.'s bedroom doorway is *C.C.* Or, to be more precise, it's the part of C.C. that is need-lessly suffering unresolved guilt and refusing to forgive herself for the fact that she and her husband were estranged when he died and her last communications with him were so strained and unpleasant.

Her second dream is her fear that her guilt and her withholding of self-forgiveness could lead her to repeat that same unhappy mar-riage with another man in order to try to finish that particular piece of unfinished business, so to speak, or do some form of pen-ance to pay off this imaginary debt. But those burdens are nothing but preprogrammed baggage that her conscious mind is lugging around. The truth is, her heart and her spirit know perfectly well that there's nothing for her to feel guilty about. She is getting stronger every day, and she learned more from that marriage than she thinks she did, including the fact that she has worked too hard and been through too much to put herself through that kind of man and that kind of mess twice in one lifetime.

And here's how I want C.C. to start programming herself so that she'll never have to dread these dreams again. In fact, she might even start looking forward to them if she'll just be diligent. Even if she doesn't believe that this will work, I hope she'll humor me and try it anyway. I promise she'll be pleasantly surprised. She and everyone who has had recurring dreams like these should do the following:

Before you go to bed, surround yourself with the white light of the Holy Spirit, picturing a pure, glowing, brilliant, warm, protec-tive white light of God's love softly wrapping itself around you from head to toe like a divine gossamer cloak. Then offer a prayer that, in your own words, expresses the following: "Dear God, should those same painful dreams come to me again tonight, please help me transform them into stories of strength, victory, and em-powerment." Then add something more specific; in C.C.'s case: "This time, when the dark figure appears in the doorway, let me face it head-on, and let me move past my fear of it to a feeling of loving, tolerant compassion, recognizing the figure as nothing but the heartbroken embodiment of my unresolved grief and guilt. Let me look directly at this sad, unhealed part of me and quietly say, 'I love you, I forgive you, and I resolve and release you into the perfect love of God's eternally healing embrace.' "

Keep asking for that kind of ending to the dreams every night, as your last thought before you sleep. Sooner or later, that ending really will happen. And it's very likely that for C.C., once it does, the second dream, in which she finds herself so unhappily married again to her late husband without having a choice, will vanish like the residual, empty fear it really is.

In case it does reappear, though, she can program a happy ending for that dream, too, just as before, with God's help through prayer. Whatever outcome to a recurring release dream you can think of that would make you wake up smiling, just keep demanding it until you get it. Maybe C.C.'s late husband demands that she remarry him, and she calmly informs him that she can't, while introducing him to her wonderful new ideal husband who is everything her late husband wasn't. Maybe he proposes, and C.C. gathers her children around her and says, "No, thanks, I love my kids too much to raise them in an unhappy home." Maybe she's walking up the aisle toward him, beautiful in her wedding gown but crying with dread, and suddenly he vanishes into thin air. Remember, it's your dream, your ending, there are no rules and no limits, as long as the ending's a happy, reassuring, confidence-building one for you. I can't stress patience enough. Keep asking, keep demanding, and eventually the "rewrite" will occur. And all it will take is one time, just one night when you and God turn your nightmare into a personal victory, and that dream will be gone forever, you can count on it.

One of my clients offered a slight, helpful addition to this "rewriting" technique that I encourage you to try if you think it will work for you. "I have a lot of powerful dreams, very colorful and beautiful. Because they seem like a movie, I can always pause, rewind, and change the ending if I don't like the way it turns out the first time. Sometimes a person introduces the dreams to me, as if introducing a play."

I appreciate the idea of pausing, rewinding, and changing the ending of a dream if the first ending doesn't appeal to you, because it's a visual any of us with a VCR can easily picture. As for the "person" who introduces the dream, that is this client's Spirit Guide.

In case you're unfamiliar with what a Spirit Guide is, it's someone we know on The Other Side who agrees to accompany us through this incarnation, gently and quietly keeping watch over us from Home to help make sure we accomplish the goals we set out for ourselves in our charts before we come here. Our spirit minds, free to express themselves while we sleep, are intimately familiar with our Spirit Guides, so it's not at all unusual for them to show up in our dreams, especially as a kind of narrator or master/ mistress of ceremonies, in proximity to the action but not a participant in it. Spirit Guides are great advocates for us throughout our lives. In later chapters we'll discuss in more detail the ways they can contribute to our sleeping hours, but for now, it's worth mentioning that asking them to help us reprogram our release dreams for more positive, empowering outcomes is an excellent habit to get into. If you don't know your Spirit Guide's name, by the way, make one up. I made up Francine's name because her real name, Ilena, didn't appeal to me, and she's never objected. Your Spirit Guide won't either. They'd much rather be acknowledged, even by an alias, than ignored completely.

"Rewriting" the endings of fearful release dreams is one of the most effective skills we can master for our own mental and emotional health, and for the clarity of communication between our conscious minds and the spirit minds alive and well in our subconscious. It's especially effective in waking up a winner from some of the most common release dreams that, with minor variations, occur to the vast majority of us sooner or later. See if any of these sound vaguely familiar to you.

Common Release Dream Themes

"TIME WARPS"

"I have a recurring dream in which I find myself having to return to high school. (I'm forty-two and have dreamed this for perhaps fifteen years.) I'm already late and unable to obtain transportation, so I begin walking. The further I progress, the more difficult it becomes to walk. All my joints become unbendable and my muscles contract in pain, and I'm reduced to a shuffle. Eventually I give up and stop . . . In similar dreams, I've ended up in an office where I'm shown to a desk and told to get to work, but I have no idea what to do."—Tamara

"I've been having the same dream for many years. I am the age I am at the present time, but I'm back in middle school. I should actually be in high school, but I had to go back because I failed to take one class."—M.

"I have a recurring dream that I'm still in high school. (I'm twenty-nine years old.) In this dream, I realize my age and am frustrated that I'm still there. All of the people I went to school with are there as well, and I'm pleased to see them, but they're all still eighteen while I'm almost thirty."—B.

"I'm by myself and back in the poor section of town where I lived from the age of nine until I was eighteen. It's always a warm day in late spring or early summer. But there's no one around. Ever. The neighbors have all moved, and everyone is gone. I walk around wondering where everyone is and feel so alone."—A.C.

These dreams, and all those like them, in which we find ourselves trapped in some situation from the past, beautifully demonstrate how aware our spirit minds are of the life charts we wrote on The Other Side before we started this particular lifetime. We all suffer from an occasional subconscious fear that we're not keeping pace with our charts, not accomplishing everything we set out to do and not in synch with the potential we designed for ourselves. That nagging concern commonly releases itself in these dreams of being lost, stranded, and inadequate in a familiar setting in which we feel impotent and inappropriate, and they tend to be most frequent at times when we're questioning the life choices we've made, times when even some level of success leaves us asking the age-old question, "Is that all there is?"

"Time warp" release dreams lend themselves nicely to reprogramming, with the revised ending of a sudden, happy announcement to everyone in the dream to the effect of "Hey, I just remembered—I don't belong here!" and a confident exit into bright, warm sunshine. But even more, they're very valuable wake-up calls (if you'll pardon the expression), a reminder to take stock of where we are versus where we know we have the potential to be, *especially spiritually.* It's a guarantee that whatever details our charts contain, we included plenty of opportunities to confront inhumanity, meanness, and negativity and, rather than being seduced or defeated by it, overcome it. I've said and written more times than I can count that we sometimes make the question of our purpose in this lifetime much too complicated. When you wade through all the confusion and all the rhetoric, it comes down to a simple "Do good, love God, then shut up and go Home." Believe it or not, when you know you're accomplishing nothing more and nothing less than that to the very best of your ability, you'll be rid of "time warp" dreams once and for all.

"CHASED BY SOMETHING EVIL"

"Most of my dreams involve trying to scream for help, or I'm trying to run away from someone who wants to hurt me. Usually it's my own screams that wake me up."—Mitchell

"I always have horrible dreams about someone chasing me, or just generally being very frightened of something I can't see."—V.S.

"In a recurring dream, I'm a child, searching a dark basement full of locked storage areas. There's something or someone behind me, chasing me, and it frightens me so much that I'm too afraid to even cry out for help."—Cora

"I was driving down a narrow, badly damaged road. On each side was swampy land, partly frozen over by a howling, icy wind. Suddenly the road tapered off and disappeared. I tried backing up, but it was so dark that I couldn't see behind me, and my car ran off the road. I was trying desperately to get the car back on the road again when the person or thing I was running from caught me. The feel of that hand on my shoulder was so terrifying that it woke me up."—T.

At some time or other, I think most of us have had dreams of something evil and threatening bearing down on us as we frantically try to escape.

To that handful of you—you and I know who you are—who are plagued with that dream as a result of you or a loved one having been victimized by violent crime, I urge you never to fall asleep without the added protection of surrounding yourself with the white light of the Holy Spirit. But with equal passion, I urge you to find a qualified professional therapist to help you through the very real horrifying trauma of post-traumatic stress. As powerful as release dreams are in bringing our fears, doubts, and insecurities to the surface and giving us a chance to face them and vent them, dreams in which we repeatedly relive a personal tragedy have the potential to keep deep wounds open that need the kind of healing only an expert in the fields of psychiatry and psychology can provide.

For the rest of you, though, who are being chased in your release dreams by a threat that's more vague, faceless, and nameless, this is a perfect opportunity to put the reprogramming technique to use. Keep praying to rewrite the ending of the dream, keep asking your Spirit Guide to help you rewrite the ending of the dream, and the night will come when you find the courage to stop running, turn around, and face your pursuer head-on. Nine times out of ten, that "monster," that "demon" you're trying to escape from is *you*—some guilt, some insecurity, some weakness, some sense of spiritual estrangement, some regret, some betrayal, some habit or addiction, some perceived flaw that you're sure will destroy you if it catches up with you. You might find yourself looking at an exact duplicate of you. You might find yourself looking at your concept of the devil, or a monster, or some person you associate with evil, or just some shape as awful and grotesque as you believe that part of you that you've been running from to be. Our subconscious minds like to speak in images, after all, and it's often easier to deal with intangible fears by attaching a face and form to them. I promise you, whatever you turn around and look at will be less terrifying than whatever you're imagining while you're running away. Just please *turn around*.

And when you do, stand firm, meet your pursuer's eyes, and say with courage, whether you're actually feeling courageous or not, "Through the grace of God's infinite love and power, I release and resolve you into the peaceful white light of the Holy Spirit, now and forever."

* * *

I'll be addressing more common release dreams in Chapter 9, on symbols and archetypes. For now, let me simply remind you that release dreams in any form, no matter how upsetting, are a blessing. In your prayers before you sleep, never pray to be relieved of your release dreams, because they're so much for our benefit. Instead, pray that, once you've let off all your pent-up emotional steam, you can end those dreams in ways that reinforce your waking awareness that, for eternity, you are a divine child of God. Thank Him for the growth, learning, and insights your release dreams provide, because even with the inevitable growing pains we have to endure, life without growth is really no life at all.

Personal Notes

To J.W., who wrote, "I keep having dreams in which I'm being picked up and moved by a very large being with very large hands. I can't see whatever it is, I just know that it feels enormous compared to me, and it makes me feel very uneasy. Can you please tell me what's happening?"

At first glance this looks like a normal release dream. But please, J.W., pay attention to how out of control you're feeling, and to the male in your life who's trying to overpower you in every aspect of your life. You can try reclaiming your power from him, but it's unlikely that he'll cooperate, in which case you really do need to get away from him as soon as possible.

S.S. wrote, "My father died on October 18, 1988. I'm still haunted by a dream in which I was in my bedroom and my father suddenly burst through the door. He was coming toward me with a knife raised as if he intended to kill me. But instead, he sat down on the bed next to me, turned the knife on himself, and slit his own throat."

I understand your horror at those images, S.S., but don't worry, your father isn't an earthbound. He's not trapped here, and he wasn't trying to torture you with violent images as some kind of cry for help. Instead, the dream was *your* cry for help, with your subconscious begging you to acknowledge and release your belief that somehow you could have stopped his death. You couldn't have. I guarantee it. As for the knife, it was simply an image you construed to depict your own unresolved pain. I hope you find peace in knowing that your father charted the exit point he chose to take long before he came here, and you had no more to do with it than I did. He's living a happy, productive life at Home and visits you often with unending love.

And finally, to T., a simple thank-you for offering such a perfect real-life example of what happens when we confront our fears in release dreams instead of running from them. In her dream, T. was being chased by a fierce dragon with a long red-and-black scaly tail. During the chase T. realized that the dragon, which had paused to eat, had spotted her and was coming after her again. "As I tried to run, the dragon lunged at me. I instinctively put up my knee to protect myself and somehow ended up knocking the dragon's lower jaw, slamming its mouth shut. There was a standoff. I was frozen in place. I felt such intense fear, wondering if I could make it to the nearby gate before it ate me and then feeling sinking despair at realizing that I couldn't, and that a slow, painful death awaited. My fear and despair were so intense that I felt myself starting to wake up, but I told myself over and over, 'face your fears, face your fears' and managed to hold myself in the dream. Still feeling incredible fear, heart pounding, I looked at the dragon. Then I really began studying it, and noticing how beautiful it was, with its brilliantly colored red and black diamond-patterned skin. The dragon stood there and let me study its beauty, as if I couldn't stop myself. And gradually my fear vanished, and the dream ended. Usually I retain uneasiness and anxiety after a scary dream. Instead, for several days after this particular dream, I felt a peaceful inner sense of accomplishment, as if I'd passed a big test."

You did, T., a test we can all aspire to learn from and pass with the same God-given courage and grace.

Chapter Five

✳

THE WISH DREAM

*J*ust as our subconscious minds act out our fears, guilt, regrets, and confusion in our dreams, they also act out our wishes. Wish dreams are exactly what they sound like: wonderful reflections of what we want, or at least what we think we want, and we usually wake up from them with a smile and a certain sense of satisfaction, because even if it was only for a few brief moments while we slept, we won our own version of the lottery.

Some of our wish dreams are sweetly literal. We want a silver BMW convertible, and we dream of driving along the beach at sunset in one. We hate being overweight, and we dream of ourselves as slender. We love baseball, and we dream of hitting the grand slam that clinches the World Series. We're in law school, and we dream of arguing and winning a case before the Supreme Court. There's no doubt about it, wish dreams can be lovely gifts from our subconscious minds and from God, not to be analyzed to death but simply to be noted and enjoyed.

Others of our wish dreams, though, are not meant to be taken as literally as they might appear, and it's important to keep the distinction clear. A dream from Mrs. D. helps explain why:

"I'm constantly having a dream about an ex-boyfriend I was totally in love with. I'm now happily married and don't understand my dream. In my dream, my ex wants a relationship with me and is very loving toward me—more so than he was in real life. When I wake up I feel refreshed, because I feel as though he does love me and always will. It's crazy. I love my husband, but I get so excited just thinking about this dream. Help!!!"

This is *not* a wish dream about Mrs. D. reconciling with her ex-boyfriend, so she shouldn't even let it enter her mind that she should try to contact him and see if maybe there's some unfinished business with that man. There isn't. By her own admission, she's even romanticizing him in her dream far more than he ever hinted at being able to deliver. No, he's not what she is wishing for, she has just understandably put his face on what she is *really* wishing for— the romance, the passion, the relative simplicity, the anticipation, the breathless urgency, and all the other unique qualities that new relationships, especially the turbulent ones, bring with them, qualities that so easily get misplaced in the everyday continuity and practicality of marriage. Everyone needs to pay attention to what, not who, his or her wish dream reveals. With some effort on Mrs. D.'s part, open communication, and reprogramming herself to exchange her husband's face for her ex-boyfriend's face when this dream comes up again, her wishes for more romance and intimacy in her life can come true exactly where she is.

It really is true that most wish dreams are more about the good feelings we're wishing for than about specific people or things we use to portray those feelings, and as much fun as the portrayals can be, it's the feelings that last and the feelings that can teach us so much about ourselves. At the risk of stating the really obvious, what we wish for in our lives is a good indication of what we think is missing from our lives, so wish dreams are a great cue for us to start filling in those gaps.

Here's a wish dream that made me smile at the very imaginative misinterpretation its dreamer, T.E., came up with by paying too much attention to trivial details and not enough attention to the bigger emotional picture:

"I'm a single mother of a twenty-month-old girl who doesn't yet speak a word. In my dream she was standing next to me, and all of a sudden she said, 'Thirty-nine.' I almost fainted. Then she went on with the numbers 40, 50, and 60. When I woke up I wondered if maybe an Angel had given me a message to play the lottery. I don't even know how to play, but off I went to get a ticket. They don't have the numbers 50 or 60, so I played 39, 40, and four other numbers. The next morning I checked the paper, and 39 and 40 were winning numbers. I only had three numbers right, so I won a free ticket, but ever since I've wondered what the dream meant. Did I misinterpret?"

Yes, T.E. did misinterpret, in a perfectly harmless way. One clue might have been the discovery that two of the four numbers she was "given" weren't legitimate lottery numbers. (I don't know the first thing about the lottery, so it's news to me, too.) And then there's the idea that Angels, who are so divine in God's hierarchy that they never even incarnate in human form, routinely check on lottery numbers and pass along tips about them, which, as I said, made me smile.

Instead, this is very simply a wish dream, expressing how much T.E. is looking forward to her daughter reaching the age when she begins to talk, which as far as I'm concerned beats winning the lottery any day. In this case, the specific numbers mean nothing. She could just as easily have been reciting the alphabet or singing "I'm a Little Teapot." T.E. is eager for her first words, that's all, and I don't blame her, it's a thrilling experience. (And by the way, T.E., when your daughter does start talking, avoid the temptation you're going to have to talk *for* her too much.)

On a sadder, more serious level, H.M. wrote, "I had a dream five nights in a row that my deceased mother-in-law told me that there's a letter hidden in my house that I need to read. Every time she'd start to tell me where the letter was, something would wake me up. I've searched this house from top to bottom, but so far I have found nothing."

There is no letter, I promise you, so H.M. can stop looking. This is a pure wish dream. H.M. and her late mother-in-law had what H.M. considered to be some unfinished business, and it's her wish that there could be one more communication with her mother-in-law in which H.M. could say those things she felt were left unsaid. H.M.'s mother-in-law is still very much around, so she can talk to her all she wants and, as she goes to sleep, pray for an uninter-rupted conversation with her, so that she can tell H.M. not where this imaginary letter is, but what she would have written in the let-ter if one existed.

A client named Nora told me a seemingly simple wish dream that I especially loved because I related to it so well. It's worth mentioning that Nora and her husband were going through some serious marital issues at the time, with Nora in particular feeling unfulfilled and very much dismissed and taken for granted. The dream involved nothing more than her riding a bicycle through a sunlit park and then getting into an argument with someone who wanted to take it away from her. It reminded me of a day during my first marriage when my husband and I had a major argument, and out of sheer frustration I ran out of the house, jumped on my bicycle, and rode as hard and fast and far as I could, until I was just too exhausted to care anymore.

Nora's wish dream was easy to take at face value, a wish to feel as free and content as she felt in that quick, quiet moment in the park, and to protect that feeling when someone tries to take it away. She was curious, though, about why she would dream about a bicycle when she hadn't ridden one in years and years. It didn't take long to unearth a couple of relevant childhood memories. One was that, at an early age, she insisted on riding her bicycle three miles to school rather than be driven there or take the bus, to make the statement to herself that she could get herself where she needed to go without having to rely on anyone else. The other was a cherished occasional bike ride with her mother, sharing the same seat with her, arms tight around her mother's waist, nestled securely against her mother's back while they rode and rode and rode. So beneath the surface of Nora's perfectly lovely dream, expressed through the image of a bicycle, was her yearning for independence, self-reliance, and a sense of comfort, trust, closeness, and belonging.

That's one of the most intriguing things about wish dreams—if we take the time to look beyond the obvious "wish," we can often unearth some deeper wishes that speak volumes about what emotional and spiritual "missing pieces" we're really searching for.

Which is one of many reasons I'm such an enthusiastic advocate of keeping a dream journal.

Dream Journals

There's nothing unique or original about the idea of writing down dreams. In fact, the idea is so ancient that a whole lot of dreams have been discovered in hieroglyphic form in the Egyptian pyramids, so it's been thousands of years since anyone, including me, could trot out the dream journal concept as if it were some kind of brainstorm. And yes, I'm also an advocate of keeping pencil and paper on your nightstand, so that you can write down key images of your dreams in any fleeting waking moments you might have during the night, to help trigger your memories in the morning.

What gets on my nerves, though, I admit, is the emphasis of so many dream book authors on keeping track of every ominous, upsetting, or prophetic dream we have, as if our happier dreams and wishes aren't as important. Granted, in our waking hours we tend to learn more from hard times than we learn when times are good. But every dream we have has something to say about us, and frankly, I happen to be just as interested in discovering what I'm truly wishing for as I am in exploring what's troubling me.

And parenthetically, if you want to learn even more about yourself from your wish dreams than you'll learn by just jotting down the dreams themselves and any of your thoughts and conclusions about them, try jotting them down and then putting them away in a safe place for six months or so. You'll be amazed at how often, as you review your wishes after time has passed, you'll find in some cases that you've made some progress, while in other cases you'll think to yourself, I wanted *what*? Our wishes change as we change, after all, and a wish dream journal can be yet another fascinating yardstick by which we can measure our emotional and spiritual growth.

At any rate, I can hear the vast majority of you saying, "That dream journal thing is a great idea, Sylvia, but how am I supposed to write down my dreams if I can't remember them?" It's a fair question, and it deserves a fair, detailed answer.

Remembering Dreams

Don't ever let anyone convince you that remembering dreams comes naturally and that there's something wrong with you if you find it difficult. Like interpreting dreams, it's a learned skill, a discipline that takes patience, practice, and reliable information to guide you along. And as we discussed in Chapter 1, dreams only occur during REM sleep, which is only part of a normal ninety-minute sleep cycle, so the longer the time lapse between REM sleep and your waking up, the harder it will be to recapture what you experienced while you slept. There's a way to help control your "dream time" that we'll go into later in this chapter, but for now, please know that if you've been having trouble remembering your dreams, you're not alone, and you can get better at it.

The only "props" you need are paper, a pencil, and an alarm clock (I'll explain the reason for the alarm clock later in this chapter) within easy reach of your bed.

Now. I hope you don't get tired of hearing me advocate prayer, because I'll never stop advocating it and I'll certainly never apologize for it. And the first step in the discipline of remembering your dreams is asking God, and your Spirit Guide if you choose (it can't hurt), to help you. I know it sounds too easy and too good to be true, but there's no such thing when it comes to praying, you have my word. Your own words will be music to God's ears. If you'd like to offer one of my favorite bedtime prayers, though, I'm happy to share it with you:

"Dearest God,
"The day is finished, a day like so many that I have lived and many more that I may live within Your blessed grace and light.
"As Your mantle of darkness falls, let peace come into my

heart and all despair be replaced by joy knowing I have completed another day in Your service.

"I call on all the blessed Angels to attend me and bring me peaceful sleep and blessed dreams that remain in my consciousness when I wake, that I may learn and grow from the ageless wisdom of the eternal spirit You breathed into me when You created me. Amen."

As you settle onto your pillow, let your mind relax along with your body. I can't suggest with a straight face that you actually "make your mind go blank," which seems to be such popular advice among some sleep, hypnosis, and meditation "experts." I'm convinced that there's nothing busier on this earth than my mind when I order it to go blank. Instead, you can put your mind to work in a positive, productive way that will be relaxing and beneficial to your entire body at the same time.

Close your eyes, take a few long cleansing breaths, and let all your mental attention focus on your feet. Picture a pure white light, the white light of the Holy Spirit, alive with protective energy, slowly encircling them. A band of sacred purple light, God's touch, and a brilliant band of healing green light swirl within the white light enveloping your feet, warming them, cleansing and relaxing them, penetrating them to unwind all those knots of tension from each tendon, each muscle. The divine tricolored glow begins spreading, up your ankles, calves, thighs, comforting, blessing, restoring, protecting, through your pelvic area, up your spine, into each organ, your lungs, your heart, cleansing your blood so that it flows red and free and rich with life, on to your arms, your wrists, each finger, one at a time, unwinding, relieving, healing, across your shoulders and up through your neck, white, purple, and green working their magic, turning tension to ease, tightness to release, on up to the top of your head, still protecting and restoring, until you're completely cloaked in sacred radiance, your body divinely relaxed and your mind not blank at all but filled with the quiet, peaceful joy of being healthy and perfect, a child of God falling asleep in the safety of its Father's arms.

Not only is this a gorgeous way of ending each and every day, but it also takes a very few minutes, prepares your body for good, quality rest, and signals your subconscious that you're receptive and eager to hear anything it has to say.

If you wake up during the night with a dream fresh in your mind, get in the habit of reaching for your notepad and pen immediately and quickly writing down whatever highlights and important symbols or people you remember, to help trigger your memory in the morning.

If you sleep through the night, get in the habit of spending your first ten waking minutes with your notepad and pen, whether you stay in bed or get up and start moving around. Jot down anything and everything you remember, beginning with six key elements: the people in your dreams; the setting or settings; the "storyline" (even if it seems chaotic and hopelessly illogical); whether it was in color or black and white and anything you especially noticed about the colors; any specific words you saw or heard; and finally, how you felt during the dream, and how you feel about it now that you're awake.

By the time you've finished reading this book, you'll also have enough information to decide which of the five dream categories each of your dreams falls into—again, those categories are prophetic, release, wish, information or problem solving, and astral visits. Ideally, you should keep a separate file or envelope for every category, put your dreams into their appropriate envelopes, and then, as you go along, see if you have a noticeable imbalance among the categories—a lot of release and information dreams, for example, and few if any prophetic, wish, and astral dreams. There's no "right" or "wrong" to the balance of your dreams in these categories, it's just one more interesting thing to learn about yourself.

Best of all when it comes to learning about yourself, though, is to reread your dreams, category by category, every few weeks. I promise, you won't need me or anyone else to point out how obvious some of the progressions of your dreams really are, how they'll actually point out your own progress in some emotional and spiritual areas and your lack of progress in others, with more hints than you might recognize at first, when the dreams are fresh, about what blocks are in your way if you're not growing as much as you might like.

One of the most effective habits to work toward when it comes to remembering dreams comes from the deeply spiritual Australian Aborigines, a culture thousands upon thousands of years old, among whom the worlds of dreams, nature, and spirits are utterly inseparable and sacredly intertwined. In fact, the Aborigines' legend of the creation of Earth is known to them as Dreamtime.

Dreamtime

According to an Aboriginal tribal elder, "They say we have been here for sixty thousand years, but it is much longer. We have been here since the time before time began. We have come directly out of the Dreamtime of the great Creative Ancestors."

Dreamtime was the beginning, that "time before time began" when the Aborigines' great spirit ancestors emerged from beneath the earth and traveled throughout its surface, bestowing it with its physical form and its laws before returning to their underground dwelling places and becoming part of the earth itself. These spirit ancestors were part human but also resembled animals and plants.

The Rainbow Serpent, for example, was an ancestral spirit in the form of a huge snake who, when it rose to the earth's surface, slithered throughout the world creating rivers and valleys with its long, massive, winding body. There was Bila, the sun woman whose fire lit the world, who was destroyed by two lizardlike men called Kudna and Muda. Frightened by the sudden darkness they'd brought about, Kudna and Muda began throwing boomerangs into the sky in all directions, trying to bring back the light. Finally Kudna threw his boomerang into the eastern sky and a brilliant ball of fire appeared, rolling its slow way across the sky until it disappeared again beyond the western horizon, and day and night were created. And when a plant or animal broke one of the very loving, humane laws of the ancestral spirits, it was punished by being turned to stone, and those stones became the earth's mountains.

Again, while my own ideas about the Creation differ from those of the Aborigines, I find their stories of Dreamtime and their continuing reverence for dreams, nature, and their spiritual ancestry to be gorgeous and inspiring. I love that their beliefs have survived for perhaps a hundred thousand years without the benefit of a written language. I love that their spiritual connections to animals and the earth make them among the most environmentally respectful cultures on this planet. And I love that when they go on wanderings through the sacred landscape created by their spirit ancestors during Dreamtime, they call those wanderings Dream Journeys, to reconnect themselves to eternity, "the time before time began."

To keep their spirits aligned with those of their ancestors, many Aboriginal tribes honor a "dreamtime" ritual of their own, taught to them from childhood, in which they set their body clocks to wake up, shortly before sunrise, and then fall briefly back to sleep before they're awake for the day. They know that during that brief "second sleep" they're most likely to have vivid dreams that they'll remember most easily, and that "dreamtime" is not only an homage to the Dreamtime that created them but also an essential form of nourishment for their own spiritual survival.

Because it's simply true that dreams are essential for our mental, emotional, and spiritual survival, because sophisticated sleep researchers completely support the concept of "dreamtime," whether they're familiar with the Aboriginal culture or not, and because I can personally attest to the fact that it works, I promise you'll be amazed at the added clarity of your dream journal if you'll create your own "dreamtime." All it takes is setting your alarm clock to go off fifteen minutes before you need to wake up and then letting yourself doze for that added quarter of an hour. You'll experience REM sleep without going into that Non–REM sleep in which memories of so many dreams become frayed or lost. After a week or two of this discipline, your subconscious mind will learn that it can count on those fifteen minutes every day to communicate clearly, and thanks to making your "dreamtime" a treasured, valuable part of your sleep cycle, you'll never say again that you can't remember your dreams.

And then there are those other night journeys that so often pass for dreams but are really so much more than that, journeys that, even beyond dreams, prove the power, the infinite potential, and the timeless eternity of our spirits, journeys that every single one of us take several times a week whether we choose to believe it or not.

Chapter Six

✳

WHEN THEY'RE MORE THAN DREAMS: INFORMATION AND PROBLEM-SOLVING DURING SLEEP

*I*t's happened to all of us. We fall asleep worried about a problem and wake up with the solution. Or we wake up knowing something we didn't know or couldn't have known when we fell asleep the night before. So where does that new information come from? And how do we so effortlessly solve a problem in our sleep that we've spent hours or days or weeks wrestling with during our waking hours? Why does the advice to "sleep on it" really seem to work?

Close-minded skeptics and other "experts" offer up a variety of explanations. The "information" we think we receive while we sleep is actually a series of lucky guesses and/or coincidences. Or, one of my particular favorites, when we hear this information while we're awake, we simply experience false memories of having dreamed about it, that's all. As for problem-solving, these experts assure us that we really had the solutions all along, it's just that during sleep we're relaxed enough to let our confusion unravel and the solutions clearly reveal themselves.

If those explanations make sense to you, congratulations. If they made sense to me, if I didn't know with absolute certainty that this world and our subconscious minds aren't that random and easily fooled, and that there are greater, higher sources at work around us all the time just waiting for us to give them access, I wouldn't waste another moment of your time with this chapter, or this book for that matter. But between my need for logic and my soul-deep commitment to those things in life that I know to be the truth, I'm compelled to share my explanations (and the explanations of countless others before me) and leave it to you to decide where your common sense and God's involvement in our lives finally take you.

Did you know that Mozart received many of his most glorious compositions through dreams? Or that the theory of relativity came to Albert Einstein in a dream? Dreams inspired everything from Elias Howe's invention of the sewing machine to Thomas Edison's invention of the light bulb. Dmitry Mendeleyev, a brilliant nineteenth-century chemist and physicist, re-created the Periodic Table during his waking hours after it appeared to him in its entirety in a dream. Robert Lewis Stevenson struggled for days over a short story that refused to take shape until a dream transformed it into the classic "Dr. Jekyll and Mr. Hyde." And if Dr. Jonas Salk had chosen to ignore his dreams, the polio vaccine might never have existed. Lucky guesses? Coincidences? Preconceived solutions that just happened to reveal themselves during the relaxation of sleep? The words "fat chance" leap to mind.

Fortunately, it's not just extraordinary people like those who are given information and answers during the night. For the last thirty or forty years I've been hearing story after story, and had the firsthand wonder myself, in which we "ordinary people" have awakened with more knowledge than we had when we dozed off. My idea of logic dictates that if it didn't come from *inside* of us, it came from *outside* of us, and each one of us is gifted enough, whether we're conscious of it or not, to retrieve that knowledge and put it to use.

There are two ways we receive information and solutions to our problems while we sleep: through telepathy and through astral travel. Both are marvelously helpful God-given blessings, and both come as naturally to us as breathing once our noisy, skeptical, chronically interfering conscious minds are at rest.

Telepathy

"Last night I had a dream that a friend of mine had killed himself and I was attending his funeral. A few hours later a phone call woke me up. It was that same friend's brother, telling me that my friend had indeed killed himself in 'real life.' My friend had never even mentioned the idea of suicide. How could I possibly have known a thing like that before the call came?"—Ellie

"Through the years I've had occasional dreams of an old boyfriend I hadn't seen or heard from since high school. In one dream I was attending his wedding. In another, a few years later, I dreamed that he and his wife had a new baby boy. A year after that I dreamed that he was getting divorced and looking for me. Through a chance encounter with his sister, I discovered that in every case, my dreams about him were 100 percent accurate, right down to their timing and everything."—T.R.

"Two nights ago I had a vivid dream about terrorists hiding out in New Orleans. I asked my Guides and Angels to validate my dream, so that I'll know it's not simply a reaction to these tense and frightening times. Each time I asked for confirmation, I've been given another reference to New Orleans, and some of the signs have been placed in the exact physical location I asked them to be. Because this vision is so clear and persistent, I'd hate to think I'd been given some insight that might be helpful and did nothing about it. At the same time, though, I can't imagine that the authorities would take me seriously. I'm hoping that by writing to you I'll feel as if I've told someone who won't think I'm nuts and who will know what to do with this 'information' if it turns out to be real."—L.M.

These "dreams" are wonderful examples of telepathy, which is simply the direct passing of information, knowledge, or feelings from one person or entity to another without using any of the five "usual" senses of sight, hearing, touch, taste, or smell. It's instantaneous, silent transference from any subconscious "sender" to any subconscious "receiver," either with or without either of them being aware of it or deliberate about it at the time it happens. Because telepathic information is often meant to have an impact on the receiver and is sometimes even meant to be acted upon, the conscious mind is usually let in on it sooner or later.

In Ellie's "dream" about her friend taking his own life, his subconscious—in this case, his spirit as it left his body—said good-bye to hers on his way Home (some suicides do make it to The Other Side, regardless of what you might have been taught). Sleep allowed her subconscious mind to be completely available to his message, and suddenly, with no cues from any of her five senses, she "knew without knowing" that he was gone.

T.R. clearly kept an unintentional telepathic connection with her old boyfriend long after the two of them physically separated. Someday she'll find out whether or not he was deliberately "sending" to her, and whether or not he was keeping the same telepathic "tabs" on her. Frankly, it doesn't really matter. Her successfully receiving the information and being able to verify it later is enough of an accomplishment.

As for L.M., I don't just *think* she's not crazy, I *know* she's not. She has received valid telepathic information about terrorists in New Orleans, and I appreciate her being conscientious enough to speak up about it. The fact is, there are several small terrorist cells throughout the United States, including New Orleans and New Jersey. While she and many others are getting these same telepathic messages, our various intelligence, investigative, and law enforcement agencies are doing some of the most brilliant, focused, and cooperative work in their respective histories. I feel safe in assuring L.M. to "let go and let God" and watch things unfold, because the information she's been given will be validated.

L.M.'s experience demonstrates beautifully that telepathy isn't limited to communication from one person to another, or from one "spirit" to another. It can be transmitted from any energy source (a city, for example, or a country, or any united consciousness) to any other energy source or sources (a person or any number of people, whether they know each other or not).

One of my favorite documented and fairly well-known stories of telepathy during sleep involved a man named Victor Samson, who was a news editor for the *Boston Globe*. One night he did a little too much celebrating after work at a nearby bar and decided that instead of going all the way home, he'd go back to his office and sleep there.

Passed out on his office sofa, Mr. Samson had a horrifying "dream" about a devastating volcanic eruption on an island that in his dream he knew as "Pele." Molten lava poured from the mountaintop, destroying all the villages in its fiery path and the thousands of helpless people who inhabited them. Deeply shaken by what he saw in his dream, he grabbed the closest piece of paper—a reporter's work sheet—the instant he woke up and wrote down every detail he could remember. Then, still shaken and more than a little hungover, he decided to head on home for a few more hours of sleep before he was due back at work again.

Very early the next morning, the *Globe*'s publisher happened by Mr. Samson's desk, noticed the work sheet, picked it up, and read the amazing story of this small island and those thousands of people decimated by a violently erupting volcano. Not having the slightest idea that the story was actually nothing but Mr. Samson's dream, the publisher breathlessly printed it and then sent it out on wire services throughout the country.

Not until Mr. Samson arrived at the office later that day did the publisher discover that the story he'd recorded for all of the city and America in general to see was nothing more than an alcohol-induced dream. And not until weeks later did a fleet of ships arrive in Boston harbor with the news that on the Indonesian island of Krakatau, an island the natives called Pele, a volcanic explosion had killed almost forty thousand people, within the same hour Mr. Samson had his dream.

It was August in the year 1883, you see, and news traveled slowly back then. Coincidence? Lucky guess? False memory after the fact? Please.

There are those who believe that some of us are "senders" and some of us are "receivers" when it comes to telepathy. An oversimplified yardstick is that if you find yourself thinking of someone and they call shortly afterward, you're probably a "sender," while if you tend to know who's calling before you pick up a ringing phone, you're probably a "receiver." I don't happen to think any of us needs to be categorized or limited to being one or the other. We come here from The Other Side, our spirits brilliantly gifted, wise, experienced, and eternal, and the ability to communicate telepathically through our spirit minds, which we use as a matter of course at

Home, extends to both sending and receiving. It's only when our conscious minds get involved that we start making a big, mystical, magical "paranormal" deal out of one of our most common, useful, innate God-given talents.

Astral Travel

And speaking of one of our most common, useful, innate God-given talents, there are few that come more naturally, or that we practice more often during sleep, than astral travel, which is simply our spirits taking a break from the confines of these limited, cumbersome, gravity-challenged bodies they're housed in and traveling to whomever or wherever we want. Like telepathy, astral travel isn't some eerie, esoteric New Age-y concept that you can only believe in or accomplish if you're too nuts to be let loose in the neighborhood. (I'm sixty-six years old and have devoted my entire life to subjects like this one, by the way, so imagine how much patience I have with the term "*New* Age.") It was astral travel that brought us here from The Other Side, when our spirits entered their chosen bodies, and it's astral travel that will take us Home again. We're born knowing how to astrally travel, we routinely travel astrally while we sleep (an average of two or three times a week, in fact), and it's astral travel that lies at the core of some of our most vivid and memorable "dreams."

Pam, for example, writes, "My dad and one of my brothers died in a car accident. I saw the accident in a very colorful dream at the exact same time it happened. It was as if I was in the backseat of the car watching the whole horrible thing."

Pam's "dream" wasn't really a dream at all. Spiritually connected to both men as she was and still is, her spirit traveled to them the instant she sensed they were in trouble. She didn't have to imagine that she saw the accident as if she'd been in the backseat with them. She really was with them, in her spirit body, and I'm willing to bet that her father and brother will tell her someday when they come to visit her that they saw her there, if they haven't already. And by the way, when I say "the *instant* she sensed they were in trouble," I mean that very literally. It takes less time than the blink of an eye to travel astrally from one place to another, no matter how far away the destination is, so no place on this earth, on The Other Side, or anywhere in God's infinite creation is beyond our reach while we sleep.

I loved a story that was sent by a woman named Martha, that was kind of a combination of information, problem-solving, telepathy, and astral travel both from here and from Home:

"I was widowed eight months ago after a wonderful forty-two-year marriage. Nothing in this world means more to me than the eternity band my late husband gave me when we renewed our vows on our fortieth wedding anniversary, so I was really distraught when somehow my eternity band disappeared from its special place on my dresser where I always kept it. I tore the house apart looking for it. I checked every pocket of every article of clothing and every purse I own. I emptied the trash, I emptied the vacuum cleaner bag, I searched every square inch of my car and trunk, I even hired a plumber to see if maybe he could find it in the pipes. It broke my heart when I finally decided it was gone forever. And then, out of nowhere, in one week, I had four different dreams in which I ended up under the bed for the silliest reasons, including one where I was working on a TV show and it was my job to lie under the bed making sure the camera didn't come unplugged. It took a few days for it to dawn on me that maybe those dreams were trying to tell me something. My bed is too low for me to reach very far under it, so some friends came and helped me move it, and sure enough, in the middle of the thick carpet under my bed, there was my eternity band. I'll never understand how it got there, let alone how I was told through my dreams where to look for it."

I love everything about this story, and I appreciate Martha's rolling so many relevant subjects into one experience. First of all, it was her late husband who left her eternity band under the bed. He visits her—astrally travels to her—often and loves letting her know he's around by moving things like car keys, the remote control, a wallet, any number of objects that keep not being where she knows she put them. When she thinks about it, she'll realize that her ring wasn't the first item she "lost" and then found in some unlikely place, it was just by far the most important, and he certainly got her attention with it, didn't he? And it was during one of her many astral trips to meet with him while she slept (she met him on an old wooden dock at the lake where he proposed to her), which she mistook for wish dreams, that he telepathically (when she remembers the "dreams" she'll recall that the two of them somehow "spoke without speaking") gave her enough information to guide her to the location of the ring he knew she treasured. Good for her for paying attention and taking the hint seriously enough to check it out.

I received many astral travel/"dream" letters after the unspeakable tragedy of September 11, all of which had the same theme. One came from a woman named Teresa: "I had this dream on the terrible night of September 11. It seemed I was flying. It looked as if it was snowing, but it wasn't snow, it was thick ash and dust and embers. There were buildings all around and so much danger. People were scared, and I was trying to help. There were several of us doing the same thing. I can't tell you what we actually did, I just know that we were helping and it was very difficult. Someone told me to go get more help. I must have still been flying as I went somewhere to get the best help I could. The next thing I remember was coming back with help, and it was Jesus who came with me. It's the clearest of all my memories of the dream, and we helped so many people. Never in my life have I dreamed anything like that, and I'll always hold it dear to my heart."

And a sweet woman named L.R. wrote, "When I went to bed on September 11, the instant I closed my eyes, faces started coming toward me, especially those of a man and a woman. Then I got a 'wider shot' of the scene and saw a lot of people's spirits passing over. I looked back at the man and the woman because I wanted so much to see who they were. They were both smiling. They came closer, until I could see her in particular very clearly. I was still able to look past them at all those spirits crossing over, and from the giant clouds of smoke billowing up I knew I'd somehow traveled to the site of the World Trade Center. What I'll always remember is that while the smoke was rising up, the spirits were moving *across*, just like you say in your books. I have no idea why I had this dream, that felt a lot more like an actual event. And I certainly can't go around telling my friends about this without their thinking I'm either lying or crazy. But I felt as if I was supposed to somehow share what I saw in the hope of assuring those who lost loved ones on that horrible, horrible day that I'm an 'eyewitness' to countless souls going safely to the peace of Home. I know if I saw photos of the victims, I would recognize that sweet woman whose face and smile are still crystal clear to me. If only one person finds comfort in my experience, it will be worth the whole thing."

As I said, these two letters describing astral travel during sleep represent so many more like them that I'll always treasure. It's a clear and inspiring fact that on that awful night, and days and nights ever since, legions of spirits from all around the world and from The Other Side as well are in constant attendance to help every victim, every grieving loved one, every member of the fire departments and police departments and every volunteer and, indeed, every person on this earth whose heart has yet to completely heal from the Godless evil of those events. Believe me, the night air is thick with concerned spirits, astrally traveling wherever they feel they can help, and the vast majority of those compassionate travelers continue to wake up in the morning with perhaps only fleeting memories of their emotionally charged, busy "dreams."

The Truth About Astral Travel

There is no limit to the people and places we can see, and *do* see, during astral travel. We routinely meet loved ones, both living and departed, from this life and past lives, as well as dear friends we don't happen to have shared an incarnation with but are very close to back Home. We routinely travel the globe revisiting places we've loved, we routinely check up on people we miss or are worried about, and we routinely go to The Other Side, that place of places we're most Homesick for of all.

"I've had a couple of dreams where I met with old friends, both living and deceased," writes L.F. "One in particular concerned a college friend I'd heard was terminally ill with breast cancer. I couldn't think of a graceful way to find out what had happened to her, so I prayed to be led to her in a dream, and my prayer was answered. She and I met in an area that seemed arid and rocky. She was walking on a series of large rocks, almost playfully, and we enjoyed each other's company without verbal communication. The message I got was that she's okay and happy. Was she trying to communicate anything else? Should I share this dream with others who were close to her, or should I keep it to myself?"

L.F. should absolutely share this "dream," which of course was really an astral experience, with the people who were close to her friend, and definitely pass along the message she got, which was all her friend was trying to tell her—that she's alive, that she's happy, and that she's in the safe, blessed peace of Home.

And there's a wonderful reminder for all of us in L.F.'s reunion: if there's someone you want to see, someone either here on earth or on The Other Side, pray to meet with them while you sleep. If it doesn't happen the first night you pray for it, or the second, or the fifth or even the tenth, keep praying. What could be more worth a few minutes of your time as you settle into bed? Remember, the best way to assure getting what you want is to believe it's possible, and then ask God. There's never a moment when He's not listening and loving you with all His perfect, infinite heart.

A Few Facts About Astral Travel

I'm sure you're wondering how you can tell a dream from an astral experience, and the good news is, there are some easy ways to spot astral travel every time, to help clear up any confusion you might have.

Any time you dream that you're flying without the benefit of an airplane, it's not a dream, you're astrally traveling. Mark writes, "All my life I've had dreams of flying. Someone is there with me, like they're teaching me. I would just like to know if this is unusual." Sherry says, "Several times a week I dream that I'm above the earth, flying on my own, looking down at my old neighborhood where I grew up, or peering in the window of my husband's and my first apartment." And Sam writes, "I love the thrill of the flying dreams I have all the time. It makes me feel so free and kind of like I have special powers or something."

Those are just a few of dozens of letters I received from people whose astral travel during sleep includes the realization of flying. It's very common, so I hope those of you who experience it don't feel there's something strange or crazy about you. And Mark, by the way, that "someone" who's with you on your astral travels is your Spirit Guide, simply seeing to it that you accomplish what you hope to while you're outside of your body taking these spirit excursions.

As for the rest of us, please take it from me, we all routinely astrally travel when we sleep, but not all of us experience flying when we sleep. I can honestly say that while I have a very active out-of-body life at night, not once have I ever had a flying "dream." That doesn't mean those of us who don't experience flying take astral trips that are any more or any less significant than the trips of those who do, it only means that the travel itself manifests in different ways.

All astral travel "dreams" unfold in a logical sequence of events, just as waking experiences do, rather than in a haphazard jumble of images, people, and locations. This seems as good a time as any to share the story of one of my own astral trips, which happened, as so many of them do for all of us, just when I needed it. I was on an Alaskan cruise with my grandchildren Angelia and Willy, getting in some relaxing family time before Lindsay and I started work on our second book, *Life on The Other Side*. There's no doubt that the book was taking shape in the back of my mind, but the vast majority of my attention was on the children, the gorgeous views, and my lifelong disdain for hiking. The last thing I was expecting, in the midst of all that beauty and nonstop activity with the kids, was to experience one of the most disturbing nights I've ever spent in my life, which I can still remember in excruciating detail.

One minute I was peacefully dozing off in our ship's cabin. The next minute I was in a place I'd never seen or imagined before, a vast, gray, dimly lit emptiness, crowded with a silent, shuffling expanse of spirits, their joyless eyes cast downward so that none of them ever once looked at me, as if they were either too disillu-sioned to lift their heads or too lost and confused to care. The age range was from early adolescence to elderly, and the air was so thick with hopelessness that I literally found it hard to breathe.

I didn't have a clue where I was, but "somehow" (which usually means "telepathically" when it comes to astral travel), even though they never did speak a single word to me or to each other, I knew what kind of desperate trouble these poor people were in and the only way they could get themselves out of it. I started frantically racing around among them, putting my arms around each of them, one after another after another, and pleading, "You need to say you love God. Please, you can get out of this place and go Home if you'll just say you love God." My almost hysterical voice was the only sound there was. I was crying. They weren't. They had already cried all their tears before they got there.

Beyond this awful void I could make out a seemingly limitless entrance, opening into what I can only describe as the blackest, coldest, ugliest, most loveless, hopeless, joyless, Godless darkness my wildest imagination could possibly conceive of. It filled me with such dread that I turned away from it and became even more frantic about these tragic spirits around me, hugging and urgently begging them again to say they loved God, because I knew if they stayed turned away from Him like this, they would end up going into that vile darkness.

I knew what that darkness was. It was the Left Door, through which those who've turned away from God and embraced evil pass when their lifetimes end, only to horseshoe right back in utero for another incarnation. I'd heard about it from Francine and re-searched it for most of my life, but I'd certainly never glimpsed its entrance before, or experienced a fraction of the horror of it.

But the space I'd traveled to, with all those poor lost spirits shuffling silently around in such deep despair, was like nothing I'd ever heard of or imagined. Just from my short time there, I was in a deep depression for days. I would love to have been able to write this whole thing off as just a major world-class nightmare, but it was much too real and certainly much too sequential in the way the action in it progressed. I remember waking up in a cold sweat, sobbing, and immediately calling Lindsay to tell her something had happened while I slept that I knew we'd have to include in *Life on The Other Side*, I just wasn't quite sure what it was yet or what it meant.

Francine and an enormous amount of further research led me to discover that I'd been to a sort of anteroom to the Left Door called the Holding Place, where some desolate spirits go after death, riding the fence between God and Godlessness, not light, not dark, but gray and lost, torn between the Left Door and The Other Side and still able to go either way, depending on whether they finally turn toward God or away from Him. I've written about it at more length in *Life on The Other Side*, but in that book I only mentioned in brief passing the astral trip that got me there.

We astrally visit The Other Side several times a month, and the experience, unlike that particular one of mine, is invariably thrilling. M.R., for example, writes, "I was in a beautiful fluffy-looking tunnel with all kinds of golden shades of color. The tunnel seemed to have its own source of light, and I felt completely enveloped in its love. I emerged from the tunnel to hear singing like I have never heard before. It sounded like hundreds and hundreds of people, each one of them with a perfect voice, and the only way I can possibly describe it is to say the music sounded as clear and sparkling as crystal. I found a place beneath the stage to listen and had the joy of listening to this amazing choir singing about God. What I'd like to know is, where was I, and what was I listening to?"

M.R. took a simple, logically progressing trip Home, to listen to a concert by the Angels in a stunningly beautiful building called the Hall of Voices. It's a fascinating fact that Angels never speak, and only communicate with us and each other through telepathic thought. Their voices are strictly reserved for brilliant hymns to God, their Creator, which they joyfully perform on the holiest of holidays. We've all had the sacred honor of hearing the Angel choir in the Hall of Voices during our lives on The Other Side, and our spirits remember exactly when they occur, so how smart of M.R. to time that particular astral visit around such an unparalleled event. I know the musical gifts he has been bestowed with in this lifetime are very important to him, and that trip was just added affirmation and inspiration to help keep him focused on his God-given talents.

One important caution about astral travel to The Other Side: don't be too alarmed if you find yourself a little out of sorts if not downright melancholy for a few days after even the most euphoric trips to paradise. Gwen's experience is not uncommon: after a visit Home while she slept, she says, "I remember feeling very depressed and sad. I felt like crying. I also remember saying out loud, in a hushed tone, 'Please don't leave me.' As I finished saying that I opened my eyes, stared at my bedroom wall, and started to cry. My depression lasted for days, and I still feel haunted by the experience."

Every one of us is here because we chose to be, in our courageous insistence on continuing to learn and grow toward the greatest perfection our spirits can achieve. We came from the impossible beauty of Home, where we live among dearest friends, the saints, the Angels, and the messiahs in the constant, tangible presence of God's divine love, and we're Homesick from the moment we leave until the moment we get back. Usually our astral visits are exhilarating reminders of everyone and everything waiting for us at the end of this rough camping trip to earth we're all trudging through. But sometimes, particularly when we're struggling, those visits only make us miss our loved ones on The Other Side even more than usual and make the differences between here and there depressingly glaring. When that depression sets in, be patient with it, keep reminding yourself that all those loved ones in that sacred, perfect place will always be right there waiting for you and visiting you here as well, and don't lose faith that you're here for a purpose you're either consciously or subconsciously determined to accomplish before you head Home again.

Not all astral trips during sleep are prophetic, but all prophetic "dreams" are really astral trips. You might have noticed that in Chapter 3, on prophetic dreams, I said they all are always in color and always progress in a logical order, and the same thing is true about astral trips. That's because there's no such thing as a prophetic dream that doesn't involve astrally traveling to a very real building on The Other Side called the Hall of Records, where every past and present chart of every one of us on earth is housed. As I mentioned in that chapter, we all write painstakingly detailed charts before we come here for another incarnation, including the five Exit Points we've designed for ourselves ahead of time for when we're ready to head Home. During prophetic "dreams," we actually go to the Hall of Records and browse through those charts, which are *the only place that information physically exists.* If your prophetic "dreams" ever include memories of a room more vast than you can comprehend, with aisle after aisle after aisle of shelves full of scrolls, all housed in a gorgeous domed building with white marble columns, you're remembering your trip to the Hall of Records.

More often, though, we're likely to forget the astral trip itself, due to our higher priority of reading the charts themselves. Sometimes our choices of which charts to read seem almost random and a bit pointless, as a man named Greg described in a recent letter: "I often have dreams about people I've seen during the day. In my dreams, I become aware of their death, and without fail, I find out the next day that they've passed away. Obviously it's too late by then to warn them, so what's the point of having these dreams in the first place?"

It's a good question, Greg, although, again, remember that we're only given information in time to warn someone if we're meant to intervene in an event they've already charted for themselves. What's being clearly demonstrated to you while you sleep is your comfortable, easy access to the charts in the Hall of Records through astral travel. Try including in your prayers before you sleep a request that God guide you to the charts of those you might be able to help ahead of time, and spare you the futility of knowing things you can't do anything about.

"How do you know the difference between a dream that's a forewarning and one that is just your subconscious trying to work something out? I often have dreams in which everything proceeds very logically, like they're really happening, and they're in vivid color, and they're usually about my friends' health problems that they don't even know about. Am I supposed to warn them to get a checkup, or am I just worried about them?"—W.M.

By all means, W.M., strongly suggest to those friends you "dream" about with health problems that they get a checkup, and even offer any details your "dreams" give you. You've been astrally traveling to read their charts in the Hall of Records, precisely because you have been worried about them, and the tip-offs are the logical progression of the action and the fact that the "dreams" are in vivid color. (There's no color more vivid than that of The Other Side, by the way, so with any "dreams" you have in which the colors seem too rich and breathtaking to exist here on earth, you can rest assured they *are* too rich and breathtaking to exist here, and you've taken a trip Home instead.) If your friends choose to ignore your suggestions about seeing a doctor, that's their decision. But at least you've shared the information you were given from a highly reliable source, in good, loving conscience. The rest is up to them.

Any dream you're not only part of but actually view yourself in isn't a dream at all but an astral experience instead. Astral travel, by definition, is simply your spirit spending time "out of body." We've all heard of and read about people who, under anesthesia or when they're otherwise supposedly unconscious, have found themselves looking down at their own bodies from some elevated vantage point, watching, hearing, and remembering everything that's going on around them. The exact same thing occasionally happens during astral travel while we sleep. Never forget that our spirits are living, seeing, thinking, hearing, feeling beings, housed in these bodies for all the obvious practical reasons but hardly trapped in them. And sometimes, when our spirits take off on outings, they can't resist the novelty of sticking around to observe the bodies they're taking this break from. Unfortunately, it's not always recalled as a pleasant experience.

"In this dream I could see myself sleeping, facing the bedroom door. It was as if I was floating above my body, and I could see everything. I heard a knock on the bedroom door. It was death. It had no face, just darkness. It wore a black cloak and held a book under its arm. I knew it was death, and I also knew that I had to tell it to go away. I remember how scared I was. I commanded it to 'go away, in the name of God,' over and over again, and it left. When I woke up I was sitting upright in bed and saying, 'Go away, in the name of God.' I was sweating, and scared. I turned on the lights and did not go back to sleep. I know that death should not be a scary thing. I guess that's why I'm still wondering what it meant."—D. W.

As we discussed in the chapter on release dreams, it's common to put dark or confusing parts of us into some kind of physical form in a dream to help our conscious minds deal with them. This dream is an excellent example, and there are actually a couple of things going on at the same time. The first is that it can be a bit of a shock to the system—or, to be more precise, to any part of the conscious mind that's aware of what's going on—to find yourself so undeniably looking down at yourself. Again, we take several astral trips a week while we sleep, but we don't consciously remember all of them, and we certainly don't always pause to look at our bodies as we take off. It's not that surprising for there to be a certain feeling of "yikes!" when even a tiny fraction of our conscious mind realizes what's happened and, for what it perceives to be the first time, experiences the separation of the spirit mind from the physical body. That "yikes!" can be very frightening, and that fear can easily take any number of equally frightening forms, including the dark, faceless image of death, as it did for D.W.

Second, don't forget that our spirits carry the memories of every moment of every lifetime we've ever had, both here and at Home. And since most of us have lived many, many lifetimes on earth, we've "died" many, many times, too. Our spirits know that when this earthly thing called "death" happens, we simply travel back to The Other Side, where we came from in the first place, leaving our bodies behind once and for all. I promise you, our spirits don't find "death" one bit sad or frightening, aware as they are that it's just a very familiar transition in a life that always was and always will be. It's only our conscious minds, tied as they are to these finite, earthbound vehicles called "bodies," that make any connection at all between death and fear. So when D.W. found her spirit separate from and floating above her body, her spirit mind calmly made the connection to death, and her conscious mind reacted with panic. As she said herself, she knows death *should not be* a scary thing. But we all have many perfectly rational "shoulds" that drop like flies when we're caught off guard as she was. And notice that invoking God's name chased away this terrifying form that she called death but was really nothing more than the embodiment of her conscious fear that if she had actually separated from her own body, she must be dying.

Another fascinating astral trip in which the "dreamer" found himself outside of him own body came from G.H.: "I saw myself as an Egyptian, in shadow form, with the familiar headdress with a single snake sticking out in front of it. A voice said, 'You are the Egyptian named Oberon, and you will be reincarnated.' Please help me understand this. I hope it doesn't mean that I will literally be reincarnated. I don't want to come back here."

G.H. has nothing to worry about as he is definitely on his last lifetime on earth, so there won't be any more reincarnating. What he saw was himself in an incarnation thousands of years ago, which frankly wasn't one of his happiest ones. As we'll discuss in far more detail in the next chapter, when I say we can astrally travel any-where we want while we sleep, that definitely includes the past. It's only here on earth that we've devised this measurement called "time." Beyond earth, and certainly in the spirit world of The Other Side, there is no "time," no such thing as "past" and "present," let alone thousands of years ago. Everything is *now*, as hard as it is for all of us to wrap our conscious minds around that concept. So G.H. shouldn't think of this glimpse of himself as an Egyptian named Oberon as a trip to another life. He can simply think of it as a snapshot of this life he's always lived and always will live, in one of its many stages and forms.

Another aspect of astral travel during sleep that can be discon-certing or even scary if you're not expecting it is described in this dream from Shannon: "I felt as if I woke up above my bed and could see everything in the room the way it's supposed to look, including myself, sound asleep. What upset me is that I could suddenly feel and hear a strong, almost roaring wind. I could literally feel my hair blowing back from my face. It really scared me, and I asked God for His help because the dream made me so frightened. The dream, and the sound and feel of the wind, suddenly stopped, and I woke up in the exactly same position I saw myself in. Obviously it was a nightmare, because I was so frightened, but what did it mean?"

Of course, it wasn't a nightmare, or a dream of any kind. It was simply Shannon experiencing astral travel *at its intermediate speed.* Again, it's something our spirits are all accustomed to; it can just create a feeling of panic when the awareness of it seeps into our consciousness while we sleep.

There are actually three speeds of astral travel once the spirit has separated from the body. The first speed is the most familiar to us and the least disorienting—our spirits move at the same pace our bodies do when they're walking. The intermediate speed is fast enough to create the illusion that we're standing still while everything around us is flying past us from front to back. (What Shannon experienced, in other words, wasn't a howling wind in her face, blowing her hair back. Instead, it was her moving forward at an intermediate pace.) At supernormal speed, our spirits can travel incomprehensible distances faster than our finite minds can even begin to imagine, to the point where we might remember our destinations and what we did while we visited, but we have no awareness at all of how we got there and how we got back.

An astral trip Alicia sent describes a typical supernormal speed experience: "I was flying over what appeared to be the landscape of a volcanic planet. Jutting up from the gaseous terrain were these massive, jagged monoliths. I was flying in and out of these spear-shaped mountains, although I had no sense of a specific direction or destination—that is, I wasn't trying to find something, or arrive anywhere in particular. At no point during the dream did I have any strong emotions, like the fear or apprehension you might expect to feel when navigating an alien terrain. I didn't feel as if I was part of the planet. I was definitely an alien there, which didn't bother me, and I was just exploring because it was there to explore. Is there any significance to this?"

It seems significant to me for a lot of reasons, although I'm not sure any of them are what Alicia had in mind when she asked the question. It's significant in how well it exemplifies supernormal speed in astral travel, because while Alicia wasn't aware of it, she was taking a tour of the planet Mercury, but you'll notice that she either didn't find the trips there and back worth mentioning or she had no memory of them. Even more, though, the experience is significant in how beautifully it expresses what curious, courageous, adventurous, and limitless beings our spirits are, no matter what physical and mental boundaries we might have chosen for ourselves this time around.

Alicia's letter and others like them bring up another fascinating aspect of astral travel that was frankly a relief to me when I first started reading about it and then actually saw it with my own eyes.

The Silver Cord

There is a very real cord, glistening silver and occasionally visible during astral travel, that connects our spirit entities to our bodies and nourishes us with God's divine love as surely as the umbilical cord nourishes us until we leave the womb. The silver cord is attached to women at the breastbone and to men slightly above and between the eyes, where the "third eye" would be. It's been known about and referred to for thousands of years. In fact, if you know the Bible well, you're familiar with Ecclesiastes 12:6–7, which reads, in part, "Before the silver cord is snapped . . . and the spirit returns to God who gave it." Until we "die" and return to The Other Side, the silver cord, limitless in its length, can't be broken, which means that no matter how far from our bodies our spirits might travel, we can and will always be "pulled back in," sometimes gently, and sometimes with such a jolt that we're jerked awake, thinking we've heard a "pop" of some kind but unable to figure out where it came from.

I mentioned being relieved when I knew beyond a doubt that the silver cord was real. There's a simple, slightly embarrassing reason for that: I don't especially enjoy astral travel. It's not so bad when I'm asleep and have little or no awareness of it. But as a waking diversion, or during meditation, it makes me feel too out of control, even though I know perfectly well that we can't just go floating off and find ourselves unable to get back to our bodies. When I first started hearing and reading about the silver cord, I thought it was a lovely concept, I just didn't pay much attention to it one way or another. Then one day during a Tantric meditation, I not only found myself looking down at my body from the ceiling, but also saw my own silver cord, glittering from my body's solar plexus to the etheric substance I had become. It was gorgeous, my one single sighting of it, and while I'll never take up deliberate astral travel as a hobby, I'm now an eyewitness to this "safety net" God's given us to maintain this attachment between our physical and spiritual beings.

The silver cord was studied in depth, and seen on any number of occasions, by a brilliant and very gifted expert in the field of astral travel named Sylvan Muldoon, whose books on the subject from the 1920s through the 1940s documented his countless out-of-body trips, which began when he was twelve years old. According to Muldoon's own eyewitness accounts, the thickness of the cord varies, depending on our spirit's proximity to the body it's temporarily vacated. When we're traveling close by, within fifteen feet or so, the cord is approximately the diameter of a silver dollar, with a sparkling aura that makes it appear even larger. But when we're as far away as the other side of the globe, The Other Side, or beyond the planets, the cord stretches, with no possibility at all of fraying or breaking, to become no thicker than a length of thread.

You might see your own silver cord, or the silver cord of a visiting entity, during your astral travels while you sleep, without realizing what you're looking at. That's exactly what happened to Peter, who wrote, "Last night I was awakened in the middle of the night to see a thick outline of a male figure standing in my room. Emitting from the top of his head was a brilliant light of white-and-gold-corded rope reaching up through the ceiling of my room. At that moment all I felt was this wonderment and curiosity. In the next moment it was gone. Then I turned on the light and thought to myself, What was that about? Was I dreaming this? It felt so real. Next, I hear a voice say, 'I'm from India.' That's it. Nothing more. Honestly, I've had bizarre dreams in my lifetime. But this is one I will not soon forget."

Peter had the pleasure of a visit from his Spirit Guide, an East Indian named Bahrat, and the added blessing of seeing his Spirit Guide's silver cord.

An argument could be made that Sylvan Muldoon and I, researchers to a fault, were aware of the phenomenon of the silver cord and kept our subliminal eyes out for it during astral experiences. But Peter saw it without having the first clue that such a thing even existed. So if you don't choose to take Sylvan Muldoon's or my word for it, by all means take Peter's.

And while astral travel during sleep is perfectly safe, because the conscious mind isn't involved and the spirit mind knows exactly what it's doing, please don't play with it during your waking hours without following the guidelines I've detailed in previous books, including *The Other Side and Back* and *Past Lives, Future Healing*. There's a story that's famous among astral researchers of a man who decided, without proper training, that he'd like to take an astral trip to the surface of the moon. Instead, he found himself hurtling through outer space, completely out of control. He panicked, his silver cord snapped him abruptly back into his body, and he was exhausted to the point of illness for days afterward.

Remote Viewing

There's a close relative of both telepathy and astral travel called remote viewing. Remote viewing is a skill as old as humankind, but it wasn't given its name and formally studied until the 1930s. In the 1970s the CIA and various branches of the military began studying its potential usefulness in such areas as intelligence and defense. In 1995 they disbanded the program and published an official report dismissing remote viewing as having no value to the United States government. If that report were accurate, objective, and unbiased, am I the only person who thinks it's odd that it took them twenty-five years of research to decide that remote viewing is useless? Even with nothing but casual observation, forget serious research, has it ever taken you twenty-five years to spot "useless" about anything when you see it? Me neither. Which leads me to believe that maybe the government, in the end, just couldn't bring itself to endorse something that even vaguely resembled paranormal phenomena. And so, on the subject of remote viewing, I guess we'll have to struggle along without them.

Remote viewing is a skill that allows us to perceive and describe details about a specific item or location that we're separated from by time, distance, or any physical barrier. It varies from telepathy in that there's no real "sender" whose thoughts we're tuning in to, and the information we receive is in the form of images, not words. And it varies from astral travel in that our subconscious can explore these "remote" places or things without ever leaving the body. But with practice at remote viewing, we can, for example, "walk" down a street in some city halfway around the world we've never been to before and accurately describe the weather there at that particular moment; "tune in" to a loved one's kitchen and see such details as what dishes are in the sink and exactly where any incidental objects are sitting on the counter right then; or even "view" the guests and the seating arrangement of a state dinner at the White House during the Lincoln administration.

The key element in genuine remote viewing is validation. Without validation, it's not remote viewing at all, it's just guesswork, logic, or a vivid imagination. If I claim to be remote viewing a friend's kitchen and describe two dinner plates and three coffee cups in the sink, and then call my friend and discover that there are no dinner plates and only one coffee cup in the sink, I've failed. If I go into breathtaking detail about a Lincoln state dinner at the White House, right down to what everyone was wearing, but historical archives prove an entirely different guest list or seating arrangement, I'm doing nothing but making noise. But if I can do a scan of your office, let's say, without your telepathically sending me any information at all, and tell you that there's a tipped-over paper clip dispenser on your desk beside a framed photo of your three children, all of whom are wearing red, and there's a Styrofoam container on your green blotter that has a half-eaten tuna sandwich and one slice of a dill pickle left in it, and you confirm that description after I've committed to it, that would be a successful remote viewing experience. That's why researchers, including me, are so drawn to this particular skill—it's either verifiable or it doesn't count. There's no gray area, no such thing as "close enough."

That's also why I'm a big believer in the importance of practicing remote viewing to help sharpen our accuracy when it comes to remembering and understanding our dreams. Mind you, some dreams actually involve remote viewing. Alicia's "dream" about exploring the planet Mercury could have been mistaken for remote viewing if it hadn't involved such a clear sensation of flying, which made it astral instead. But frankly, when it comes to the journeys we take while we sleep, I don't happen to think it's worthwhile, or even very interesting, to spend valuable time trying to distinguish between telepathy, astral travel, or remote viewing. For me, it's one of those "who cares?" distinctions.

However, as a form of "mental calisthenics," remote viewing is an easy, fascinating, and even relaxing way to help the conscious mind and the subconscious mind work together as a team, and to improve the communication between the two, since both are important participants in successful remote viewing. The subconscious mind does the actual viewing, but in order for it to be effective, the conscious mind has to tune out its usual "noise" on command and stay out of the way so that the subconscious mind can receive a clear "signal" from the object or location it's focusing on. And while the subconscious mind is doing its work, the conscious mind needs to be able to express what the subconscious mind is receiving, either verbally or through writing or sketching, and express it accurately, without interfering or trying to edit the information. A researcher named Ingo Swann, who was one of the leading experts on the subject of remote viewing in the 1960s and 1970s, wrote that developing this skill can "expand the parameters of our perceptions." He's exactly right, although when it comes to the world of sleep, I would add "and help our conscious and subconscious minds learn to cooperate with each other so that we can get the most possible value from our dreams and other sleep journeys."

Remote viewing is something we can practice every single day if we want, even if we only have a few spare moments when our conscious minds can take a nice safe break. During a shower or over the morning's first cup of coffee or in a quiet break between meetings at the office are good opportunities. On the other hand, practicing while driving, performing surgery, or let's say, trying out a new table saw could be dangerous or at the very least just plain stupid. As with any other exercise involving the mind, be responsible.

Wherever you are as you begin, I want you to take a few deep, rhythmic breaths, releasing negativity and self-doubt with every exhale. If you're sitting, place your hands on your thighs, palms upward, in a position to receive. If you're standing, take a moment to simply extend your hands in front of you with the palms facing upward, just a quick acknowledgment of your openness and will-ingness to be a receiver. Let a sense of quiet peace drape itself over you, soft, deep, and rich as a veil of velvet, shutting out the noise and confusion and distractions around you and letting the God Center inside you fill you with loving silence as your eyes close. Feel an easing, a loosening, a relaxing move slowly through your feet, your ankles, your calves, your knees and thighs, all through the pelvic area and on up through the whole trunk of your body. This divine ease, this God Center, moves into the shoulders, down through the upper arms, the lower arms, the hands, the fin-gertips, then up through the neck, around the mouth, the nose, the eyes, the forehead, every inhale deepening the relaxation, every exhale cleansing and releasing all stress and anxiety. Thank God for this beautiful moment of peace, this time, no matter how brief, that you've claimed just for yourself, in the infinite, perfect love of His embrace.

Without alerting anyone ahead of time, and without doing any reading or investigating of any kind, in this exquisite state of relax-ation, I want you to calmly select a target location in your mind that you want to explore. Don't choose a room in your own home, where your conscious memories could interfere, and don't choose a place that you have no way of validating later. Make it easy on yourself at first, somewhere familiar—a friend's car as they drive to work, for example.

Send your mind out from wherever you are, like a silver shaft of sparkling light, piercing the air, making a direct line, strong and straight, from you to your target. I want you to start with the big picture, a "wide shot" so to speak, of the car itself as it makes its way along the street or freeway or road, and begin asking yourself questions, ignoring what you think you know and instead just taking the first impressions your subconscious mind receives. Is the car in sunshine or shade? Is there traffic around it? If so, is it light or heavy? What color is the car in front of it, or the car behind it? Is your friend's car clean or dirty? Are there any dings or marks on it at all? Which windows are open and which are closed? Keep making note of every detail you can about the car and everything around it as you slowly "zoom in" on it, and with that same silver shaft of light connecting your mind to this car, enter it through the passenger window and start scanning the interior, keeping the questions coming.

Another way that remote viewing differs from telepathy is that the senses are very relevant and important. So as you begin looking around inside the car, in addition to asking questions about what the speedometer reads, whether the ashtray is open or closed, whether the visors are up or down, whether or not your friend is talking on the phone, whether or not there's a cup holder and what if anything is in it, what specific items might be lying on the seats and the floor of the car, what the interior temperature is set to, and whether or not there are any items on the dashboard or hanging from the rearview mirror, ask yourself sensory questions as well. What smells do you notice? Can you smell leather, or coffee, or perhaps a fast-food snack? Has someone smoked in the car? Is there a deodorizer of some kind that you can smell, or the distinctive odor of a recent trip to a car wash? And listen closely. Is the radio on? If so, is it tuned to the news, or music, or a talk show? If not, is your friend listening to a tape or a CD? If your friend is talking on the phone, see if you can make out a word or phrase, and stop to notice which hand the phone is in, or if the phone is hands-free. From inside the car, looking through the windshield, notice a few street signs along the way, or turns your friend takes—anything you can call your friend later and validate is worth noticing, and if you have paper and pencil handy, make notes or sketches as you go along, the more detailed the better.

It really is that simple an exercise, and it takes no longer than you want it to. Whatever you do, don't get discouraged if your accuracy leaves something to be desired at first. One or two "hits" is an accomplishment and a great starting point to work from, and remote viewing really is a skill you'll get better and better at the more you practice. If nothing else, again, any attention you devote to the connection between your conscious and subconscious minds and the clarity of their communication with each other is guaranteed to help you integrate your dreams into your waking life. This is a worthy goal under any circumstances, but I'm especially eager for you to become adept at it for the sake of all the loved ones, both here and at Home, who are visiting you and receiving visits from you while you sleep—and just waiting for you to fully appreciate them while you're awake—visits so real and so powerful that they're more than worthy of their own special chapter.

Chapter Seven

✳

ASTRAL VISITS:
THE MIRACLE OF REUNIONS
WHILE WE SLEEP

We now know that while we sleep there's no limit to what we can learn about ourselves, our world, and even the future, no limit to where we can travel, from the far reaches of the universe to the intimate closeness of The Other Side. But my own experiences and the sheer volume of "dream" letters I received convince me that there are few things we cherish more than the reunions we're blessed with in those lovely hours when our conscious minds are resting and our spirits, alive and thriving in our subconscious minds, are set free to touch those other spirits, other places, and other times they're yearning for. Skeptics call it wishful thinking. My soul knows better, and so does yours. That's not to say that every dream about a deceased loved one is an astral visit and nothing more, but by the time this chapter has ended you'll be able to easily tell the difference.

I want to stress something before we start. Many of you wake up with memories of time spent with people you've lost whom you miss terribly. Many others of you don't. Please believe me when I tell you that the difference isn't in the existence of those reunions, it's only in the ability to remember them. There's no question that we're at our most accessible for spirit visits while we're asleep. And we all pay and receive those visits, every single one of us, many times a week. So if you're one of those people who wake up unaware that some loving spirit was with you as you slept, don't feel left out as you read this chapter. Instead, just let it help fill in some blanks for you and explain why there are certain mornings when you open your eyes and feel a little more loved and at peace than usual for what seems to be no reason at all.

Visits and Messages from Loved Ones

"My close cousin Jim was killed in Cambodia in June, 1970," writes Bobby. "Even though all these years have gone by, I'm suddenly having frequent, pleasant dreams that are very realistic. Usually we're talking and walking along streams or on the beaches of Los Angeles. Nice dreams. There is nothing sad about them. I'm a healthy fifty-five years old, but sometimes I think that my time's almost up and Jim is just getting me used to the idea of crossing over. I wonder if this is a common occurrence for so many years to pass before a close friend or relative finally shows up."

The answer is yes, it's very common, and there's an explanation that might help a lot of readers, so I would like to thank Bobby for sharing this experience. His "dreams," of course, are actual visits between Jim's spirit and Bobby's, always near water, which they both love. Remember that on The Other Side, where Jim went instantly, there's no time, only a complete awareness and understanding of eternity. And in the context of eternity, "all these years" are as quick as the blink of an eye. Jim, like so many victims of trauma deaths, went immediately into Orientation when he arrived back Home, a common and very comforting process that helps spirits through the shock of their sudden departure from earth. I describe it at great length in my book *Life on The Other Side*, so I don't want to be repetitious and long-winded about it again here. But suffice it to say that he's very happy and healthy, as Bobby has seen for himself. As for his getting Bobby used to the idea of crossing over, he's just eager for him not to be one bit afraid of it, because *according to Jim's time*, i.e., eternity, he'll be going very soon. By our time on earth, though, Bobby is exactly right about how healthy he is, and he is going to stay that way for a very long time to come.

An astral visit sent by S.G. reads, "I dreamed that my late husband came to see me. He spoke to me. He's been gone for over ten years, but he told me he'd been in a coma that whole time. He looked very good and happy, and he gave me a hug."

Here again we have someone who's just come out of Orientation, who described it as being in a coma, and who S.G. had undoubtedly been wishing for visits from for ten years—an endless amount of time to her, but no time at all to her late husband. Orientation involves an enormous amount of sleep, rest, and relaxation, and again, it's such a normal way to help some newly arrived spirits become acclimated to being Home again. My Spirit Guide Francine describes it as being like helping deep-sea divers through a case of "the bends" when they surface too quickly. So if you've lost someone and are afraid you're never going to receive a visit because it's been too long, be patient. There's no such thing as "too long" in the spirit world. They'll come sooner or later, and all you have to do is be open to receiving them.

J. sent this fascinating experience. "In 1992 a very close friend—an ex-fiancé, actually—died. His name was Ronnie, and he was only twenty-five at the time. He never visited me until around January or February of 2000, just after my third child was born. I'd always thought about Ronnie over the years, but not nearly as intensely as I started thinking about him then. Suddenly he seemed to be everywhere. I missed him terribly, and he consumed my thoughts. And then one night while I was asleep I received a 'visit' from him. I was in an old house, on the second floor. I got this feeling in my stomach and looked out the window, and there he was, riding up to the house on his motorcycle. I ran outside, unable to believe it was really him. He held my hands and told me to stop crying for him—he's okay, and he has never left me. He took my face and said, 'Don't miss me anymore. I am coming back to you. We'll be together again.' I kept asking him how that was possible, and he kept repeating that he's back and we are together again. Then he kind of floated away. I was so confused when I woke up. And ever since that dream, I don't feel him around me anymore. I miss the memory of him, but I don't feel like there's any reason to miss *him*, and I don't hurt for him anymore. I want to know what he was telling me. He said he's coming back, but as who? How will I recognize him, when he's someone else?"

I think J. knows this, but Ronnie is already back. The reason J. doesn't miss him or hurt for him anymore is that she's with him all the time now, not just spiritually but physically as well. Ronnie is her son, her third-born child, and he couldn't bring himself to wait any longer to share the news with J. If you think we adults astrally travel a lot during sleep, we look like rank amateurs compared to babies, who have just arrived from The Other Side, find these silly bodies they're suddenly living in to be fairly boring and inconvenient, and spend almost as much time out of those bodies as they spend in them for their first several years on earth. And it shouldn't surprise J. to know that her baby's spirit, which is Ronnie, appeared in adult form. First of all, he wanted to be sure J. would recognize him. Second of all, never forget that inside those tiny preverbal infant bodies live spirits as eternal, ancient, experienced, and "mature" (such a relative term, let's face it) as we are. J. should watch her son as he grows and she'll see some of Ronnie's subtle mannerisms. She'll also see how especially protective her son will be of her, just as Ronnie was. I only caution J. to remember that while Ronnie's spirit has come back in her son's body, her son wants his own identity, and she'll be doing him a great disservice if she tries to re-create Ronnie in him. As many of my readers know, my beloved grandmother Ada came back to me in the form of my granddaughter Angelia. Same spirit, two separate people, with two separate charts, two separate purposes and life themes, and two separate and unique relationships with me, both of which I treasure beyond words and each in its own distinct way. So J. should enjoy the pleasure of Ronnie's presence, but she shouldn't shortchange her son or herself by inadvertently trying to encourage him to be a duplicate of a man he has no conscious memory of at all.

L.S. had a similar but much more difficult astral experience while she slept. "I was going into my third month of pregnancy when I had a dream that two figures were carrying my baby away with them. It seemed as if the three of them were following a beam of light away from me. I couldn't do anything but watch it happen, and I felt so helpless. I woke up shaken, and that dream still haunts me to this day. About a week after I had that dream, my coworkers asked me if I was feeling okay. I told them I felt great, like I wasn't even pregnant. Shortly after that I started spotting and went for an ultrasound. I found that my baby had died at about the same time I had that dream. I was heartbroken. Sylvia, I heard you say once on the Montel Williams show that some miscarriages try to come back. I was so happy to hear that! I gave birth to my son Daniel almost a year to the day of the miscarriage I saw in my dream. Is it the same spirit? And why would I see my child being taken away from me? It was a horrible thing to witness."

I'm so happy to tell L.S.—to *promise* her, in fact—that yes, her son Daniel is the same spirit who went Home a year earlier. That's not always the case with miscarriages, but it's absolutely the case with L.S.'s. She needs to understand what it was she saw in her "dream." That first child wasn't a healthy, thriving entity who was "taken away" from her against his will. Through no fault of hers or anyone else's, he would never have made it to full term, because of countless physiological problems, and he chose to go early in the pregnancy. What you saw were his two Angels, there to take his spirit Home lovingly after he passed away in utero. It's not a sad memory for Daniel, so when he's learning to talk, L.S. should ask him if he remembers his Angels. I'm guessing he'll say yes, and mean it.

Another L. shared an experience that I know a lot of you are struggling with, and I hope this helps all of you put the issue to rest once and for all: "My mother died of a self-inflicted gunshot wound in August 2001. She suffered for over seventeen years with a chronic medical condition that caused her constant pain that was not relieved by medications. She was unable to do many activities she'd previously enjoyed and hated being unable to walk without assistance. This situation made her quite bitter and difficult to be around. Two months after her death, I had a very vivid dream of being with her in a large store that had long aisles, like a huge home improvement store. My aunt and uncle were with us. My mother was walking very fast through the aisles, and we couldn't keep up with her. She was laughing and joking and seemed quite free.

"Suddenly my mother decided that she was finished shopping in that store and walked through huge automatic glass doors. I couldn't quite get to her and was yelling for her to stop and wait for me. As I was running to get through the automatic doors, I suddenly noticed that my aunt and uncle were collapsing. I was torn between following my mother and trying to catch my aunt and uncle before they hit the floor. I was angry because I knew they'd cost me my chance to follow my mother. As I looked up from this chaos, I saw my mother standing on the other side of the glass door and she just smiled at me, waved and turned away to leave.

"I'm really hoping that this was my mother's way of letting me know that even though she committed suicide, she found her way to The Other Side and is finally relieved of pain. I feel torn between dismissing the dream as just 'wishful thinking' and other times finding comfort in the hope that my mother was sending me a message that she's happy now and knows that I forgive her."

Let's get something straight about suicide. It's *never* written into our charts as an Exit Point, which means it's *never* part of the contract we make with God before we come here. I pray that none of you ever let it enter your mind as an option without immediately thinking, Don't! And if it does, please, please, *please* talk to a qualified professional—a doctor, a counselor, a therapist, someone who's trained to help you—and give yourself every possible opportunity to regain your bearings and get reliable relief from the depression that invariably creates thoughts of suicide in the first place. Suicides that are motivated by revenge, or self-pity, or cowardice, or laziness, or selfishness go into that horror of the Left Door I described earlier and come right back in utero again, without so much as a glimpse of the divine peace of The Other Side.

However, there are suicides, as in L.'s mother's case, that are the result of mental illness (and L., your mother's endless unsuccessful battle with her physical problems did lead to devastating mental illness, as I'm sure you know), severe chemical imbalances, and a handful of other causes that are far beyond that person's control, and I promise you those spirits are embraced by God's love on The Other Side as surely and completely as the rest of us will be.

As for L.'s question about whether or not this was "real" or just wishful thinking, I want you to notice how logical—downright clever, in fact—the sequence of events in L.'s "dream" was. That's a tip-off that this was an actual astral experience, designed by her mother, with her aunt and uncle participating to make a point. It's wonderful that L. not only got to see her mother laughing and happy and moving around freely and painlessly, but also that her mother chose a brilliant place for all of them to be together. For one thing, home improvement stores tend to be populated for the most part by the physically fit and aren't much fun at all for anyone who's exhausted from severe chronic pain. And then there's the fact that, as we'll discuss in Chapter 9, "Archetypes," a house or home is very often symbolic of our bodies, so a "home improve-ment" store is loaded with messages of the strength, health, and physical and emotional well-being L.'s mother is enjoying on The Other Side.

I know it was frustrating for L. to have to tend to her aunt and uncle rather than catch up to her mother, but again, what a clever way for her mother to tell her that it's not time yet for L. to follow her. She's fine. She's happy. She doesn't need L. to take care of her anymore. She assured her of that with her final smile and wave, as L. stayed behind to focus on earthly concerns, which is what she is meant to do and where she's meant to be. As for her mother knowing that L. has forgiven her, L.'s mother never doubted it for a moment.

E.S. also had a very sweet astral experience that seems to hap-pen to a lot of us, and maybe by clearing up her confusion about it, I can clear up some of yours as well: "Five years ago, I dated a guy whose brother had died in a car accident the year before. The entire family talked often about Tony, the deceased brother/son, and I often found myself wishing I could have met him. And then one night I had a dream that haunts me to this day. I was aware of the darkness of my immediate surroundings as an entrance of some kind, emitting a beautiful bright light, opened some distance in front of me. It was as though I was standing outside of a tunnel, although I wasn't conscious of seeing an actual tunnel at the time. Tony stood right in front of the entrance, framed by the gorgeous light so I could only see his silhouette, although I knew with absolute certainty that it was him. He held out his hand to me, palm up, and spoke my name. It was as if he'd spoken directly into my ear, because it woke me up at that instant. To this day I want to believe that Tony contacted me, although I can't imagine why he would have chosen me."

Tony did contact E.S., and she was a perfect choice. He knew she'd welcome him, he knew she'd be open to the experience of a visitation, and above all, he knew that, unlike some of his family members and closest friends, she wasn't too blocked with grief to be aware of his presence. If she hasn't done it already, E.S. should tell those who miss him so terribly, especially his mother, about her visit from him. He wants them to know he's alive and well at Home, and he chose exactly the right person to convey the message with the respect and credibility it deserves.

And it's true for all of us that our grief, our guilt, our anger, our fear, and those other powerful emotions that so often accompany the "death" of a loved one can interfere with our ability to clearly receive their spirits and the messages they're trying to give us—which almost always boil down to nothing more and nothing less than the thrilling news that they're not dead at all, they're thriving on The Other Side and watching over us. Our own pain, understandable and normal as it is, often puts us in a daze that's difficult to penetrate even for people here on the same plane we're on. So imagine what a tough time the spirit world can have getting through to us until our pain subsides.

It's because of our conflicted emotions surrounding loss that we sometimes manage to blend astral visits into other kinds of dreams, with results that can be very confusing and upsetting if we don't understand what's happening.

Astral Visits within Dreams

I don't want it to sound more complicated than it is to work a very real astral visit into a dream we're having at the same time. It's really no different than when we work a very real ringing phone or some other earthly sound into our dreams, and I think we've all had that experience at some time or other. I've even picked up a ringing phone while I was sound asleep and started chattering away in the midst of some conversation I'm dreaming about, so the blurring of reality and the dream world is really perfectly common and is all that's happening when astral visits and dreams seem to be one and the same.

"My husband passed away a year and a half ago in an ATV accident," L.Y. writes. "Since that time I've experienced two recurring dreams that are really upsetting me, and I hope you can help me understand them. In one, I'm standing talking to some people when I'm touched from behind. My late husband puts his arms around me, but it startles me, and as a reflex I push him away. Then I realize who it is, and I scream for him to come back, but he just keeps walking away without ever turning around again. In the other dream, he's sitting in the middle of a group of friends. I'm struggling to get through the crowd to see him, but when I finally get there he's gone. Everyone is walking away laughing and talking about how good he looks and how happy he is, and I just stand there screaming his name. In both dreams I only see the back of him or hear his voice. Never do I see his face. I hope that someday I'll be able to talk to him. He left so suddenly. One morning he just walked out of the house and never returned."

I couldn't have given you more perfect examples of astral visits combined with release dreams if I'd written them myself. What's really going on here is that L.Y.'s late husband is visiting her while she sleeps, and she's absolutely seeing him, which is thrilling and not something everyone's able to do, so that part is cause for celebration. What's preventing these from being happy encounters is the fact that L.Y. is still trying to recover from the shock of the sheer suddenness of losing him, still trying to come to terms with the tragic illogic of waking up with her husband one ordinary morning and going to sleep that same night widowed and alone, unable to remember what "ordinary" even felt like. And if you look at the scenarios of both of these dreams from an emotional point of view, they represent exactly what the circumstances of that last morning felt like to her—he left, he never came back, and she was powerless to do anything to change it. Working him into release dreams that express how abandoned she feels is so understandable, and a natural part of grieving when you lose someone with no way in the world of seeing it coming and being able to prepare for it.

L.Y.'s husband will keep coming while she is asleep and while she is awake, at all hours of the day and night, and as her shock and depression continue to fade, even though it's taking longer than she'd like, she'll find that the release-dream part of his visits will fade. She'll see him walk toward her, not away from her, and she'll hold him, and she'll wake up knowing they've been together while she slept. Until then, she'll need to talk to him. Tell him all about what she's feeling and how she misses him and loves him and even how angry she is at him for leaving her if she wants. He'll hear her and understand, and it will help her feel less separate from him, which will lead to many gorgeous visits with him as time goes on.

Mary had a similar experience. "My husband has been on The Other Side for two years. I always talk to him and ask him to come to me in dreams. It's rare that he does this, but when it happens he never seems to acknowledge that I'm there. I get so sad that we don't talk to each other on these rare visits. Is there a reason for that? I want to know for myself that he's happy, and I have so much to tell him."

It must be exciting for Mary that she is able to see her husband when he comes to her while she sleeps. And the fact that he shows up when she asks him to, no matter how rarely, tells her that he can hear her. She can tell him all those things she wants to. He'll hear that, too, and there will be lots of visits in the future where he assures her of that himself, when her healing is farther along. For now, Mary can take heart in knowing he comes and that she can actually see him, and rest assured that her perception that he's ignoring her is just her natural release-dream way of working through her grief over losing him, which can so often feel like a form of abandonment and even rejection. As with L.Y., the more Mary embraces the reality that her husband is not gone at all, he's right there, the more joyful her reunions will be.

An experience from D.L. has a similar theme with a slight variation. "Both of my parents have passed. I have very vivid dreams. What bothers me is that when I dream of my mother, she is never smiling and doesn't talk. But when I dream of my dad he makes me laugh and is full of life. I don't know why my mother never seems to be happy with me, or for herself. She always talked of being happy when she got to heaven. Why isn't she?"

She is, D.L. The unhappiness you're seeing in your mother is actually yours, not hers, and it comes from your fear that she hasn't found the happiness at Home that so often seemed to be beyond her grasp throughout this particular lifetime. In this case you're working your parents' visits into release dreams that reflect the unresolved, and quite complicated, relationship problems you've had with your mother throughout your life, in contrast to the uncomplicated and fairly easygoing bond between you and your father. I know it's easier said than done, but I hope you'll let your mother, and yourself even more, off the hook for the conflicts that went on between you. They were inevitable, considering the differences in your personalities, not to mention the similarities, which sometimes were even harder for the two of you to deal with. Let it go. She has. And when you do, when you've forgiven yourself and her and started focusing on the real bottom line of how much love there was between you, hidden under all that mutual stubbornness, you'll be pleasantly surprised to discover that your visits from her are every bit as happy and lighthearted as those lovely visits from your father.

I'm sure you're all wondering at this point how you can reliably know that astral visits from deceased loved ones who seem unhappy or displeased or dismissive or resentful are just release dreams, and not a reflection of how they're really feeling. The answer is simple, and you don't have to be psychic, just logical. The fact is, and please always remember this, all negative emotions are human and earthly. We come here to feel them, confront them, and do our best to overcome them. But *they don't exist in the spirit world*. The Other Side is bliss, perfect love in the immediate presence of God, the Angels, the Messiahs, our soul mates, and countless magnificent kindred spirits we've always known and always will know, throughout the timelessness God has given us. Unhappiness at Home, or from anyone visiting from Home, is an impossibility. So rest assured that anytime you're visited by a spirit who's offering anything less than complete and unconditional love, joy, and peace, that spirit has simply become part of a portrayal of your own unre-solved emotional pain. As with all release dreams, you can use this information to clarify where the pain is coming from and what you need to do about it, and no one will be happier for you than those dear spirits who are surrounding you at the very moment you're reading this, who'll wait as long as it takes for you to look back at them while you sleep with the same pure adoration with which they're looking at you.

Too Good to Be True

It's fascinating and a bit sad to me how reluctant we are to be-lieve good news. No matter how obvious it is, or how simple, we almost seem programmed to be skeptical when something good happens and immediately start thinking, What's the catch? or I probably just imagined that. So when the best news of all comes along, when we discover that a "deceased" loved one isn't "de-ceased" at all, and that in fact they're very much around, loving us and watching over us, we seem almost determined to believe any-thing *but* the truth. I've asked this question a million times in my life, and I'll probably keep right on asking it: If we accept that the spirit survives the death of the body, why wouldn't we accept that those spirits can interact with us? Spirits are powerful enough to overcome death, but they're not powerful enough to come to us and say hi? Does that make sense to you? It doesn't make sense to me either. When it comes to the spirit world, what in the world is the "downside" to believing?

I can hear you pointing out that you've been tricked before, and that some things on earth really are just plain too good to be true. You're not wrong. Fortunately, "too good to be true" doesn't apply to the spirit world. How can I be sure? Well, I've seen and heard proof with my own eyes and ears for about sixty-six years now, and what I haven't personally experienced, fifty years' worth of clients, friends, and viewers have. But you don't have to take my word for it, or even theirs. Instead, remember something you already know yourself if you have any spiritual beliefs at all, something we've seen over and over again in this book alone—when spirits transcend earth, with all its cruel inconsistencies and imperfections, they also transcend our nonsense and our negativity and our laws and our physics and our limitations. So the bottom line is, on earth if something sounds too good to be true, it probably is. In the spirit world of The Other Side, from which spirits travel to visit us, there simply is no such thing.

"Shortly after my dad passed away," writes G.B., "I had a very vivid dream of him standing next to my bed. He very gently touched my right cheek and I immediately awoke. I could feel his presence and still feel his touch on my face. Was he really there reaching out to me, or was it just a dream? I have been wondering about this for eighteen years and would be so grateful for an answer."

You see what I mean? G.B. has spent eighteen years wondering, and afraid to believe, instead of celebrating this simple, beautiful visitation from her father and taking heart in the proof it offered that he's very much alive, and so real that she acknowledges herself that, even wide awake, she can feel his touch on her face. I'm really glad G.B. asked about this, and there's no such thing as a "stupid" question, especially on this subject. I am not criticizing her reluctance. I received dozens of letters similar to hers, so she is certainly not alone in wondering.

For example, here's a letter from K. that I had to read several times, thinking maybe I missed something: "I had a dream about my dad after he passed away on December 6th of 2001. He had a heart attack, I took him to the hospital and he didn't make it. In the dream I was telling him how sorry I was and how I felt like maybe it was my fault. But he said everything was okay. I really don't know what that meant."

I am sorry to be so blunt here, but what part of "everything is okay" don't you understand, K.? Your dad is happy and healthy and was assuring you that there's nothing for you to be sorry for, you did exactly what you should have done when you took him to the hospital. I say this to K. and to everyone (including myself, since I occasionally have trouble remembering this, too, in my conversations with my Spirit Guide Francine): Unlike us here on earth, ten times out of ten spirits say what they mean and mean what they say. Nothing more, nothing less. That much simplicity can throw us when we're not accustomed to it, but it's a refreshing break from all the guesswork we go through in conversations with other humans, don't you think?

Louise received a message in a visit from her grandfather that was equally simple, although I can understand why it might have seemed a little abrupt. "In August of 1999 my grandfather passed on," she says. "We were very close, and shortly after he passed away, on that same night, I had a very vivid dream. I was walking down the hall of the hospital he was in, and when I entered his room he was standing by his bedside removing the tubes that had helped him breathe. He looked at me and said, 'I am not going to worry about you anymore.' It felt so real."

It was real and I hope Louise didn't think her grandfather meant that his "death" ended his caring about her. Louise knows that her grandfather hated knowing how sad she was because of him in his last days and hated knowing how much she was going to miss him. But the glorious fact is, the moment our spirits reach The Other Side they regain all the wisdom and knowledge and awareness of eternity that we lose sight of here on earth. As a result, they don't spend another instant worrying about us, because they know there's nothing to worry about. We'll all be together again, in no time as far as they're concerned, and we'll literally be living "happily ever after." Tell me, if you knew that with the spirit world's absolute certainty, how much time would *you* spend worrying? By telling Louise he wasn't going to worry about her anymore, her grandfather was telling her he was Home safe and sound and will be with her, watching over her, from now on.

A.V. sent a variation on a spirit's visit that I don't run across very often. She was clearly disturbed by it, as any of you might be if you had the same experience without enough information to appreciate what was happening. "I've been having dreams about my maternal grandmother, but they're not always comforting. They're usually in a dark place, and she tends to ignore me. She passed away twenty-one years ago, both in the dream and in real life, and in the dream she said she was coming back for another lifetime, although I don't remember either one of us saying a word to each other. I don't understand why my dreams about her aren't light and happy like they used to be."

I can tell A.V. exactly why, and it's really interesting, but actually, her grandmother already told A.V. herself. Her spirit is so strong, as is the bond between the two of them, that she visited her from where she is right now, which is in utero, waiting to be born. That's why it was dark. She wasn't ignoring her, as she seemed to be during her visit, it's just that once the spirit has entered the fetus to prepare for birth, it begins the process of the most difficult transition any of us ever go through—birth is much rougher than death, and if you've ever been taken through both transitions in regressive hypnosis, you know firsthand how true that is. It took great determination for A.V.'s grandmother to come to her from the womb so close to her rebirth, and A.V. can reliably tell her family, if they'd be receptive to the information, that her grandmother is officially back on earth.

* * *

A dear departed friend of mine, whom I lost to AIDS, used to say, kidding and always at the exact right time to make me laugh, "But of course when you cut through all the trivia, everything is really about *me*." And let's face it, astral visits our loved ones pay to us are thrilling and nourishing and comforting and a true gift from God, but visits *we* pay are every bit as thrilling a gift from God, if for no other reason than that they prove it's not just everyone else's spirit that transcends the mortal body, it's our spirits, too. We're all equally powerful, equally gifted, and certainly equally blessed, just as able to touch as we are to be touched, just as able to see as we are to be seen, and all equally able to conquer time, space, and physics with, as the saying goes, one hand tied behind our backs— probably with even more dramatic results than we're aware of at the time.

Visiting the Past

For as long as she could remember, Lily had been having recurring dreams of a big, sprawling Victorian house with a wraparound porch, dormer windows, and a massive wooden front door with heavy black iron hinges. She knew every square inch of the inside of that house, from the formal dining room to the narrow back stairway leading to the servant's quarters to a small, bright bedroom with generous lace-curtained windows that she knew was hers. Nothing special happened during her dreams in that house, other than a feeling of being happy and belonging there, and while she didn't recognize them, she felt the older man and woman and the young boy who were often there with her were her family. She talked often about finding that house someday in "real life." She was sure it existed, she was sure it was in the English countryside, north of London, and she was equally sure she could find her way there if she were ever anywhere near it.

As a gift for their twenty-fifth anniversary, Lily's husband Walter took her to England. He neither believed nor disbelieved her insistence on the reality of this house she'd dreamed about throughout their marriage and long before, but he was more than willing to indulge her curiosity, and even if she were wrong, they'd have a lovely time exploring London and its environs.

On the fourth morning of their trip, they rented a car and set out for the countryside north of London. For quite some time, Lily had no particular sense of familiarity, and their leisurely drive seemed lovely but unsuccessful. But then, slowly but surely, Lily began giving Walter tentative directions, uncertain at first and then gaining in confidence as they approached a village nestled in rolling hills. Lily's heart was pounding harder and harder when she realized that she knew her way around this charming little town, and she guided Walter through a series of turns that led them onto a tree-lined street.

Suddenly she gasped, "Stop the car! There it is!" Tears filled her eyes as she gazed up a stone driveway to the house she'd spent so many happy hours in while she slept. From all her descriptions of it, Walter recognized it, too, and was impressed with her accuracy.

Lily was torn between her curiosity and her reluctance to disturb whoever lived in this mystical-seeming house, especially knowing they'd undoubtedly think she was crazy. But it was too irresistible, and with Walter's encouraging hand holding hers, she eventually let herself be led up the driveway to the massive wooden front door with heavy black iron hinges. She hesitated, very nervous and excited, then rang the bell.

An attractive, well-dressed woman in her early fifties answered the door. Lily took a breath, trying to think of a rational way to introduce herself and Walter under these most irrational circumstances.

It turned out not to be necessary. The woman at the door took one look at Lily and shrieked, "Oh, my God, it's the ghost!"

I heard that story from Lily herself, many years ago, and I admit that, while I loved it, I wasn't sure I entirely believed it. (I'm telling you, when it comes to skepticism, I'm hard to beat.) But then, on a trip to my hometown in Kansas City I had a sudden urge to visit the house where I grew up, a house I'd had nostalgic dreams about many times, and virtually the same thing happened to me. Not only did the owner recognize me instantly as her "ghost," but she knew which of the many bedrooms had been mine because she'd heard my laughter coming from it so many times during the night.

Lots and lots of research and clients later, I know that these experiences aren't nearly as uncommon as I thought they were—in all those astral visits we take while we sleep, it's not unusual for people to see us and hear us and, for all I know, become instant believers in ghosts thanks to us. Just because we're not "dead" doesn't mean our spirits can't be seen by our unwitting hosts and hostesses while they sleep, as easily as the spirits of deceased loved ones.

The biggest difference between Lily's experience and mine is that I was making astral visits at night to a house I lived in starting in 1936, while Lily was making hers to a house she lived in starting in 1712 and shared with the parents and younger brother she saw so often in her "dreams."

Never doubt for a moment that while we sleep we can astrally travel to past lives just as easily as we can travel to anywhere on earth, or to The Other Side or to outer space if we want. Again, hard as it might be for us to grasp, there is no such thing as time anywhere but on this plane we're living on right now. A life we lived in, let's say, 1450 B.C. is as current, present-tense, and "now" as today in the spirit world we pay astral visits to.

So when a "dream," particularly a recurring one, seems real, and haunting, and the elements in it inexplicably familiar, and it doesn't seem to fit any of the other dream categories we've talked about, there's a very good chance you've traveled to another era of this eternal life you're living.

"For as long as I can remember, starting when I was very young, I've had dreams of something chasing me down a hall in a white house. Whatever is chasing me can't catch me, but I'm very scared. Then I find myself looking out the kitchen window, and there is a hill in the backyard with plush green grass. I keep looking to the top of the hill to see if it's been disturbed, because I know someone is buried there. There's also a very dark cellar. I'm crouched in it, near the stop of the stairs. Someone is telling me that they will still find me, even in the dark, and I'm so scared my voice is just noises when I try to speak. The dream always ends with my husband waking me up and telling me I'm crying a terrible sound in my sleep. I hope you can tell me why I've been having this dream year after year after year."—Carla

This is a classic past-life astral trip, to a life in the Pacific Northwest in the mid-1800s. Unlike those dreams we've talked about in which we're being chased by some unseen monster, the "monster" that was chasing Carla was very real—it was her father, named Franklin, who, even in the rare moments when he was sober, was mean as a snake and horribly abusive. He literally abused Carla's mother to death, and it's her body that was buried at the top of the hill behind the house. Carla was an only child (a boy, actually, named James) and lived with a combination of terror of this brutal man and guilt over not being able to protect her/his mother from Franklin's homicidal rage. That same terror and guilt, unresolved in that life, are what's causing Carla's terrible "dreams," which are really a reenactment of very real memories of a life she keeps traveling to in an effort to make peace with it. Carla still has a tendency in this life to take on more than her share of guilt. She should recognize it as a carryover from a time that's already passed and let it go.

"I had two recurring dreams when I was a child. In one I was a young boy, running for my life down a hill on a cobblestone street with houses on either side. I had dark black hair and was dressed in nice clothing—black knickers, with a black tie and white shirt, shiny black shoes and white stockings. It seemed as if a group of people was chasing me. I never saw them, but I knew the danger and felt my life was going to end. In the other dream, I was an Indian squaw, and I was pregnant. I was running away from someone, and I was hit in the stomach with an arrow. I fell to the ground holding my stomach, and the next thing I knew I was me in my current life, alive and just fine."—Lucy

Lucy's first astral visit was to a life in Germany in the 1700s, as a boy who accidentally caused the death of a small child. The mob chasing the boy actually caught him and, in escalating mob hysteria, did in fact beat him to death. Lucy's second visit was to her life as a Cherokee squaw in the 1850s. If Lucy is having stomach problems in this life, or feels terror when people jump out at her, even if it's to yell "Surprise!" at a party, those are carryovers, too, from times she's already moved on from, that have no relevance in this lifetime she's currently living.

"When I was a little girl, I had a disturbing recurring dream. The setting was a luxurious home, and it felt like I belonged there. I was a woman, dressed in a flowing white nightgown, walking through a spacious foyer, up a long winding staircase to the second floor with an open hallway enclosed by banisters. There were many doors, including French doors that led outside onto a small balcony. One of the doors in the hallway opened, and two women emerged. One I don't remember well, but the other was dressed casually and had long dark hair. I sensed that I knew them and it wasn't unusual for them to be there. Suddenly, the dark-haired woman became very angry with me and started to attack me. We fought, and she pushed me through the French doors. I fell over the balcony toward the ground below. But as I fell from the balcony, I was somehow outside that body instead, watching myself fall."—Bryon

This was an astral trip to a past life in Louisiana. The dark-haired woman was Bryon's sister, who was insanely jealous of her. The woman with her was her best friend, who loved to instigate fights between Bryon and her sister by telling lies about Bryon. On that particular night, just before Bryon went upstairs, the best friend had convinced Bryon's sister that Bryon was trying to seduce her lover away from her, and Bryon's sister, in a blind rage, pushed Bryon off the balcony and killed her. Bryon exited her body during the fall for the simple reason that, since she was only there on an astral visit and knew what happened anyway, she had no need to actually experience hitting the ground. Her fear of heights and her difficulty in trusting people in this lifetime have their roots in that life.

"In this dream I'm somewhere in the Bible Belt. I'm around four or five years old. It's a hot and muggy day, and I'm riding my trike on the balcony of the second floor of my house. Below, through the window, I can see a big tree, and my father is hanging a black man. I am aware that my mother is somewhat removed and is playing the piano in another part of the house. I feel as though I was a 'Daddy's girl,' and seeing my father do this just breaks my heart."—M.H.

M.H.'s father was a town marshal in northern Mississippi in that life, and her mother was a weak, submissive woman with an uncanny ability to separate herself from anything she deemed "unpleasant." Later in that same life M.H. became an attorney, devoted to defending minorities and the poor, and she astrally returns to that scene occasionally not to relive the hideous trauma of it but to remind herself where her compassion and insistence on fairness come from in this life.

"My dream is exactly like the movie *Sophie's Choice*. I was fleeing a country when I was stopped by an officer and told that I had to choose which of my two children could go with me. I begged, cried, and pleaded, but the officer didn't care. He insisted again that I choose, and all the while he was smiling this cruel, evil smile, truly enjoying my pain. He finally forced me to make a choice. I chose to leave my younger daughter behind and cried uncontrollably as they took her away, screaming and sobbing. I was still crying uncontrollably when I woke up."—H.H.

This was a visit to a past life in Russia, during the cruel ethnic cleansing of the Stalin regime, and H.H. really was forced to make that impossible choice. She's always been afraid in this lifetime that her fear of losing a child might be some kind of premonition. Instead, it's a memory, a fear she can now release because the truth is, she's afraid of something that's already happened to her.

"For several years I had recurring nightmares about being raped. In the dreams it was never the same person or situation, but the awful act itself was always the same. I became afraid to dream at night because I couldn't stand the thought of going through it again. Like all women, I'm extremely afraid of rape ever happening to me, but it didn't become an 'active' fear until these dreams started. I'm now twenty-one years old, and these dreams haven't happened for about a year now. Why would I dream such a horrible thing over and over again, and how can I stop these dreams from coming back again?"—Catherine

Catherine *was* a rape victim, in a life in England in the early 1900s. A group of thugs in their late teens abducted her one night as she walked home from her aunt's house. Two of the boys raped her while the others watched. She was so frightened and deeply humiliated that she never told anyone what happened, and while her life was essentially destroyed from then on, there were never any consequences at all for the vicious bastards who did this. The dreams won't come back for Catherine. The reason she stopped having them is that she was twenty years old when the rapes occurred in that lifetime. Now that she has reached and passed that age in this lifetime, her spirit has been able to recognize the memory as just that and nothing more and release it once and for all.

"I have a frequent recurring dream about being poisoned. My mother is going out and leaves me with this nasty woman I hate. The woman is an angel when my mother's around but a real witch when I'm alone with her, and she scares me so much that I'm afraid to tell my mom what's going on. I see the woman's face very clearly as she forces me to take a pill. She says it's just a vitamin. I take the pill and don't wake up until just before my mother arrives to pick me up, so she never knows what happened. I'm now afraid of anyone being near my food and drinks. What does this mean?"—J.

The woman and the situation J. keeps revisiting were very real, in a lifetime he spent in Belgium in the eighteenth century. This deeply disturbed woman was J.'s tutor, and she routinely gave J. a sleeping potion to keep him quiet for the duration of the time they spent together. She actually despised children but found that the tutoring money she could earn from unsuspecting, trusting parents was her most lucrative possible source of income. J. can relax about his food and drinks in this lifetime. This is an old fear, not a current or future threat.

"I frequently have a dream that involves tidal waves. I'm usually on the shore and know that this giant wave is coming. I desperately try to warn everyone around me, but they don't listen, and they end up getting caught in the wave. I end up in the water, too, but I don't drown, I just keep trying to help everyone. People, animals, and houses all seem to float around me. Some people disappear,

but I don't know if this is because they drown, and I wake up before the dream is resolved."——S.W.

S.W. is having the fascinating experience of revisiting the end of
an idyllic life on Atlantis, and she's still recovering from the trauma
of witnessing and "dying" in that magnificent continent's demise.
S.W. would find it very enlightening to have a session with a reputable, qualified regressive hypnotist. She'll be amazed at how much
more about Atlantis she remembers than just the cataclysmic earth-
quakes and tidal waves that destroyed it.

"I'm sixteen years old, and I just had a very disturbing but good
dream. I went to someplace in India. I don't know why India. I
went to a house and walked in the door. There was a presence of
my mother, father, and sister. There was also a new presence of a
little boy. They said it was my brother, who I'd never seen. In real
life I don't have a brother. Anyway, he was the only one I saw
vividly. The others were just presences. They said if I wanted to
know what I looked like when I was a little boy, just look at him. I
feel so confused. I can't stop thinking of this dream, and when I do
I just cry."——Joshua

You're right, Joshua, this is a good "dream," in which you traveled to a very happy past life in India in the 1780s. Your Spirit
Guide (whose name is Simon, by the way) went with you, specifically to show you what you looked like when you were a child in
India (which is why the little boy is the only one you saw vividly)
and more generally to give you proof that you've had many lifetimes (forty-two, to be exact) in the course of this eternal life
you're living. I hope you'll travel to India someday, particularly to
an area around fifty miles or so northeast of the city of Chennai,
and experience during your waking hours how oddly familiar it
seems to you.

For all of you whose astral visits to past lives I've just discussed,
for the dozens more of you who sent such wonderful accounts of

past-life visits, and for everyone reading this who is routinely visiting past lives while they sleep, I want to explain how and, more importantly, why it happens.

I've written at great length in other books, particularly *Past Lives, Future Healing*, about a phenomenon called cell memory. It's a pet subject of mine, very dear to my heart, and my publisher finds it riveting, too, but he'll chase me up and down the hall with a cleaver if I repeat myself by going into it in too much detail here. And so, briefly—our spirits carry with them every memory of every lifetime they've lived on earth and every moment they've spent on The Other Side. The instant we enter another human body for another incarnation, the familiarity of having a body again kicks in, and our spirits' memories, safely housed in the "hard drives" of our subconscious minds, infuse the cells of our bodies with this flood of information that the cells naturally respond to. "Last time I was in a body," a spirit might say to itself, "I was shot in the stomach with an arrow. Here I am in a body again, so obviously my stomach must hurt." Or, "When I'm in a body, I get raped at the age of twenty. I'd better be braced for that until that age has come and gone this time around, and after that I'll feel safe." Or, "I enjoyed being in a body when I was in India, and now that I'm back in a body, I'm fondly remembering India all over again."

Whether the cell memories we revisit while we sleep are positive ones or negative ones, they're very powerful, without the interfering clutter of the conscious mind, and they're also incredibly helpful. Astral trips to happy past lives are lovely reminders of our immortality, and of how temporary any current unhappiness really is. Astral trips to past life traumas, upsetting as they can be, serve the same purpose as release dreams, throwing a spotlight on any pain, fear, and confusion we might be going through and giving us a firsthand view of where they came from, so that we can let go of them once and for all, subconsciously *and* consciously.

Starting tonight, and every night from now on until it becomes a habit, I want you to add the following, in my words or your own, to your prayers before you sleep:

"Father God, if I should travel to a time or place from my past before I wake again, please help me witness but not relive any moments that brought me pain or fear, so that I might understand and then release them into the white light of the Holy Spirit any negativity I've brought from another lifetime into this one, so that it can be resolved forever in Thy divine, perfect peace. And just as I release that past negativity, let me embrace the joys, the wisdom, the love, and the gifts from other lifetimes, that I may awaken tomorrow with a renewed sense of confidence and self-respect and an abiding awareness of the eternity with which You've blessed my spirit."

It really is that simple—just pray to release the negative and embrace the positive from any past incarnations while you sleep. If you don't believe me, try it anyway. In fact, try it to prove me wrong if you want, and then write to me and tell me what results you did or didn't notice. Just promise to be honest about any pain, fear, or confusion that might have vanished from your life in the process, and in return I promise not to say "I told you so."

Visits to The Other Side

There's no doubt about it, we very often get Homesick for The Other Side and our loved ones over there while we're here on earth, slogging our way through this bad camping trip that was our bright idea to begin with. As a result, as I've mentioned before, we counteract that Homesickness as best we can with astral trips to The Other Side on an average of two or three times a week while we sleep. If you have no conscious memory of these frequent trips Home, don't worry, it doesn't mean they're not happening, and your subconscious *always* remembers them. It could mean you learned things on your trips there that you're not meant to consciously be aware of yet. It could mean that other, more pressingly urgent dreams and messages got in the way. Or it could just mean you remember the trip perfectly, you just didn't understand where you were.

"I'm standing in front of the building with a lot of windows, a huge building that is kind of like a library. People are walking in and out, but they're not speaking. I'm very happy there, but I have no idea where I am or why."—Ted

Ted was on The Other Side, at the Hall of Records, where all of our life charts are housed, so it really is very much like a library. It's a favorite place of Ted's and many people's, and because of that, I hope Ted will start jotting down his dreams—I'd be very surprised if they don't have a tendency to be prophetic.

"In this dream I'm standing on a cobblestone path. Everything around me is a sandy, terra cotta color. The buildings behind me are kind of an adobe style. There's a wall on the other side of the path. I look over it and see a small pond with an island in the middle that has a swing set on it. I look behind me and there's a man, black hair, tan skin, wearing a white shirt and black pants, looking away from me. I feel I should say something and finally, apprehensive, I put out my hand and say, 'Hi, I'm Dawn.' He reaches for my hand and the next thing I know all I see is bright lights flashing, like if you closed your eyes and tapped lightly on your eyelids. I hear myself nervously giggle and say, 'I'm kind of nervous.' In reply I hear, 'Don't be, it's okay.' I end up in my childhood bedroom with my journal next to me, and in it I write the word 'Ihea.' "—Dawn

On this trip to The Other Side Dawn was simply having a quick reunion with her Spirit Guide, who's the man she met there. It goes without saying that the two of them know each other, but it's very common for us to get amnesia about Home for the most part while we're here. (Let's face it, if it weren't, the stampede of all of us trying to get back there would be completely unmanageable.) Her Spirit Guide told Dawn his name telepathically. She heard it as "Iheah." It's actually "Isaiah," and in his one incarnation on earth he was a great scholar and teacher in Israel.

"I was napping, and my dearly loved but departed dog hopped up on my bed next to me. I petted him and was pleased to find that his form was solid. The room I was sleeping in had actually changed. It was better somehow, with blinds instead of curtains, and the view out the window was so beautiful."—S.M.

Make no mistake about it, every animal who's ever been on earth makes an instant transition to The Other Side, including every pet we've ever owned in every lifetime we've spent here. S.M. took an astral trip Home to visit her dog, and I'm so glad she wrote to reinforce the fact that we're not just blobs of vapor floating around when we're in spirit form, we're all perfectly solid, as she experienced herself when she petted her beloved dog. I've said it before, and I'll say it again: if there are no animals on The Other Side, it can't be paradise. Just point me to wherever it is they are and I'll go there instead.

"I dreamed that I was running along a fence, and on the other side of the fence was a hill. I knew that I was running to see someone special to me, and this person was running down the hill on the other side of the fence to see me as well. Both of us reached the break in the fence at the same time and embraced like we had not seen each other in ages. The strange thing is that this was a male I don't know, not very tall, with a mustache and beard. Yet we seemed to know each other and love each other very much. I've never had another dream filled with so much excitement, love, and euphoria. It's hard to describe the love that I felt in that dream, and yet it was very familiar in some way."—Jana

This was a trip Home for a reunion with Jana's soul mate.

(Admit it, all of you who are familiar with my work just groaned, didn't you?) We each have one soul mate and only one soul mate, a twin spirit God creates at the same moment He creates us. Our soul mates are not "the other half of us." Each and every one of us is already whole, thank you very much. The chances of our soul mate incarnating at the same time we do are maybe one in two or three million. The vast majority of our soul mates are on The Other Side having a great time, waiting for us and enjoying these occasional reunions.

Thank you to Jana for putting into words that the excitement, love, and euphoria she felt in that "dream" defied description but somehow felt familiar at the same time.

That's exactly the Home we came from.

That's exactly the Home we'll return to someday.

And that's exactly the Home our spirits visit while we sleep, renewing God's promise of eternity over and over again.

Chapter Eight

✳

Astral Catalepsy: Temporary Paralysis and Loud Noises While We Sleep

"I've had something happen several times that really scares me, and I'm hoping you can help. I'll be sleeping, and then I half wake up and feel as if I can't breathe, can't move, can't open my eyes, and I feel as if I'm being pushed into my bed by some force. I try to yell for help but I can't make a sound. Finally I start feeling lighter and kind of normal again, but I'm too scared to go back to sleep. What is that?!"—Greg

"More than once I've had this dream that it was pitch black, and I felt someone sitting on my bed, and suddenly I realized I was paralyzed. I couldn't move or even open my eyes, and something was on top of me, keeping me pinned to the bed."—T.L.

"I'm sometimes sound asleep and awaken to deafening noise of no particular description, just absolutely mind-numbing noise. It is as though my brain is tuned into every single radio station and airwave transmission all at the same time. I'm paralyzed during this, and next thing I know I feel weightless and I'm involuntarily leaving my body."—M.H.

"For as long as I can remember I've had the same recurring dream. In this dream I'm unable to move from the neck down, and I can only slightly move my head. There's nothing going on in this dream, it's just sort of black, and I know that there is a heavy presence, a force of some kind, almost sitting on me, holding me down. And I know in my conscious mind that if I don't wake myself up from this dream, I'll never wake up."—K.C.

"I always feel like I'm paralyzed during a nightmare, and it takes a while when I first wake up to be able to move again."—W.S.

I've been reading and hearing stories like these from clients for more than thirty years, and because this is such a common and scary problem, I think it deserves a chapter of its own. Questions about it range from "Could I die from this?" to "Is this an evil force that I can feel holding me down?" to "So far the paralysis has always gone away after a few minutes, but what if it doesn't next time?" to "Does this happen to other people?" And unanimously: "What causes this? Is there a name for it?"

What Is Astral Catalepsy?

It was astral travel researcher Sylvan Muldoon who coined the term "astral catalepsy," around 1930 or so. A simpler but less accurate name for it is "sleep paralysis"—true enough, but it fails to take into account the fact that, whether more traditional sleep researchers agree or not, this experience is *always* associated with astral trips. Obviously, astral travel can and does happen without an episode of astral catalepsy, but astral catalepsy doesn't happen and can't happen without astral travel.

Sylvan Muldoon was twelve years old when he took the first astral trip during sleep that he was aware of. He woke up in the middle of the night to find himself unable to move, see, or hear, with a feeling of some kind of severe pressure on his head. And then, as his senses returned and his temporary paralysis subsided, he realized that he was floating above his bed and able to look down and see himself sound asleep. He was even aware of his spirit, once it was completely outside of his body, being pulled from a horizontal position to a vertical one. He toured his house, passing through doors and walls with the greatest of ease, and even tried to shake his parents awake because he was so frightened, but his "spirit" hands kept passing right through them as well, and they slept right on without ever feeling him touching them. And then, back above his own sleeping body again, he went from a vertical position to a horizontal one again, experienced the same paralysis and inability to move, see, or hear that he'd gone through earlier, and jerked very abruptly back into his body again, where he woke up in a panic, clearly remembering everything he'd just been through. Starting that night, he began writing down every detail of the hundreds of astral trips he took that he could recall, but, just as with the rest of us, there were many trips that only came back to his conscious mind in brief, frustratingly incomplete memories.

Sylvan Muldoon was hardly alone in his lifelong curiosity about astral catalepsy. Cultures throughout the world have been so fascinated with this phenomenon for so many hundreds or even thousands of years that they've created some very colorful folklore around it. Ancient Europeans theorized that sleep paralysis was caused by witches who abducted unwitting sleepers and took them for long broomstick rides to distant, mystical places. The Japanese referred to astral catalepsy as *kanashibari*, in which a gigantic devil would sneak into bedrooms throughout the country during the night and pin the sleeping people to their beds with its foot. Newfoundland came up with the legend of the Old Hag, a hideous witch who would sit on sleepers' chests and very often wrap her gnarled, clawlike hands around their necks in an effort to strangle them. China called it *gui ya*, to describe a ghost who, they theorized, was sitting on sleeping people and assaulting them, and the West Indians arrived at a variation on *gui ya* that they called *kokma*, which was actually a baby ghost, jumping up and down on sleeping people's chests. And ardent UFO believers throughout the world have reached the conclusion that astral catalepsy is obviously caused by aliens who abduct sleepers while they're at their most vulnerable and take that opportunity to perform examinations and experiments on them.

No matter what the culture and what the explanation, the characteristics of the experience the sleeper goes through are universal and, to put it mildly, really startling. If you're someone who suffers from astral catalepsy, chances are it includes one or more of the following symptoms:

- paralysis
- a feeling of being pressed or pinned down by an unseen evil presence
- loud noises, ranging from buzzing or humming to an insane, chaotic clamor
- a pervasive, overwhelming vibration
- a sense of something or someone threatening sitting on the bed or moving the bedclothes
- shortness of breath, usually from some sudden pressure on the chest
- the appearance of strange lights

- a sensation of being touched by a lewd, menacing, invisible phantom

If anything on that list sounds like a familiar part of your sleeping hours, please rest assured that you're not alone, you're certainly not crazy, and as real as the sensations feel, you're not in any actual danger.

I'll tell you exactly what's going on. It's not as colorful as witches or baby ghosts or UFOs, but it's the truth, it's logically consistent with what we already know, and if you look at it from its most spiritual angle, it's really very affirming for an experience that's so momentarily unpleasant.

The Cause of Astral Catalepsy

We know that several times a week our spirits take brief vacations from our bodies while we sleep, to go visiting and exploring throughout the world, the universe, and The Other Side. We also know how natural, exhilarating, and nourishing these astral trips are for our spirits. And we know that astral travel during sleep can be great for the overall health of our conscious minds, too, not to mention a frequent, God-given reminder that our spirits can and do thrive with or without these bodies they're housed in while we're here on earth.

Another thing we know, though, is that when we're sleeping, even the slightest disturbance can jar us into some level of consciousness, and when our conscious minds are startled during sleep, we can easily get very confused and very frightened. On the rare occasions when the conscious mind "catches" the spirit leaving or reentering the body, it panics, in the semiconscious belief that if the spirit is half in and half out, the body must be dying and literally unable to function. Think of the paralysis, the inability to breathe or scream, and all the other sensations of astral catalepsy as a kind of temporary mental and neurological "short circuit" in response to a realization that the spirit is in the process of either coming or going, which the physical body instinctively interprets as "death."

It's also important to remember that the spirit world we join when we astrally travel lives in a different dimension than the earthly dimension we're living in here on earth. The spirit world has a much higher vibrational frequency, and gravity and other earthly laws of physics are irrelevant there. So the fact that a clamor of noises and a sudden, distressing feeling of heaviness and pressure sometimes accompany those moments when our spirits change dimensions isn't all that surprising, especially when the semiconscious mind is jolted awake by them. Frightening as it's happening, don't get me wrong, but in the cold, logical light of day, not all that surprising.

Battling Astral Catalepsy

I wish I could promise that if you follow my suggestions, you'll never, ever experience astral catalepsy again, but I won't make promises I can't keep. What I can promise is that you can believe me when I tell you what astral catalepsy is and that it's upsetting but neither permanent nor life-threatening. And I can absolutely promise that at the very least, these suggestions will help.

First, when you talk to God before you fall asleep, as I hope you do every night of your life, I want you to surround yourself with the pure, protecting white light of the Holy Spirit as always, and mix that divine light with swirls of rich, healing green. Then add the following to your prayers, in either my words or your own: "Dear Father, if my spirit should travel tonight while I sleep, please help it exit and reenter with divine, peaceful ease, without the awareness or interference of my easily frightened conscious mind." Say it as many times as it takes to let you drift off calm and confident, but never worry about God, He'll hear you the first time, even before you've expressed it in words.

And then, if you should find yourself in the throes of astral catalepsy anyway (God always listens—the conscious mind can't necessarily make that same claim), pray again, the instant you feel it coming over you. Ask for God's protection, and your Spirit Guide's, and your Angels', and keep right on praying until it's passed, as it will. This will serve a couple of purposes. For one thing, it won't summon God and your Spirit Guide and your Angels, but it will just help remind you that *they're already there*. And for another thing, it will help you become fully awake and restore your conscious clarity, which will ease the sensations you're feeling and the sounds you're hearing and put an end to that episode of astral catalepsy. You'll be reassured one more time that your spirit is safely back in your body again and you're still safely in God's loving arms, as always and always and always.

Chapter Nine

ARCHETYPES: THE SYMBOLS IN OUR DREAMS

*L*et me say this right up front: I hope you won't read this chapter expecting that I'm going to give you *the* true, actual, one and only meaning of the symbolic entities and objects that appear in our dreams. As I said in the chapter on release dreams, our minds, both conscious and sub-conscious, and our vast bodies of experience are much too complex and unique to reduce to simplis-tic, one-dimensional definitions of what things in our dreams really mean *to each of us.*

That's not to say that there aren't some gener-alities that can be made, especially since a lot of the same imagery and symbols are common to so many of us. I'm just asking that as we go along, you'll keep in mind that your dreams are intimate, deeply personal, and all yours. As we explore the various possible meanings of dream symbols, be flexible, always look first for something that might apply to and be a comment on some current situation in your life, and remember that interpreting our dreams is an art, not a science. There's no right or wrong. All that counts is what resonates in you as the truth.

Please also remember that the same first step we discussed earlier still applies when it comes to understanding dreams and the imagery in them: start with deciding what category applies to the dream you're trying to interpret. Was it prophetic, a release dream, a wish dream, a dream that provided information or solved a problem, or an astral experience, perhaps a reunion with a longed-for person or place? Defining the category you're dealing with can help the symbolism come into sharper, more meaningful focus, because once you understand the dream's purpose, you can then kind of work backward and see how the images in it might contribute to that purpose. For example, remember the story of the woman who kept dreaming about peaches without understanding why, or what they meant, until we uncovered the fact that she associated peaches with the death of her mother? If she'd started with the realization that all those dreams involving peaches were release dreams, she could have begun asking herself what unresolved issues she might be trying to release, which could have led to the pain of losing her mother, which could have solved the mystery of the link between that tragedy and the peaches her mother kept craving before she died.

To give you an idea of how intriguing some common symbols can be, though, I want you to get paper and pencil and draw five objects (don't worry if you're a terrible artist—I am, too, and it truly doesn't matter): a house, the sun, water, a tree, and a snake. In fact, stop reading right now and don't read ahead until you've finished that.

*   *   *

Take a look at what you've drawn, and let's see how much of it might reveal a few things about you and your life.

The house represents you. Did you draw a door, or doors, to easily allow and invite access, or did you draw a house with no doors, designed to keep other people out and you isolated inside? Is there a path leading to the house you drew, to make it easier for people to get to you? Did you draw windows, for openness and a view from both the inside out and the outside in, or are there no windows, as if you don't want to take a chance of anyone looking inside and you're not interested in who or what might be around you? Is there a chimney, for warmth? Are there shutters, or other decorations, indicating pride and an interest in appearance? Is it a big, expansive house, or a tiny house that looks as if it's hoping not to be noticed?

The sun represents your father. Did you draw it close to the house (you), or far away? Is it prominent in your drawing, or is it fairly inconspicuous? Does it have rays, so that it looks like a source of light and warmth? If there are rays, are they long and generous, or are they short and limited in the light and warmth they have to offer? Or did you draw the sun as a simple, ineffective circle with no rays of light and warmth at all?

The water represents your mother. Did you draw the water so that it's close to the house, or far away? Is there easy access between the house and the water, or did you draw them so that they're completely separate from each other? Is the water you drew enclosed, like a pond, or is it more expansive, moving and lively, like a lake or river? Is it in the foreground of your drawing, or the background? Is it prominent, or trivial in relation to the other objects you drew?

The tree is your intellect—not your IQ, but the general relationship between you and your mind. How big or small is the tree you drew in relation to the house? Is it near the house, or distant from it? Does the tree have many branches, or only a few? Does it seem to be thriving and strong, or is it sickly, parched, and in need of water and other nourishment? Is it in a position to provide shade and protection to the house, or does it seem to be isolated and fairly irrelevant?

And finally, the snake is your sexuality. How important or trivial is the snake in relation to the other objects you drew? Does it have any proximity to the tree (your intellect), or are they completely separate from each other? How close is the snake to the house, and what is its size relative to the house? Does it seem to overpower the house, or is it in fairly realistic proportion to it? Does the snake look healthy, or does it look like it could use a trip to a good veterinarian?

Now that you've studied your drawing and the symbols in it, it's up to you to decide whether the relationships between the objects are in any way accurate to the relationships the objects represent. And let me stress, please don't do too much generalizing about the five objects you drew and their relevance in the dream archetypes we'll be discussing. Every dream about water isn't necessarily about your mother, you can have dreams about a tree that have nothing to do with your intellect, and we've examined enough past-life dreams to know that some houses in dreams actually represent houses. If you happen to be terrified of snakes when you're awake, and you have a terrifying nightmare about a snake, there's no reason to jump to the conclusion that you're terrified of your sexuality. And a brightly shining sun in a dream doesn't always have anything at all to do with your father. Instead, this little demonstration is simply to illustrate how readily our minds think in terms of symbols, and how worthwhile a discussion of dream symbols, or archetypes, really is.

Dreams of a House

As I just mentioned, some houses in dreams really do represent houses—a house from a past life, for example, or a house from our childhood, or a house we'd love to live in. But if you're having trouble interpreting a dream in which a house plays an important part, it's always a good idea to start by trying out the possibility that the house in the dream is you.

That possibility has several variations, all of which can offer enormously helpful insights into any number of issues we might be consciously or subconsciously struggling with. For example:

"I have a frequently recurring dream," writes P.A. "I dream that the second floor of our house is completely different from the real house. In the dream, the second floor is reached by a long, straight staircase. At the top there is a very long hall to the left that has bedrooms with baths on each side, at least eight or ten of them. The first room across from the staircase is the guest room. I only go up there to get that room ready for guests. None of the other rooms are finished. They need wallpaper, paint, and furniture. I wander through them and think it would be a fun project to finish them, but I never do because they're all haunted, so I would never have anyone stay in them. I don't think I've ever seen the ghosts, I just know they're there. The guest room isn't haunted, but I usually don't have it ready by the time my guests arrive, so they end up having to help."

One of the interesting possibilities in dreams about two-story (or more) houses is that they can indicate health concerns, with the location of the potential problems in the body correlating to the location of the disturbance in the house. The upstairs areas can represent the body from the waist up, while the ground floor and below can represent the body from the waist down. In her recurring dream, P.A. keeps sensing something wrong with the second story of her house. It needs work, but she keeps not getting that work done because of unseen ghosts—in other words, she has an uneasy feeling about what's going on "upstairs" even though there are no specific symptoms she can see or point to. If I were P.A., I'd go get a complete physical, and have them pay particular attention to the chest, lungs, and the chambers of the heart. I don't want to alarm her and I'm not saying there's anything serious going on with her health. I'm saying she is subconsciously worried about her health in her upper body, and I want her to do something about it. As soon as her doctor gives her a thorough checkup and tells her either that everything's fine or that she and the doctor can fix whatever's not fine, this uneasy recurring dream will stop.

Likewise, dreams of a house with plumbing problems, especially in the basement, can indicate a concern about the intestines; heating or air conditioning problems in a dream house can be the subconscious mind waving a flag about the circulatory system; a leaky or faulty roof could be a hint about oncoming problems from headaches to sinus infections to potential mental health issues, particularly depression. Again, these dreams don't necessarily mean you're in some kind of health trouble. They can mean you're simply sensing something "off" in the area of the house/body you're dreaming about, and it's worth checking out, if for no other reason than to get it off your mind once and for all and move on to other dreams.

Just as often, though, dreams of a house can offer clues to what's going on with us in the deepest parts of our minds and hearts, bringing our fears and joys and changes and longings into the light so that we can fully explore them.

Amy's recurring dream is a terrific example: "I keep dreaming of large *old* houses. Some have splintery wooden floors, are probably three stories high, and have a square hole in the center of the top floors with a railing so that I can look down on the bottom floors. I see no staircase. I watch people on the lower floors and enjoy the lookout position where I am. I never go down to the bottom floor."

There are a couple of interesting and conflicting feelings going on with Amy that are spelled out so conveniently in these dreams. On one hand, Amy feels isolated, not comfortable about it, and not at all sure what to do about it—notice that the houses aren't luxurious and well maintained but instead have splintery wood floors, and there's not a stairway in sight, no way to connect with the people below. On the other hand, Amy isn't self-confident and trusting enough to be sure she wants to join the group downstairs, which is why this lookout position feels kind of safe and enjoyable. In other words, this is a release dream, and it would lend itself beautifully to that experiment we talked about in the chapter on release dreams. I want Amy to pray and program herself that next time she has this dream, and every time from then on, she'll see a gorgeous spiral staircase, strong, safe, and secure, extend itself from her vantage point on that old splintery third floor right down the middle of that opening to the first floor where all the people are. I don't just want her to walk down that staircase as the people look up, see her, and smile warmly, I also want her to have her favorites among those people come up the stairs at the same time, extend their hands to her, and escort her into the crowd, which has now turned into a party to welcome her. The more sure of herself and included she demands to feel in her dream, the more she'll let herself venture out with confidence in her waking hours and the less she'll believe that the only way to feel safe is to be alone.

Another very common release dream in which a house is prominent was described very articulately in a letter from Nancy: "There has been a recurring dream throughout my life about a house. The situations in which I enter the house differ, but the experience of being inside is always the same—at some point I become aware that this is my 'dream' house because there is a malevolent feeling emanating from the house, and as I go through the rooms I feel that I can't get out without confronting this evil presence. Sometimes I feel it when I'm upstairs, and sometimes it seems to be in the basement with me. It seems to actually speak to me, threatening me not with just physical annihilation but with actual absorption, growling that it will take me over completely."

Like so many others who have similar dreams, Nancy is going through a classic internal struggle we can all relate to. And by the way, let's get it straight that no one or nothing can "absorb" or "overtake" or "possess" us, not ever, so if that's among any of your fears, I assure you you're afraid of something that's literally impossible. At any rate, with the exception of the mentally ill, we all know that we should be living lives full of honesty, integrity, kindness, compassion, hard work, generosity, and God-centered, nonjudgmental tolerance. We also have to admit, if we're completely truthful with ourselves, that sometimes it looks as if it might be easier, more profitable, and frankly more fun to just give in to temptation, throw our values out the window, and stop trying so much harder than those around us seem to be. It's the battle we all came here from The Other Side to take on: not to avoid negativity, which is impossible, but to confront it and overcome it. It's hard. And because it's hard, we all have our "what's the point?" moments. Thank God the vast majority of us are able to regroup and remember very clearly what the point is. But that battle, the very essence of why we're here, is exactly what's being played out in Nancy's recurring dream: good confronting evil in a house that symbolizes us, our release of the fear that evil will absorb us. But notice that in the end, it doesn't, because it can't.

There are wonderfully exciting house dreams, too, and I wish you many of these. A lovely example came from T.H.: "For many years I've been dreaming of a house. It's huge, it needs some fixing up and it's full of surprises. I'm always discovering new rooms or whole other parts of the house that I had no idea existed. In real life I have a house I love and couldn't care less about finding another one."

In this fairly common dream, it's obviously thrilling that the house represents us, and we don't even have to worry about running around collecting moving boxes. Dreams of huge houses indicate that we're becoming aware of our limitless potential. (Don't panic if you typically dream of tiny, cluttered houses, though. Those are usually release dream signals that we're feeling stifled and claustrophobic, like we've outgrown our lives and ourselves, our behavior and belief systems and thought patterns, and that subconscious acknowledgment through dreams is almost always followed by periods of great emotional and spiritual growth.) Houses that "need some fixing up" mean that we consider ourselves works-in-progress, and who in the world wants to ever feel "finished"? As for all those surprises, and newly discovered rooms and whole unexplored parts of the house we never knew existed, those are definite messages from the subconscious to get ready for surprises in our lives, newly discovered interests and goals and potential ventures and unexpected possibilities, and whole unexplored parts of *ourselves* that we never knew existed.

When a house plays a significant part in your dreams, then, it's almost guaranteed to be an astral trip to a house you remember from this lifetime or a past one, or it's symbolic of you, and your feelings about the physical, mental, emotional, and spiritual issues your subconscious mind wants your conscious mind to be aware of. It's not always easy to tell which is which. But a good rule of thumb is that when the house is simply the setting for the action that takes place, and the action is in some kind of sequential order, you've astrally traveled back in time to revisit good memories or bad ones. When the house seems to be the "star of the show," though, or itself the real subject of the dream, ask yourself what that house and everything you find inside might be able to teach you about *you*.

Cars in Our Dreams

Like houses, cars are very common in dreams, and they have a variety of meanings. They can be past-life memories, or early memories from this life. Because the primary purpose of cars is to get us from point A to point B, dreams of being in a car can indicate a transition in our lives. And since cars are the vehicles in which our bodies travel, and our bodies are the vehicles in which our spirits travel while they're on earth, it's not unusual for our subconscious minds to use cars, much like houses, as easily recognizable symbols to represent *us*.

"In this dream, I was in the front seat of the car and my husband was in the backseat. I was turned around facing him completely and buckled in. Then the car started to go, and I told him he would have to be my eyes while I got turned around. I unbuckled my seat belt, knowing it was dangerous to do so, and tried to turn around. The dog kept getting in the way, and I couldn't see except for brief flashes. Then I woke up."—M.C.

See what I mean? How many times have we all felt as if our lives were going, or not going, exactly like this release dream of M.C.'s, where we're trying to move forward, and not only do our loved ones sit idly by without helping, but we actually find ourselves having to work around them? Dreams like this one are especially common among people who have overdeveloped senses of responsibility, when it begins to occur to them that taking on so much is starting to immobilize them. I'll tell M.C. what I've told countless clients who've had similar "car/driver's seat" dreams: program yourself to rewrite the dream so that from the very beginning, someone else, someone you trust, is at the wheel of the car, so that you can learn to just relax and go along for the ride, and to recognize that sometimes other people would appreciate the opportunity to be in charge.

We spend so much time in cars, in fact, that it's not surprising how often we use them in release dreams to act out our fears. Here are two letters that represent dozens I've received on this very same subject in just the last few months:

G.M. wrote, "In one dream I was in my car with a three-year-old. We went off the road into a huge pit of snow and couldn't get out. In the other, my child was run over by a car, but he didn't get hurt. In the latest one, though, the same thing happened and I found him dead."

V.N. wrote, "I dreamed I left my house and put my baby in the backseat of my car. About halfway to wherever I was going, I turned around to check on the baby and he wasn't in the car. Just then I spotted my father in his car and asked for his help. I don't know what happened with that, but next thing I knew my car broke down and I had to wind up a gadget to make it go just a few meters. I knew that my baby was back at that old house, and the only way I could get back to him was a few slow meters at a time."

First of all, both G.M. and V.N. can exhale about any fear that these dreams are somehow prophetic. Remember, prophetic dreams, which are actually the result of astral travel, always have a basic, logical sequence to them. Release dreams, on the other hand, invariably have some element of absurdity to them—like a child getting run over by a car and not getting hurt, or a car you suddenly have to wind up in order to retrieve a baby that's vanished from the backseat and been magically transported to the house you took it from. So, as with every release dream, start with the fact of release and then, based on the elements in the dream, work backward to see what it is you're trying to release and let go of. In the cases of these letters and so many others like them, any responsible, loving parent will back me up on the fact that it's a fear we've all felt, whether we express it or not. Put simply, it's "I'm afraid that something will happen to my baby and it will be my fault." (And obviously, by the way, being at the wheel in any dream means being in charge, being responsible, or bearing any potential fault or blame.)

Please be assured of something I've had to remind myself a million times about my children and my grandchildren: all we can do is the very best we can do. There is absolutely no greater priority on this earth for any parent than the mental, emotional, and physical welfare of our children. As long as we live every day acting on that priority instead of just making noise about it, a point comes where we have to accept that no matter how present, vigilant, and adoring we are, the day will never happen when we won't worry about our children at least a little. So, frightening as this particular form of release dream can be, keep it in perspective as best you can, understand that it's an occupational hazard of parenthood, and recognize that, rather than a warning, it's a simple subconscious fear of losing a love and connection unlike any other we'll ever experience on this earth.

Here's a recurring car dream that could easily be misinterpreted, though. It's from Teresa. "I'm driving a large car I can barely handle on a perilous mountain road. There's a terrible storm. I can hear the rain pounding on the top of the car, and I can barely see the road ahead of me. My three children are in the backseat, crying, huddled together with fear, and I keep promising that we'll be okay even though I'm not really sure I believe it myself. (Oddly, in real life I only have one child, but in the dream there are three and I know they're mine and that I love them and would give my life for them.) I can't see lights ahead or any other sign of help, and I'm very frightened, but I know I have to keep going because at the end of this journey is safety. We start across a very old bridge near the top of the mountain, and just as it begins to crumble beneath the weight of the car and I realize it's too late to save us, I wake up, crying and shaking."

This is an astral trip to a very valid past life in the mountains of Appalachia in the late 1700s. Teresa was fleeing to her parents' home in Pennsylvania with her three children after her deeply disturbed husband had tried to kill them for being "possessed." The "large car" was actually a buckboard with a makeshift cover on it, and the reason Teresa wakes up just as the bridge is beginning to crumble is that she doesn't need to reexperience her own death and the death of her children in that lifetime. As soon as Teresa recognizes that she's remembering a lifetime that's long since passed and has no relevance to this one except to give her glorious proof of her immortality, she'll release the leftover grief and guilt and never have that dream again.

And then there was this lovely letter from Claire: "This dream happens several times a month. There are three people involved— me, my father, and my aunt. The feeling is one of serene peace and love. We're always in a car, not traveling anywhere in particular, just being together in this car and looking around at beautiful fields and occasional cities. In real life I have no idea where this is, but in the dream it's all so familiar. Again, I have no idea where we are or where we're going in these dreams, but I never care or even think about it."

Never doubt for a moment that we get together with loved ones during the night to take astral trips together, and Claire simply uses the symbol of a car to travel with her father and aunt instead of the sensation of flying that so many astral travelers experience. Very often, especially when we're feeling more stress than usual and are yearning for sanity, security, and serenity, we find it while we sleep, with those we look to for those exact things during our waking hours. In Claire's case, she and her father and aunt enjoy visiting The Other Side together at night, which is why the landscape seems so beautiful and remarkably familiar even though Claire can't quite place where it is. I have a dear friend named Bernie whom I very rarely get to spend time with in the course of our busy waking lives, and it's become a running joke between us how often we make up for it at night, hanging out together astrally a few times a month without ever planning it ahead of time.

Again, then, when you wake up knowing you've spent time in a car since you went to sleep, it's safe to assume that you've been astrally traveling to the past or to loved ones you need to connect with, or that your car trip during sleep was your subconscious using a familiar symbol to represent you and the issues that are more on your conscious mind than you might even know.

Storms, Tidal Waves, and Tornadoes

Sometimes the archetypes in our dreams mean exactly what they seem to, and unless they're past-life memories, storms, tidal waves, and tornadoes are good examples. They indicate emotional turbulence, feelings of helplessness and being overpowered and overwhelmed, fear of the unexpected, and a general sense of life spinning out of control no matter how hard we might try to stop it. So it's understandable that those symbols have been showing up in our dreams more often than ever following the September 11 horror, a day when every sane, compassionate, God-centered person on earth felt all those emotions and far, far more.

"I had a horrible dream about a tsunami threatening the coast," says J.A. "Everyone was leaving by airplane, but I couldn't leave. I kept going back to my house for things I had forgotten. This dream happened shortly after the 9/11 attacks."

Marilyn writes, "I constantly dream of trying to escape either a flood or some other major catastrophe. I'm usually trying to gather my pets and personal items. I've had these dreams for years, but they became much worse after 9/11."

It's worth repeating that September 11 was a human-made tragedy. God was nowhere to be found in the cause of it. But as so many people have pointed out in the aftermath, it was still a "sucker punch," as are so many of the natural disasters that appear in our release dreams, reminding us that life's trials are tough enough when we participate in causing them, but few things make us feel more vulnerable than getting hit with a "sucker punch" we can't see coming, didn't do anything to deserve, and seemingly have no way to defend against.

There's a message to be found in a dream from D.G. "At the beginning of my dream I'm in a large garage with my two closest friends. There is a storm brewing outside and we suddenly notice that a tornado is headed our way. Both of my friends hurry to get underneath some furniture in the garage, and I'm trying to shut the garage door. It's too late for me, though, and the tornado sucks me up. As it's carrying me into the air and I'm looking back at my friends, I'm crying and praying to God to save me. A few minutes later the tornado sets me down on the ground, almost gently. I'm crouched down and still crying from relief when I sense that someone or something is behind me. I turn around and realize that the tornado has turned into a large black man. He reaches out his hand and, in a very comforting way, places his hand on my shoulder and tells me, 'Your faith will be rewarded.' That was all, the end of the dream."

What I love about this release dream is its clear statement that even when life is as overwhelmingly chaotic as the tornado that swept D.G. away, faith and prayers are what ultimately see us through safely, whether that safety is found here on earth or on The Other Side. And what I'm sure D.G. didn't realize but somehow felt, as evidenced by the sense of comfort and the promise of faith being rewarded, is that the "large black man," who is quite beautiful and has translucent brown eyes, was his Spirit Guide, whose name is Conroe. In his dream, D.G. made a terrifying tornado turn into one of his greatest protectors. It was a very smart thing for his subconscious to do, and a wonderful "programming" hint for the rest of us, to rewrite our own natural disaster dreams in such a way that every storm, every tidal wave, and every tornado is ultimately transformed into an embodiment of love, protection, safety, and a reminder that, in the end, we really are indestructible.

Animals in Our Dreams

Now here's an area in which your own symbolism is going to be every bit as accurate and specific as anything I can tell you. As I mentioned in the chapter on wish dreams, your emotional reactions to the archetypes that show up in your dreams count far more in understanding your dreams than whatever definitions Jung or Freud or "dream dictionaries" or I might come up with. Classically, for example, doves in dreams are a sign of peace and purity—peace of mind, some idea or person you've made peace with or want to make peace with, the immaculate image of pure white wings, and so on. But if you're terrified of birds, doves in your dreams aren't likely to inspire thoughts of peace and purity when you wake up in a cold sweat with your heart pounding.

I do think, though, that I can offer some new perspectives on animals that are showing up in your dreams, confusing you, and as a result, making you miss some lovely signs.

Totems

"For as long as I can remember, I've had occasional dreams of a bear chasing me. There doesn't seem to be much more to the dreams than that, just me running and looking back to see this huge bear right behind me."—Gary

Believe it or not, Gary, you're running from a beautiful creature you yourself handpicked to watch over you and protect you for this particular lifetime. The bear isn't "chasing" you, he's running to stay close to you so that he can keep an eye on you as you asked him to. Next time that bear is chasing you, stop running, turn around, and face him. You have my word that not only will he not hurt you, he'll embrace you.

When we're on The Other Side, preparing to come here, we choose a team of protectors for ourselves to help us through this rough trip on earth and make sure we get Home again safely. Included in that team is our Spirit Guide, our Angels, and the animal of our choice, since animals are pure spirits, among God's most sacred creations. That animal, in spirit form but often visible to us in our subconscious minds while we sleep, is our totem. Chances are there's a certain animal you feel oddly interested in or drawn to for no apparent reason. If so, I promise that's your totem, and it's with you right now, never letting you out of its sight, watching over you and loving you with that amazing, uncomplicated, unconditional love animals elevate to an art form both here and at Home. As you try to figure out what your totem is, don't try to apply logic or convenience or what you'd choose as a pet. My totem is an elephant. My friend Bernie's is a rhinoceros. One of my ex-husband's is a panther. Not exactly pet potential, any of them, but I have to admit, you get me near an elephant and it won't be easy to tear me away from it.

A.B. would agree, I'm sure. "I'm thirty-one years old and the mother of three boys," she says. "All my life I've had dreams about whales. I'm always on the shore of some ocean with huge whales swimming and breaching alongside of me. They are so close, right next to me, but I have no fear of these beautiful, amazing creatures. Why do I keep dreaming of whales?"

I could do a whole paragraph about whales representing freedom, grace, power, and awesome beauty. And in some dreams, to some people, that's exactly what they mean. But in A.B.'s case, she's been dreaming of whales all her life because the whale is her totem, and her spirit, while she sleeps, holds that knowledge dear, and takes every opportunity to go visit her beloved protector.

C.K., on the other hand, describes regular tangible contact with her totem without understanding what's going on: "Very often when I'm half awake and half asleep, I feel a cat lying beside me. Sometimes I feel it walking on me and curling up to sleep beside me. What's weird is that I can clearly see the shape of a cat, but at the same time it's invisible."

As good a description of a cat in spirit form as you could ask for, and a nice reminder that spirits really do have form and shape and are only "invisible" because they live in a different dimension with a higher vibrational level than ours.

Here again, cats in dreams have a variety of "traditional" meanings, but they depend on the dreamer's subjective experience. To many, cats mean stealth, grace, independence, intelligence, and ancient wisdom. To some, dreams of cats indicate betrayal, fear, sneakiness, and arrogant dismissiveness. All of those meanings are valid, they're just not all likely to be valid *to you*, and nothing matters more than that as you examine and learn from your dreams.

And then there's J.S., who wrote, "One night I dreamed of myself as an eagle standing on top of a castle. A few seconds later, the eagle I knew was me flew above the huge plain and disappeared into the forest. What does it mean?"

One indication that you've experienced an encounter with your totem while you sleep is if you identify so closely with the animal that you can't clearly tell the difference between yourself and it. J.S. has the joy of having an eagle as his totem. "Traditionally," though, dreams of eagles, and of most birds, mean a yearning for freedom, for independence, and for escape from something that seems to be confining or limiting us. Unless, of course, birds are frightening to you, but I'm sure I've long since made my point about the importance of what all these archetypes mean *to you*, and I'm afraid I might be on the verge of clubbing you over the head with it.

Not all animals in dreams are our totems. I wish I could offer you a guaranteed way to know for sure, but there just plain isn't one, other than to consider the possibility and see if it seems to resonate as the truth deep in your spirit, where the truth is held safe and dear.

Even when they're not our totems, animals are very useful in our dreams to embody issues that our conscious minds are either trying to avoid or haven't become fully aware of yet.

"I often have dreams where I have one or more of my cats with me away from home, and I'm terrified that they'll get out of the car or I'll lose them somehow. I even hide one of them in a zip-up case, with a person to hold him there. The fear of losing them is intense, and I wake up feeling I did lose them somehow, it's my fault, and there must have been something I could do."—Barbara

In this recurring dream, cats are being used to represent loved ones in general, to help Barbara address her fear of separation and her self-imposed burden of believing that it's her sole responsi-bility to keep loved ones from leaving her. What her subconscious is begging her to learn from these dreams is that the only relation-ships worth having are ones in which all efforts are mutual and re-ciprocal, and that holding on too tightly to those she loves is a sure way to make them start looking for escape routes. As tired a cliché as it is, it's still valid to urge that if you love something, let it go, and if it comes back to you willingly, it's yours forever. Remember, Barbara, sooner or later all hostages, even those who are suppos-edly well cared for and even "loved," come to resent their captors.

S.J. shared a release dream that made very clever use of the fre-quent archetypes of rats and mice: "I was in a grand mansion with all of my dear friends. We were enjoying each other's company, but we were waiting for the musicians to come so we could start danc-ing. All of a sudden, these freakishly huge, vicious rats with grue-somely sharp teeth appear from out of nowhere and start chasing me. I'm not afraid of them. In fact, I think they're quite cute. But I run anyway, because they're chasing me, and I suddenly fall down a long chute to another level of the mansion. Now I find myself sur-rounded by tiny, adorable mice that seem to be in a state of sus-pended animation, waiting for something. There's an orchestra, my arrival starts the music, and that reanimates the mice. The rats are still chasing me, and to escape them, I find several platforms that go up and down and seem to disappear into the ceiling."

Very often, rats and mice in a dream indicate an unpleasant feel-ing of being overrun by something or someone. That's the case in S.J.'s dream, but with the interesting twist that the creatures who are overrunning her have clearly endeared themselves to her. The mice are "adorable," and even the huge, vicious rats are "quite cute" and not at all frightening. S.J. is lucky enough to be surrounded by some pretty terrific family and friends, and it's no wonder they are endeared to her. The fact that she sometimes feels as if she needs a little privacy and time to focus on herself isn't an indictment of them or her love for them, it's just a signal that she'll be doing herself a huge favor if she learns to start setting some reasonable, loving boundaries to make some space for herself that's hers and hers alone, so that she won't feel this stampede of loved ones can just "appear from out of nowhere" or be so dependent on her that her presence "starts the music and reanimates" them.

Both E.M. and her husband used the archetypes of wolves and coyotes in release dreams to illustrate another very common parents' fear: "In my dream, my husband and I were sitting on lawn chairs beside a hill with our five-year-old son. All of a sudden, a pack of wolves appeared. They didn't harm my husband or me, but they took our son and were slinging him around and dragging him away. I don't remember even getting up. The next morning my husband and I were eating breakfast and he said he had the weirdest dream last night. He and our five-year-old were hunting for coyotes and my husband went into a tree to watch for them, leaving our son on the ground. All of a sudden there was a loud stomping noise and a huge wolf came out of nowhere and starting chasing our child, but my husband couldn't do anything about it from up in the tree."

Wolves and coyotes in dreams generally represent stealth and being pursued by something cold, emotionless, and predatory. They're a looming threat of impending danger, not only to our physical well-being but to our emotional health as well. In E.M.'s case, and her husband's, these release dreams are a reaction to the fact that, after years of their being able to have the vast majority of control over his environment, their son is starting school, where he'll be affected by all sorts of influences whether they like it or not, which is why each of them had dreams of being powerless to help him. And it's no coincidence that they both used wolves and coyotes as archetypes to illustrate their feelings of "throwing their son to the wolves" of these new influences. It's very common for people who are emotionally close to each other to share telepathic images, especially during sleep. In this case, whichever of them started using the wolf symbol in his or her dreams simply transmitted it to the other one, as surely and clearly as if they'd spent that night watching the same subconscious movie.

There are almost as many animal archetypes in dreams as there are animals. Again, as you read the above "traditional" meanings and the ones of the most common animal symbols that follow, don't forget to add your own very personal and therefore very valid definitions. Many of my clients keep lists of archetypes, not just of animals but of all categories, in their dream journals, with two lists of meanings beside them—"traditional" and "mine." I'm sure they'd recommend it as strongly as I do.

Frogs can indicate a feeling of being overrun and "plagued" by too many people or too many demands and expectations. They're also a frequent sign of being jealous of someone or being the target of someone else's jealousy.

Foxes often mean the temptation to take either a sly or sneaky approach to something you want to accomplish, or the concern that someone around you is being sly or sneaky toward you rather than straightforward, so that you feel you need to "watch your back."

Birds, in addition to signaling a yearning for freedom and lack of confinement as we discussed earlier, can also be a sign that good news is coming.

Owls can hint at a yearning to achieve deeper spiritual wisdom. Also, because they're such skilled predators, they can be a warning flag about someone around you who means you some kind of harm, more often emotionally than physically.

Horses are great archetypes of strength and a yearning for some-one with whom to share burdens. They're also classic symbols of a need for or a feeling of having accomplished a new level of earthly wisdom.

Elephants, too, are wonderful symbols of physical strength, as well as tenacity and fierce loyalty.

To my amusement, dreams of *donkeys* have nothing to do with the Democratic party. Instead, they classically mean either point-less stubbornness or a fear that you've recently made a complete jackass of yourself.

Next comes a category of dreams we've probably all had at some time or other and looked back on with a shudder, thinking, There *must* be something wrong with me!

Nudity and Other Public Embarrassments

The good news is, those dreams in which we find ourselves naked in public or making some other spectacle of ourselves are al-ways release dreams. So let's pause to celebrate that they're not wish dreams or, worse yet, prophetic. They're also very common, and I've never in my life met anyone who enjoys them, including me.

Here's just a tiny sampling of a stack of dreams my clients and readers shared on this particular subject:

"I have a recurring dream about not being able to find a private toilet to do my business."—V.O.

"I keep dreaming of being in a hotel, trying to find a room. Sometimes people give me wrong directions. The elevator doesn't work. I get stuck in it, or it goes to the wrong place. There's always a bathroom involved. Sometimes I'm taking a shower in a locker room, and I've forgotten my shampoo or given it away, and somebody else is there that I can't hide from. Then, every time, I have a problem with the commode. It's either 'under construction,' it's just a hole in the floor, or it's been detached from the wall. Last night I was on the roof of the hotel trying to crawl in the bathroom window because apparently I forgot my key."—M.W.

"All my life I've had a recurring dream about being in a bathroom and sitting on the toilet. And there was this man looking in the door. I think the door had been opened or taken off. I was screaming and crying, but he just laughed at me and would not leave."—B.B.

"In real life, I'm pregnant with my first baby. I keep having dreams that I'm breast-feeding him and I suddenly realize that no milk is coming. Then I realize that I'm sitting on a public bench in a wide-open park. There are people watching me, and even though I know them, it makes me nervous and embarrassed."—Tanya

"In my recurring dream, I'm awakened by an earthquake. It terrifies me so much that I jump out of bed, race out my front door, and run for several blocks. I'm standing there in the middle of the street completely naked when all around me people start coming out of their houses and apartments, calm and normal and dressed for work and gaping at me like I'm insane. I'm completely humiliated, and from the looks on their faces I get the feeling that no one else even felt the earthquake but me, which makes me look even more inappropriate than I'm already feeling."—Denise

Release dreams like these aren't exactly apt to make us leap out of bed in the morning with a spring in our step, but again, because they're so common, they're not to be taken as signs that we're secretly disgusting or that we should check ourselves into the nearest psychiatric hospital as soon as possible.

You've probably heard or read that these dreams indicate a fear of exposure, and that's true for the most part, although we can go a little deeper than that. They can also hint at a feeling of being unprepared, or too vulnerable, without enough internal defense mechanisms to protect ourselves. And then there's a fear of being a target of ridicule, or of people catching us with our guard ("pants") down, without the facades we've all developed for "public consumption," which dreams like these bring into sharp focus. "Fear of exposure" also encompasses the fact that we all have a secret or two, something about ourselves we keep hidden out of the usually correct belief that it's no one else's business, and if our "business" is ever thrown open to public scrutiny, we'd lose any dignity, respect, and credibility we've worked so hard to establish.

Fortunately, this is another release dream that lends itself perfectly to programming a new ending, so that once you've experienced the release of the fear, you can wake up with the sense of control these dreams make us feel so incapable of. In your pre-sleep prayers, demand that the next time you have a fear-of-exposure dream, no matter what the specifics, when it reaches its most embarrassing moment, you'll look around to discover that everyone who's been watching you in past versions of the dreams is now doing exactly the same thing you're doing. If there's a witness to your using the toilet, have them walk in and join a whole group of people on either side of you who are using toilets as well. If you're breast-feeding on a very public park bench, become one of a whole crowd of women on other park benches for as far as you can see who are also breast-feeding. If you're naked in the middle of the street, simply make sure that all those people who are gaping at you are naked, too. You'll be pleasantly surprised at how empowering it is to refuse, even in your dreams, to be made to feel exposed and inappropriate.

Losing Teeth or Hair in Dreams

"I keep having the same dream over and over. My dream always starts with flossing my teeth. Then they start to get loose. Then, one by one, they fall out, and within seconds, I have no teeth left."—F.R.

"I have a lot of dreams where it feels like my teeth are falling out. Sometimes they all end up in my hand, shattered and crumbled into dust."—L.C.

"I have a recurring dream that my teeth are falling out and I'm in a panic and everyone else seems to be going on with their normal business."—M.Q.

"I frequently have dreams where my teeth are falling out. I'll be talking and they just crumble and fall into my hand. There is no pain, just my teeth falling out."—W.B.

"In this dream, I woke up in the morning feeling great, and then I sat up in bed and looked back to find that all my hair had fallen out on my pillow."—S.O.

"I dreamed I was in the shower, getting ready for work just like always, and I stepped out of the shower and looked in my bathroom mirror and I was completely bald. I looked back into the shower, thinking maybe my hair had fallen out when I washed it or something, but it wasn't there. I panicked and started to cry, and then I woke up."—J.F.

In my completely informal, unscientific poll over the last thirty years, I would say that about 95 percent of those who have dreams of losing their teeth or hair are women. I'm not quite sure why that is, although based on what these dreams usually mean, I can make some completely informal, unscientific guesses.

A majority of the time, a dream of teeth falling out means we regret something we've said, or regret that we've talked too much.

It could be that women have these dreams more frequently than men because we do tend to talk more, and God knows we remember everything we've ever said in our lives, and everything anyone's ever said to us, especially if it was insulting. Frankly, I think we could learn a lesson or two from men, who are better at what I'll politely call "selective memory" and, when quoted verbatim even just a day or two later, will often say and truly believe, "I never said any such thing." (What I really think is that both sexes would do well to find a happy medium between remembering every word and remembering not one word at all, but that will simply never happen.)

In addition to regretting something we've said, though, dreams of teeth falling out can indicate as simple a vanity concern as a fear of getting old, or as simple a dental hygiene concern as knowing it's been too long since you've been to the dentist and being afraid that losing all your teeth might be the price you have to pay for the neglect. Your subconscious might even be signaling you of an oncoming dental problem that you haven't consciously picked up on yet.

Only you know which of these explanations are most likely to be behind these release dreams. Happily, each of them can be addressed if you'd like to get rid of the dreams once and for all. If it's vanity, take it from a sixty-six-year-old woman, with the help of the brilliant cosmetic dental procedures available today, it's possible to have prettier teeth in your sixties than you had in your twenties, and worth every penny and the temporary diet of soft foods. If it's fear of losing your teeth from years of neglect, don't think about going to a dentist, just do it, or look forward to more of those same dreams in the future. And if it's regret over something you've said, even if you do it for the selfish reason of putting these dreams behind you forever, *apologize*. Never doubt for a moment that an owed but unspoken apology does a whole lot more damage to us than it could ever do to the person we owe it to, and the proof lies in the obvious fact that it can be powerful enough to disturb our sleep with some very unpleasant and very unattractive dreams.

As for dreams of hair loss, they most often involve fears of exposure or embarrassment. They can also include obvious vanity issues and fear of old age, and in men, there are typically added concerns about losing their strength and virility. I make no secret of the fact that the finest, strongest, bravest man I know happens to be completely bald, so men, I'm sure most women will agree with me when I urge you not to worry about it.

A recent client who's going through some serious marital problems had a lovely experience with a hair loss dream. After years of feeling disrespected and controlled by her husband, she informed him, and meant it, that she wasn't going to tolerate his behavior toward her any longer and that if things didn't dramatically change between them, she would leave him. She found a great therapist, started doing some great work on her self-confidence, and found ways to leave no doubt in his mind that she meant business. In the midst of all this growth on her part, some of which was very difficult and took a lot of courage, she had a dream in which her hairline receded several inches, so that from the top of her head forward she had no hair, only very soft, fine, pale fuzz. She happens to be a steadily employed actress on a popular television series whose living is partially dependent on her appearance, so it surprised her as she thought back on the dream that she wasn't even slightly upset about how silly she looked with only half a head of hair. Instead, she found it interesting and couldn't figure out why, in some odd way, it actually made her feel good and even a little exhilarated. It finally came to her as she continued telling me about the pale fuzz that had replaced her own hair and heard herself say, "It was so soft, like the hair of a newborn." We both agreed that someone who's working very hard on growing and changing and expanding their self-knowledge couldn't ask for a more obvious sign that their efforts are paying off than to look in the mirror and see hints of a newborn looking back at them.

Makeup, Masks, and Faceless Strangers

"I have recurring dreams in which I'm constantly trying to entertain people who have no faces."—Janice

"I've been seeing masks on people's faces in my dreams, similar to party masks or masks right out of *Phantom of the Opera*. Most of the faces are very scary. The sights were intense for about a month, and I saw them everywhere, at the mall, at the beach, anywhere crowds were gathered. The appearances went away for quite a while, and they've returned now, but not nearly so intensely."—Kara

"I keep having almost obsessive dreams about makeup—putting it on, buying it, sharing it with friends, talking about it, etc. I know it doesn't sound like that big a deal, but it happens so often that it's getting a little scary."—Alexandra

These fairly common variations on an archetype are fascinating because they often indicate two sides of the same coin, with that coin being the word "identity." If we feel there's a huge disparity between the face we wear in public and the person we "really" are, it can seem logical to assume that those around us are doing the same thing, and actually start viewing the world as a sea of masks disguising true identities. If we feel faceless and easily ignored, why wouldn't we project that same lack of identity onto everyone we encounter? And what could be a clearer way of asking not to be ignored than a dream of trying to entertain an audience of faceless people? Makeup, of course, is another identity statement (and I for one thank God for it every day), just like masks and no faces at all, or anything connected to the concept of hiding our true and invariably flawed personas.

Another frequent cause of dreams in this particular archetypal category is a fear that we can't trust our own judgment when it comes to the people we let into our lives, so that, in our dreams, no one seems genuine and it's impossible to tell who anyone really is or even tell them apart. If you've been betrayed by someone in whom you invested an enormous amount of trust, or if there's someone around you you're trying to trust despite some evidence that your trust might be misplaced, these dreams can be very useful in pointing out a huge part of life you might want to work on. I hope you won't ever be offended when I recommend a professional counselor or therapist if you need help with issues as important as identity, self-confidence, trust, and character judgments. I work with the mental health community on a mutual referral basis, I place great value in the work of qualified psychologists and psychiatrists, and I've turned to some wonderful therapists myself in rough times and know firsthand what a profound difference they can make.

So please pay attention to the frequency of these dreams and the extent to which they seem to be affecting your waking hours. If it starts to feel as if they're getting too frequent or too "real," I do hope you'll seek good, reputable professional help, and if you have trouble finding someone, call or e-mail my office and we'll be happy to refer you to one of the hundreds of doctors we work with throughout the country. A world full of masks, disguises, and no faces at all might be an interesting place to visit in your dreams every once in a while, but not for one moment do I want you to live there.

And a special note to the woman who wrote about her boyfriend's recurring dreams of finding his ex-girlfriend's face beneath his own: please don't take his fear lightly that he might end up, as you put it, "doing the same thing to me that his ex did to him." He's holding on to more guilt, pain, and anger than is healthy for either of you, and I want you to make it a condition of your continuing to be with him that he get into therapy immediately.

More Archetypes, More Possible Meanings

Not all common dream symbols fall into convenient categories like the ones we've already discussed, but that doesn't mean they come up any less often and can't be just as confusing. I refuse to call this section a "dictionary" of dream archetype definitions. Instead, please consider it a *guide*, nothing more, nothing less.

Moving hands in a dream usually indicate a concern about work and career-related issues.

Idle hands in a dream usually indicate issues dealing with unemployment, boredom, a lack of progress, depression over not accomplishing things.

An arrow pointing toward you in a dream usually indicates that someone is on their way to you.

An arrow pointing away from you in a dream usually indicates that someone is leaving.

Luggage in a dream usually indicates travel, obviously—sometimes upcoming physical travel, but sometimes an impending emotional journey as well.

A pine tree that's prominent in a dream usually represents a particularly strong character who's either important in your life or will be soon.

Books in a dream usually represent education, learning, and wisdom but can also reveal an inhibited nature due to too much self-doubt and self-criticism.

The moon in a dream usually indicates an especially strong connection with the power of one's feminine side, one's emotional side, and one's psychic, intuitive aspects.

Garbage cans in a dream usually indicate an excess of gossip, either too much indulgence in it or the fear of being the subject of it.

Bells in a dream are usually connected to a celebration of joy or a victory, often a victory of the spirit over some moral dilemma.

A mountain in a dream usually concerns a struggle, either physical or emotional, or the satisfaction of having triumphed over a struggle.

A lit candle in a dream usually symbolizes a connection to one's faith and spirituality. *An unlit candle* indicates a yearning for that connection.

A rose in a dream usually represents love, appreciation, and a sense of thriving, physically or emotionally.

A cross in a dream usually represents the obvious—a strong connection to one's religious beliefs—but also an exploration of those beliefs, as well as either a need for protection or a desire to protect.

A circle in a dream usually indicates a sense of completion, as well as a growing connection with one's development of psychic gifts.

A key in a dream usually represents a new opportunity or an upcoming change in one's career or personal life.

An open door in a dream usually signals potential new situations. *A closed door* often symbolizes a feeling of rejection, isolation, or loneliness, or just as often, a sense of being safe and secure, depending on whether you're outside or inside that closed door.

Stairs in a dream usually symbolize a challenge or aspiring to a new level in some area in your life or, when you climb and climb and climb with no apparent progress or destination, a sense of futility, often indicating a need to change jobs, location, or a relationship.

Tickets in a dream usually indicate a sense of being included in something that was previously unavailable or off-limits.

Your signature in a dream usually indicates issues regarding a promise, a commitment, or a business agreement you've either just made or are about to make. If the signature is bold and strong, you're optimistic about it. If it's unclear, shaky, or looks as if you ran out of ink, you either are or should be having second thoughts.

Sunflowers in a dream, interestingly, usually reflect an interest in or a special affinity for American Indian history, often unrealized and eager to be pursued.

A sword in a dream usually signifies an interest in world history.

A triangle in a dream usually signifies an interest in metaphysics.

A blue cross in a dream usually spotlights the presence of a spiritual leader or your potential to become one.

A yellow cross in a dream usually spotlights the presence of a philosopher or your potential to become one.

A hike or walking excursion in a dream usually symbolizes a period of disorientation and loneliness, or a sense of disorderliness, or a decision-making process.

An old woman in a dream usually represents security or a yearning for emotional maturity and wisdom.

An old man in a dream usually represents a yearning for intellectual growth and wisdom.

Heroic dreams are usually subconscious compensation for a general feeling of inferiority, ineptitude, or being underappreciated.

The sex act in dreams usually indicates a need for emotional intimacy, an overdependence on others for reassurance and self-confidence, or a discomfort with verbalizing repressed emotional issues.

Flowers in dreams, contrary to old-fashioned superstition, do not foretell the death of a family member. Granted, odds are that when you dream of flowers, sooner or later some family member or other is going to die. When you dream of *anything,* some family member is undoubtedly going to die *sooner or later*. Instead, flowers in dreams usually signify vitality, a reawakened appreciation for life, or the giving or receiving of respect.

Pregnancy in dreams usually has nothing at all to do with biological pregnancy but instead indicates the impending birth of a new aspect of you, a previously hidden or inaccessible part of yourself that's about to be born. The frequent fear in pregnancy dreams that those around you will disapprove of the "baby" is usually an insecurity that this "new you" won't be accepted by loved ones who might be resistant to the changes in yourself you're about to make.

The devil in dreams usually signals an unfounded, unfairly programmed sense of inadequacy and unworthiness.

Death in dreams usually signals the exciting demise of an old attitude, belief system, approach, structure, habit, or situation that has outlived its usefulness, making way for your own important "rebirth." Please don't ever be afraid of dreams of your own death. They *never* mean your own *physical* death, I promise you.

As I said earlier, I really would love for you to write your own list of archetypes and their meanings in your dream journal, because no one can do it better than you for your own purposes. I know it can be frustrating to read the definition of a dream symbol and realize it doesn't apply to you by any stretch of your imagination. But look at it this way: if there were only one meaning, etched in granite, for every archetype found in dreams, that would mean all of us who dream are nothing but mental, emotional, and spiritual carbon copies of each other, and that all the mysteries in our dreams were solved thousands upon thousands of years ago when humankind first began interpreting them. I'm not sure which of those two concepts would be more horrible, but I'm eternally grateful that none of us will ever have to find out.

Chapter Ten

✳

THE POPULATION OF OUR DREAMS: FROM LOVED ONES TO ODDLY FAMILIAR STRANGERS

I'm not sure anything enriches and confuses our dreams more than those people we choose to "cast" in the tragedies, occasional comedies, historical dramas, and travelogues our subconscious minds produce for us while we sleep. The oddest collection of characters can show up, some we recognize, some we don't, some we're not sure about, appearing and disappearing, sometimes for the most obvious reasons and sometimes for no apparent reason at all, leaving us to wake up feeling fairly sure someone we spent time with during the night was trying to tell us something, if we could just figure out what it was.

Adding to the mystery and the intrigue is the fact that the people we summon, seek out, meet with, and envision during sleep are there for our purposes, at our insistence, as themselves and as archetypes, not just because of who they are but because of who they are *to us*.

Loved Ones with Messages

"My deceased grandmother came to me out of nowhere," writes R.F. "She took my arm to stress the importance of what she was about to telepathically tell me. I was to contact Sylvia Browne to ask her about 'him.' Alive, my *abuelita* only spoke Spanish, but telepathically she spoke perfect, non-accented English. I got the feeling that 'him' was a reference to the boyfriend I recently broke up with, but I'm open to any other thoughts of who 'him' might be."

This is a wonderful example of bringing in the heavy artillery while we sleep to make a point we're reluctant to consciously accept. R.F. knows perfectly well that the "him" her grandmother was concerned about is her ex-boyfriend. She knows he's emotionally dangerous to her and potentially physically dangerous as well, and that he has no intention of staying away permanently. Most of all, she knows that, left to her own devices, she might not have the strength of will to continue resisting him if he's relentless enough and manipulative enough, especially since he's so familiar with her weaknesses and how to use them against her. And so, rather than rely on her own sometimes clouded judgment (like all of ours from time to time, let's face it), she summoned her grandmother, her *abuelita*, the person she trusted most, someone who'd always had R.F.'s best interests at heart, someone whose wisdom, strength, and love she knew could empower her, someone who would never let something as trivial as "death" keep her away. Like the vast majority of messages received while we sleep, R.F.'s experience wasn't a dream. It was an astral meeting between her and her grandmother, as real as any of the frequent conversations she'd had about her ex-boyfriend with "living" family and friends, with the advantage that she and *Abuelita* could speak volumes with the simple telepathic message about "him."

And for the record, R.F., I know it won't surprise you to hear that I support your grandmother's position a thousand percent. Please stay away from this man. You have too much to lose and nothing to gain from giving in to him again.

If a woman named A.B. ever doubted that loved ones keep an eye on us whether they're "gone" or not, it was erased in one quick recent astral trip to a cemetery. "My father and I were driving along in the graveyard where my late uncle is buried, when suddenly my uncle appeared and warned us about something being wrong with our car. I told my father about this dream, and how real it seemed, when we were at dinner a few nights later, and even though he's pretty skeptical about things like this, he decided to have the car checked out just in case. I don't know who was more surprised, me or him, when it turned out there was something seriously wrong with my dad's brakes."

A quick note about cemeteries: You've probably heard me say about a million times that your deceased loved ones aren't there. I can't tell you how often spirits have told me about taking the car trip to the cemetery and back home again with their families and friends. They only care about your visiting their graves if it brings you comfort. So please don't get the mistaken idea that A.B.'s astral meeting with her uncle happened at the cemetery because that's where he was. It happened at the cemetery because that's where *she* was, astrally traveling to see him in a place where she feels particularly close to him in her waking hours.

Now, don't start getting annoyed with your deceased loved ones for not giving you clear warnings like that one about car trouble and other practical matters. They try more often than we give them credit for—our most typical response, whether we're awake or asleep when the messages are given, is to either ignore them or give ourselves a pat on the back for our "intuition" about something being wrong. Yes, sometimes our sixth sense absolutely warns us. But other times, the warning comes from someone we think we've lost, who met us while we slept, to share information with our subconscious minds that our conscious minds are far too noisy and cluttered to hear during the day. Credit goes to A.B. for hearing and remembering the warning, and to her father for heeding it despite his skepticism.

K.C. also chose an astral meeting place with a deceased loved one where she felt secure about being able to find her. "I had a dream three or four months after my grandmother died in which she arose from her casket and looked at me. I kept telling her that I loved her, and she just looked at me with this kind of amused stare. It was as if she was asking me why I was repeating it over and over again, when I'll have forever to tell her that. I also remember she wasn't wearing her glasses or hearing aids."

First of all, never doubt what good sports our deceased loved ones are about where we ask them to meet us while we sleep. This astral experience happened fairly soon after K.C.'s grandmother went Home, which is why K.C. still associates her with a casket, the last place she saw her. As time goes on, and K.C. starts remembering her grandmother's life more clearly than she remembers her death, they'll find hundreds of prettier, more inspiring places to get together.

Second of all, when you have an astral encounter during sleep, keep in mind that nine times out of ten the words "it was as if" can be accurately translated to mean "I was given a telepathic message." It's not unusual to look back on an astral meeting in the "rational" light of day, have an impression that we were involved in a conversation with a departed loved one, but then dismiss it as *only* an impression, since we're fairly sure no actual words were exchanged. Our conscious minds are so addicted to verbal communication that we don't pay nearly enough attention to the stunning, eloquent efficiency of telepathy between two spirits. In K.C.'s case, it wasn't "as if" her grandmother was assuring her that they'll have forever to say "I love you." That's exactly the telepathic message her grandmother gave her. K.C. was repeating "I love you" as a form of good-bye. Her grandmother was simply responding with a reminder that there was no need for good-bye, because this "death" process isn't an ending at all.

Third of all, if K.C. had any doubts before this experience that her grandmother made it safely to The Other Side, the absence of glasses and a hearing aid should have eliminated them. Illness and infirmities are earthly, human afflictions. There are no such things at Home, where we're all in divine, perfect health.

Pam received a beautiful, crystal clear message, with the added bonus of validation from hundreds of miles away, that's stayed with her for more than thirty years. "My father died in 1966. I was fifteen. My sister was almost eighteen. One night in 1971 I had a dream. My father was with us all again, in the house I grew up in. We were all so happy, but he couldn't stay. He said he just wanted us to know he would know our children. My sister and I lived in different states by then and hadn't spoken in a while, but on the phone the next day we discovered that we'd had the exact same dream at exactly the same time. It happened to us again—same dream, same night—about a year later. How could our dad visit both of us at the same time? And why haven't we had any more visits from him ever since. Also, our mom died in 1990, and neither of us has had a single visit from her. Is she okay? And if so, what's keeping her away?"

This is a great opportunity to remind us all how hard it is to think "outside the box" of the earthly laws of physics and picture the spirit world, where none of those laws apply. What could be more natural than Pam wondering how, with her and her sister living in two different states, their father could visit them both at the same time? And yet, she answered the question herself without realizing it, when she said that they were all together in the house she grew up in. She and her sister didn't have the same "dream," they had the same astral experience, "flying in" from their respective earthly locations to meet their dad at a place full of mutually cherished memories. If you've read *Life on The Other Side*, you know that spirits actually can bi-locate, i.e., be in two places at once. But in this case, Pam's father didn't have to, any more than she and her sister did in order to meet at their former family home.

Pam says her father "just wanted us to know he would know our children" as if confirmation that he was alive and well and looking forward to watching over his grandchildren was pretty much of a yawn as news goes. After fifty years of passing spirits' messages along to clients, I still never cease to be fascinated by the frequent nonchalance, and even occasional disappointment, with which those messages are received. A supposedly deceased loved one says some version of "I didn't die after all! I'm fine, and I'm right here!" and it's not at all unusual for a client to reply to me, a little annoyed, "That's it? That's all they had to say? That they're here?" It always sounds comparable to "Yeah, yeah, eternal life, big deal. I was hoping to hear something interesting, like lottery numbers or why she left the good china to Aunt Dorothy instead of me." Sorry, but ninety-nine times out of a hundred, the message our departed loved ones are so eager for us to hear is that *there is no death*. I know it's simple, but I can't really think of a more thrilling message than that.

At any rate, back to Pam's questions—and I really can't stress enough how understandable they are, I just needed to vent that one occupational frustration. Pam's father is still very much around. Pam has continued to visit with him during her sleep from time to time, it's just that her memories of the visits haven't been as vivid as those early ones were. And during her waking hours, I know she has had occasional electrical problems around her house without realizing that he's causing them to get her attention, and I also know she has felt someone in the backseat of her car while she is driving and even been a little surprised when she checked the rearview mirror and didn't see anyone. Pam needs to talk to her father, to tell him how much she loves him and misses him, and by all means suggest specific meeting places in her prayers every night before she goes to sleep. Sooner or later she'll see him again, and this time wake up remembering it.

As for her mother, patience is the key. She's fine, she's just been in Orientation. Before the end of 2002 Pam will have a crystal clear visit with her while she sleeps. In anticipation of that first meeting, Pam should start talking to her now. Fill her in on everything she has wanted to tell her over all these years and let her know how much she is looking forward to being with her. Not only will she hear Pam, but she'll find a way when both of them are together to confirm that she heard her.

Lynn is in a confusing situation that left her a little unsettled after an astral visit she mistook for a dream. "My sister died in the autumn of 2000. Not long after her death I started having feelings for her husband, whom I didn't particularly care for while she was alive. May of the following year he and I got involved in a long distance relationship. And then recently I had a dream about her. She was at my house. I remember waking up to find her sleeping beside me in my bed, just like when we were children. I started walking around trying to understand why she was here. I knew she had died, and yet it seemed normal to be with her. Her husband walked into the room as though everything was just like it was when she was alive. I remember watching them together and thinking, Okay, this is fine, they're husband and wife, they're meant to be together. When she and I were alone again I said, 'There's something we need to talk about.' She replied, 'Not now. We'll talk about it later.' Just as I nodded agreement, the dream faded away."

Lynn's relationship with her late sister's husband is fine with her sister. Lynn's needless guilt colored her interpretation of her sister wanting to postpone the conversation about it. The truth is, Lynn's sister completely understands. She also knows that Lynn is going to have some of the same problems with her husband that she did, but it would be too easy for Lynn to mistake her caution for disapproval, so she'd rather say nothing at all. Just notice the setting and the dynamics of this astral experience—Lynn and her sister sharing a room and a bed together, just like when they were children, while the husband only puts in a brief appearance. In other words, being sisters is far more important to both of them than either of their relationships with this man. And the moment Lynn found the three of them in a room together again, she didn't hesitate to respect her sister's marriage, exactly as she always would have if her sister were still here. It's also interesting to note that on The Other Side, Lynn's sister has complete access to Lynn's life chart and her husband's. She knew both of them were going to be together before the two of them did, she knows exactly why both of them charted this relationship into their lives, and she knows exactly what's going to happen. Next time she sees her sister, Lynn should not waste time on guilt. She and her sister have far more interesting things to talk about, don't you think?

Kim took a gorgeous astral trip to The Other Side for a fairly uncommon moment I'm sure she'll never forget. "I had a dream that I'm holding a child in a very holy church, and the most beautiful strong voice told me that the son I'm holding should be called Daniel. In that moment, two angels without wings flew around us."

As you might know from my previous books, among the countless details we write into our life charts when we're preparing to come here for another incarnation is the identity of our parents. We choose them, and they choose us. There are no accidents, even when there's a parent or a child it seems no one in their right mind would deliberately pick out. Kim had the gorgeous astral honor of attending a church blessing at Home in final preparation for her child's trip to earth, before Kim had even conceived him. The "beautiful strong voice" was that of her Spirit Guide, whose name is Timothy, and the two Angels attending the blessing were the Angels the child had chosen as part of his team of protectors for the lifetime he was about to embark on.

And then there's the name Daniel. I really want to stress that we don't just have form and personas and physical characteristics when we're here on earth. We're every bit as viable, solid, and distinctly individual, if not more so, in our real Home on The Other Side. We have height, weight, eye and hair color, physiques, and even names, which God gave us at the moment of our creation an eternity ago. On The Other Side, the person who'll be born to Kim in infant form is named Daniel, just as he'll be called here, and it might even surprise Kim and the others who'll be around to love and care for this child from the moment he arrives how remarkably quickly he seems to respond to his name.

"When my son was five years old," writes J.D., "he had a dream in which God and the Angels told him something, and he was sent to tell me. Unfortunately, he can't remember what it is! Can you help?" I can help J.D., but in this case I have a feeling that what his son was sent to tell him is something he's already discovered: that while he'll have a very full, active, and independent life, he's really here for J.D. this time around. They've had no fewer than four past lives together, two as brothers, one in which his son was J.D.'s father, and one in which they were in battle together and J.D.'s son saved his life. There are some very specific things J.D. has come here to learn, and J.D. and his son made a pact on The Other Side that his son would be the one to teach J.D. No one on this earth knows J.D. better than his son does, which means he'll test J.D.'s limits more expertly than anyone else possibly could. When he does, J.D. should try to remember, in the midst of his frustration, to say thank you. His son is living up to a promise he made to J.D. long before he was born.

Sometimes the message a loved one comes to deliver simply boils down to "I know you're confused, and I'm here to help." A dream from Nancy illustrates that experience beautifully: "I was in a large log structure on a huge mountain. One whole wall was glass, facing the ledge of the mountain, so that when you looked down from it you couldn't see the ground beneath you. There were a lot of people with me, maybe thirty or forty of them. Suddenly I heard a voice, and I knew it was God. I knew everyone else had heard it, too, since they were all crying, as I was. He told us to go outside, and we did, still crying. I was so happy to hear Him. I remember thinking, He hasn't forgotten me after all. As I was walking outside, I saw my deceased grandmother walking toward me. I fell into her arms, crying, and she told me that everything was all right, just listen to Him and listen well. Then God started talking again. He told us to look out over the edge of the cliff, and when we did I saw a few people scattered on ledges below. As I looked at them, God said, 'These are the people I'm giving knowledge to, so that you can learn from them. Listen to them. They know.' The next thing I saw were these deep blue tornadoes, coming down from the sky and hitting each of these chosen people in the chest, while God explained, 'I am now giving them the knowledge that you seek.' The whole time I was still crying, and my grandmother was still by my side, holding my hand. Then the dream got a little fuzzy, and then downright dumb, with God giving lists on how to improve ourselves and other self-help advice. I woke up crying like a baby."

This is a wonderful example of a loved one making an astral appearance in a release dream, with a glaring archetype thrown in for good measure. The archetype is the mountain on which the dream takes place, and its meaning is the classic one we discussed in the previous chapter: the mountain represents a struggle, in this case the spiritual struggle Nancy was going through when the dream began, feeling as she was as if maybe God had forgotten her. We know that this is a release dream because of the glimmers of absurdity in it, culminating in the idea of God Himself gathering a group of people together to listen to Him dispense "dumb" self-improvement lists. It's a very safe bet that when we do hear His voice, the word "dumb" won't be among the adjectives we come away with.

So what was Nancy's deceased grandmother's role in this release dream? She was there for comfort and support, obviously, to put her arms around Nancy while she cried and to hold her hand as the rest of the dream played itself out. But she also was there to reassure her that everything was all right, and to tell her to listen carefully as God spoke. At first glance that might seem like the most rhetorical piece of advice ever offered. It's hard to imagine any of us having to be told to listen carefully to something God in His own voice has to say. In this case, though, what Nancy needed, because of the struggle she was going through, was to listen to what the God she was in the process of constructing had to say—a God who might be capable of forgetting one of His children, a God who picks favorites to dispense wisdom to while deliberately leaving out others, and ultimately a God who by her own description isn't even all that bright.

I happen to think it's a brilliant exercise that Nancy's grandmother accompanied her through, and an inspired approach to those times when you're feeling confused about or disconnected from God: create a situation in which you're encountering who God would be if He were like what you've started imagining Him to be, and then play it out to its logical (or, in this case, inane) conclusion. By the time Nancy was finished listening to a forgetful, elitist, dumb "Supreme Being" offer self-improvement techniques, you can bet the contrast between him and the all-knowing, all-loving God she was finding her way back to had made its point, and as a result her faith became stronger than ever.

When Dreams of Loved Ones Are Disturbing

It would be so nice if we could count on leaping out of bed feeling excited and rejuvenated after experiences with deceased loved ones while we slept. But life is too complicated and we're too complicated to expect that to happen. Instead, if nothing else, maybe the biggest lessons to be learned from the downside of dreams of loved ones are that it's imperative to keep our emotional business current as best we can while we're here, and that we've got to stop and think before we inflict pain of any kind, because we have no control over how deep the wounds will be or how long it will take them to heal.

"When I was a child, I had a dream that my father took me to the park and abandoned me there. I cried so hard, and I ran toward him, but he ran away. When I got to where I thought he was, it was like a jungle, full of wild animals, and I couldn't get in."—J.H.

You see what I mean? This wasn't just a dream J.H. had, it was the cell memory of an actual past-life experience in Nigeria in the mid-1600s. J.H. was born into that lifetime with a severe disability. His father was humiliated to have an imperfect son and, when J.H. was six years old, took him deep into the jungle and left him there, where J.H. couldn't and didn't survive. Centuries later, on finding himself in a body again, J.H. was still associating "father" with "abandoned" and "jungle" and still trying to release through dreams the heartbreaking terror of an egomaniac's inhuman cruelty. As I do to anyone who has had a dream like this, I suggest saying the prayer in Chapter 7 and repeat saying it every night before sleep, in my words or your own, because I don't want anyone to spend one more moment under the weight of that pain. Here is a slightly altered version of the prayer I know will help: "Father God, please help me release into the white light of the Holy Spirit any negativity I've brought from another lifetime into this one, so that it can be resolved forever in Thy divine, perfect peace. And just as I release that past negativity, let me embrace the joys, the wisdom, the love, and the gifts from other lifetimes, that I may awaken tomorrow with a renewed sense of confidence and self-respect and an abiding awareness of the eternity with which You've blessed my spirit."

Not all cruelty is deliberate or motivated by malice, of course. Sometimes it comes from selfishness, or loneliness, or a combination of both. "My oldest sister had the same dream repeatedly after our father died. They had a stormy relationship. My father loved us, but he seemed to have set up my sister as more of a wife to him than a daughter, on a purely psychological level. (There was never any physical or sexual abuse.) He was seventy-nine when he died, and my sister was forty-one. She was still having vivid, disturbing dreams about him until recently, when she took Daddy's photo down and put it away. If Daddy was contacting her during sleep time, why were all the dreams 'bad'?"—Kay

Before I even start, I want to mention how much it always touches me when someone contacts me on someone else's behalf. Your sister is lucky to have you, Kay.

Kay's father isn't contacting her sister while she sleeps. Her sister was having release dreams about him, over and over again, repeating their relationship in her sleep in the hope that somehow, finally, it would come out okay, and she'd be allowed her childhood just once, instead of being expected so young to have the emotional maturity of a woman. I know she expressed her resentment toward her father hundreds of times during their "stormy relationship," and I also know he refused to accept the fact that he was wrong in using her to indulge his neediness. He put her in an impossible situation by taking advantage of her natural love for him, so that she found herself in a classic love/hate position, and because he was such a stone wall about it, she wasn't able to work through it with him while he was around. I'm glad that putting his picture away helped, but a few months of therapy to release the residual anger she's been trying to release while she sleeps would help her even more.

And then there are completely well-intentioned but misguided actions that have cruel, potentially long-lasting results. "I'm a junior in high school," writes Laurie. "My father is gone, and my mom and I are living in the southwest now after moving here from the midwest. I started having horrible dreams about family members dying, so my mom took me to a therapist who gave me sleeping pills to make the dreams stop, but it didn't help. Now I'm having dreams about the boyfriend I broke up with when we moved. It makes me think there's some unfinished business with him back in the midwest, and that I won't be able to go on with my life unless I take care of it, I just don't know what it is. Can you help me?"

Laurie's mother tried to do the right thing by taking her to a therapist. I hate to second-guess things based on so little information, but I hope that, maybe through a school counselor, she will get a referral to a different therapist who'll see her on a regular basis without being so quick to prescribe sleeping pills that can severely disrupt her need for the release of healthy dream cycles. And though I *definitely* don't prescribe any medication, ever, because I'm neither qualified nor licensed to do that, I think Laurie should discuss, with either a new therapist or with her family doctor, the possibility of taking an antidepressant to help her through this very difficult time she's going through. The dreams she's having, both about family members dying and about a boyfriend she is now separated from, are all about feeling terribly abandoned and isolated. She is dreaming of her ex-boyfriend not because there's unfinished business there but because he's familiar and when she was with him she didn't feel so alone. She is not yearning for him, she is yearning for the feeling of belonging, and believe me, the right therapist can help her a lot. Laurie needs to remember that she didn't create her current situation by herself, so she shouldn't take on the responsibility of trying to fix it by herself. Best of luck, Laurie. You'll be in my prayers.

People in Our Dreams as Archetypes

Laurie's dreams of her ex-boyfriend illustrate a very common device our subconscious minds use to make a point: enlisting a familiar face to symbolize the emotional issues we're working on. There's no doubt about it, it can be hard to distinguish between dreaming about a specific person and dreaming about the feelings with which we associate them. I'd love to give you a hard-and-fast rule for telling the difference, but there isn't one, and I'm certainly not going to mislead you by making one up. I can tell you, though, that as you look back on dreams of specific people, it's worthwhile to at least consider the possibility that you weren't meant to take those dreams literally, and that you'll learn more about yourself if you step back for a wider view of them. Don't stop at asking, "Who was that person?" Ask, "What does that person represent to me?" and see where the answers to that question take you.

Take a dream for M.E., for example: "I left Jamaica last year to start school in Barbados. My grandmother died in New York that same month, and I was extremely upset because I didn't get to visit her before she died. Not long after she passed away I had a very upsetting dream. I was in what seemed like a black cloud coming out of nowhere, and I saw my grandmother walking down the path to get to my town house in Jamaica. I screamed out her name to try to get her attention. She turned around and looked at me very blankly. I wanted to tell her that I love her, but she quickly turned and proceeded on down the path. I kept screaming her name and she continued walking away, and I actually felt a stinging pain, like electrical shocks, from her obvious angry dismissal of me."

I hope it's obvious that this is definitely not an astral visit from M.E.'s grandmother. Instead, this is a release dream in which M.E. used her grandmother as a symbol of her guilt and grief. M.E. is very angry with herself for being so involved with her own life that she didn't get to her grandmother in time to say good-bye. She shouldn't be, of course—it's happened to all of us, and no good-bye was necessary, since her grandmother is around her all the time and is enormously proud of her. In order to dramatize that anger at herself while she slept, she had her grandmother act out that anger toward her, just as she felt she deserved.

What we know as an absolute, guaranteed, no-exceptions fact, though, is that no one on The Other Side is even capable of being angry with us, ever. So that is one hard-and-fast rule you can count on when you're trying to figure out if you experienced an actual person in a dream or if you're meant to focus on what that person might symbolize to you: if anyone from The Other Side ever seems angry or upset or unhappy or displays any other negative emotion of any kind, it wasn't really them at all. Period. You simply used them while you slept to demonstrate your own emotional issues, to help you know what you need to work on during your waking hours.

Not all people who act as symbols in dreams are brought in from The Other Side, and here's a letter from Linda to prove it: "I recently dreamed that Sylvia Browne was talking to me about my love life. A little background—I recently got together with an old boyfriend I consider to be the love of my life. He doesn't call me very often, but last week he called and I saw him twice. But in this dream, Sylvia told me that he was evil and that I should stay away from him. There's another man I've been seeing, and she said I should keep going out with him instead and just enjoy him for the short amount of time we would have together. Afterward, I'd be able to carry on with my life the way it should be, with my old boyfriend in the past where he belongs. I guess my question is, could Sylvia really have contacted me in a dream like this, and should I really follow the advice I dreamed she gave me? I love my old boyfriend so much that two years ago I sought counseling because I was feeling suicidal without him. I'm better now and glad to be alive, but I can't stop feeling that he and I are meant to be together someday."

There are certainly times when I astrally visit people while I sleep. This is not one of those times. Linda should notice that I didn't tell her that her old boyfriend is not ultimately the man for her and she should put him in the past where he belongs, and I didn't tell her that her relationship with this other man will be brief and of no real consequence. *She* told *herself* that. She simply used me to tell her something she already believes, probably because she is familiar enough with my work to feel confident that I really am psychic and I don't believe in lying just to make someone feel better for a few minutes. Her old boyfriend isn't evil. He also isn't capable of offering her the happy, stable, secure life she deserves—he's never been committed to her and he never will be. If she and he did get together someday on a full-time basis, she'd be miserable. I guarantee it, and she's already subconsciously sure of it, too. The man she has been seeing isn't for her either, which she is also sure of, or she wouldn't have had me stress how temporary that relationship is. There's someone else coming who'll be wonderful for her, but only if she'll let herself be completely available emotionally instead of reserving a part of her heart for someone whose real purpose in her life is to teach her to walk away when she is getting anything less than the best.

T.S. shared this experience: "In August of 2001 we moved from New Mexico to Arizona, and I was unsure if I should continue in real estate. That was very much on my mind one night before I went to sleep, and I had a surprisingly vivid dream. Sylvia came to me wearing a blue flowing dress. Her hair was shoulder length. She sat across a table from me and said, 'Of course you should continue in real estate, you will be very successful and very happy in this field. That's why all the doors open for you.' It was so real that I expected you to be in my house when I woke up. I didn't get a chance to ask you to confirm this when I attended a lecture of yours a few weeks later, but I really didn't need to—you already gave me the answer."

I'd love to take credit for this, T.S., and I'm so honored that you and so many others over the years have given me such a special role in your dreams. Again, though, I'm not the heroine of this story. You are. You're completely confident that you're pursuing exactly the right career for you, and I was only a symbol of your own intuitive certainty that you're on track with your life chart. There's nothing for me to add but my applause.

In case you're wondering, this isn't false modesty on my part when I insist that I'm only an archetype, not a messenger in these dreams. I just want to be sure with all of you that when your own psychic instincts and subconscious powers are so obviously working like well-oiled machines, you give yourselves, and God, every bit of the recognition you deserve.

And by the way, a little off the subject, but just to validate a letter from Jenna: "I dreamed I was at Sylvia's house. I was in her bedroom, saw her bed, and a very large-screened television. Her granddaughter was there, about eight to ten years old, with shoulder-length dark hair. In what seemed to be a living room was a very elderly man whom I thought might be Sylvia's father, but it was strange, because he was just sitting in a comfortable chair and seemed to be oblivious of what was going on around him. Sylvia didn't acknowledge me, which was fine—I didn't want to be rude, because in a way I felt I was invading her private space."

I often work in my bedroom, so it makes sense that Jenna would picture me there. I do have a large-screened television. My granddaughter is eight years old, with shoulder-length dark hair. I know exactly the chair Jenna saw my father sitting in. He passed away a few years ago, but that's his favorite chair when he comes to visit. As for "invading my private space," anyone is welcome to pay me astral visits anytime they like, as long as they come with love and keep the noise level at a minimum.

The "Strangers" in Your Dreams

Not every stranger who shows up in your dreams and in your astral experiences while you sleep is really a stranger at all. Don't dismiss these "strangers" too quickly because you didn't recognize their faces or you don't think you know anyone who looks like that. As with so many things in sleep journeys, it's the essence of that person you need to focus on, not the physical characteristics, and if the essence seems oddly familiar, or like someone who might have a message you should pay attention to, stay focused until your heart tells you who that stranger actually was.

L.T. had a visit from a "stranger" with a message a few years ago, if she could just figure out what on earth he was trying to say. "Eight months after my father passed away, I had an experience while I was asleep that seemed too real to be a dream. I was actually asleep and dreaming when my dreams were interrupted by everything becoming foggy or smokey, as if I was on the inside of a cloud. Out of this white foggy cloud came a black dot in the distance, the size of the tip of a pen. It came toward me in a rather smooth, gentle glide, but extremely fast. As the 'black dot' approached me, it became increasingly clear that it was the face of a man (no body), coming right up into my face. I didn't recognize him. He looked Greek, or maybe Middle Eastern, with dark curly hair and a round face. I was asleep but awake, as strange as that sounds. He said five words to me, telepathically but loud and clear. The words were 'You will win the lottery.' I somehow internally spoke back to him and asked him what he meant by that. He immediately moved away from me exactly the same way he approached, back into the fog, into the distance, becoming a little black dot again, and then he vanished. As he did, the fog disappeared, and everything returned to normal again. I kept yelling louder and louder, upset, asking him to please come back and explain what he meant, but he was gone. I felt elated and optimistic about the future when I woke up the next morning, but to this day I still don't know what he meant. It's been almost four years now, and I certainly haven't won the lottery. In fact, not only am I too broke to buy a ticket, but my life has deteriorated so much that sometimes it's almost unbearable to be alive. Please tell me what happened and what I'm supposed to make out of all this."

For some reason it amuses me no end—and believe me, I'm laughing with you, not at you, L.T.—that through all your curiosity about the message you received, not once did you ask, "And by the way, who was that man?" Not to worry, I'm going to tell you anyway. The man who astrally visited you that night was your Spirit Guide. His name is Tyrone, and his message was as hopeful as you first felt it was, it just suffered a bit in the translation and understandably led you to think he was predicting your winning a financial lottery. While that's not the lottery he was referring to, I do promise your financial situation is going to start turning around within the next sixteen to eighteen months. The lottery, or enormously valuable win, Tyrone was referring to is the only kind The Other Side knows or cares about. There's no question that you've been going through a very rough period. Possibly without even realizing it yet, you're growing more spiritually from this rough period than many people do in an entire lifetime. You're going to emerge from these troubles a truly extraordinary person, to the point where, hard as this is to believe right now, you'll actually look back on these last several years and say, "If that's what it took to get here, it was all worth it." If you're reading this thinking that spiritual growth is lovely but it won't pay the rent, I understand. In fact, I've been there. I'd love to tell you that your financial relief will come first. In your case, though, it will essentially be a tangible reward for the amazing spiritual evolution you know is already under way. Please don't even think about checking out of this lifetime by your own hand for any reason, ever, but most especially when there's so much joy, and the money to celebrate it, waiting for you right around the corner.

A.C. astrally traveled to a "stranger" to learn the source of some of the serious emotional issues that were nagging at her to be solved. "In this dream, a male I neither knew nor recognized had a very serious head injury. (I believe he was shot in the head.) For some reason, I was constantly at his bedside in the hospital, helping and encouraging him, and assuring him everything would be okay. He was very dependent on me and didn't want me to leave. His family was very resentful of me because he only wanted me with him and would send them away when they came to visit. I remember some reference from one of his family members that I was just a golddigger. Toward the end of the dream, I went to my place of employment and filled them in on this man's condition. They understood why I would be away from work for a while. At the end of the dream, I returned to the hospital. The man's family was gathered outside his room, trying to keep me from going back in. He became so upset that the doctor had to scold the family about it, and they left, furious with me, while I went back into the hospital room to calm the man down."

I don't doubt for a moment that A.C. has had a lifelong feeling of never being really accepted, no matter how hard she tries or how much effort she makes. I also don't doubt that this feeling is holding her back, both personally and professionally, because she sometimes rejects people or opportunities without giving them a chance, to avoid giving them the opportunity to reject her, as she's sure they will if she drops her defenses and lets them into her life. Her spirit took this astral trip to her past to show her where this problem comes from so that she can finally start to heal from it. It was the early 1900s, and the man in the hospital bed was her husband. He was much older than she was, and his family had hired her as a part-time live-in caretaker when he suffered a debilitating stroke. His family—three sons and a daughter—was nasty and abusive toward him and hired A.C. so that none of them would have to take care of him themselves. They occasionally went through the motions of visiting him because he was wealthy and they felt entitled to inherit his money. A.C. never fell in love with him, but she was fond of him, devoted to him, and protective of him, especially around his children. He proposed marriage to guarantee her some security when he was gone, and she, a widow with no family of her own, accepted. His children were livid when they heard that he'd changed his will and left everything to her. A.C.'s astral trip was to his hospital bed on the last day of his life. He hadn't been shot in the head, but the brain aneurism that killed him had essentially the same effect. His children's cruelty toward her after his death was relentless and ultimately successful. They ended up with his entire estate, and she ended up alone and virtually broke, despite her legal entitlement to a considerable fortune. The desolation, and even beyond that the unfairness of it, has carried over into her lifetime this time around, and by astrally traveling back to it she's trying to release it once and for all. She'll be successful at it when she realizes that this cell memory from a hundred years ago is only relevant to the life she's living now to the extent that she allows it to be.

Gary had a marvelous experience with a "stranger" at a time when he really needed a reminder that none of us has to get through these rough lives without some very powerful help. "A few weeks after my wife took off and left me and our three children, I had an odd, very real dream. I was working late in the high-rise where I work in real life. The building seemed completely deserted when I left my office and walked to the elevator. I can still hear my footsteps echoing on the marble floor, like I wasn't just the only person in the building, I was the only person on earth, and I remember thinking if it wasn't for my children I wouldn't care about living anymore. I was almost to my car in the parking garage when I saw a man leaning against the garage wall, like he was waiting for me. I was a little nervous because he and I were the only two people around, and mine was the only car on the whole parking level.

He had light-colored hair, a slender build, and a kind of ordinary face, and I don't know what it was about him that made me think he'd seen a whole lot in his lifetime. When I got to my car, he took a step toward me, not threatening, and there was this kind of fog all around. He didn't talk out loud, but telepathically he spoke in a beautiful language I've never heard before, that I can only describe as very smooth and fluid. I couldn't understand the words, but I felt comforted by them. I woke up in tears. What's interesting was, over the next few days I realized I was putting in a lot of overtime at work to keep from being in the house that reminded me of my wife leaving, but in the process I was being unfair to my kids, who needed me more than ever, and I've been spending a lot more time with them ever since. Do you know who the man in my dream was, and if what he said to me was about my children?"

I'm so glad Gary wrote, because he reminds me of something I really want to mention. This wasn't a dream, it was an astral visit from his Spirit Guide, whose name is Marcus. And yes, he did talk to Gary about his children, simply telling him that he'll recover more quickly from the pain of his wife leaving if he focuses on helping his children through the pain and confusion of losing their mother. What will be interesting to so many people who are reading this is that, without realizing it, Gary really did understand every word Marcus said to him. He spoke to you in Aramaic, which is the universal language on The Other Side. We have temporary amnesia about much of our lives at Home during our brief lifetimes here, including our conscious ability to speak fluent Aramaic. But our spirits retain it, and it's not all that uncommon for us to have conversations in Aramaic during astral experiences with spirits from Home while we sleep.

For the record, by the way, shortly after Gary starts divorce proceedings, his estranged wife will want to come back to him. He shouldn't fall for it. It's not him and his children she'll be missing, it's the stable, secure lifestyle he provided, which she's now discovering she can't provide for herself. She has problems he can't begin to fix, and she'll cause far more heartache than he and his children deserve.

Some strangers in dreams are there to wave flags about something in our lives that we already have concerns about but aren't paying enough attention to, either because we don't want to or because we don't know what to do about it. A dream from Jean-Marie illustrates that point: "I had to fly somewhere with two other people. I was the pilot, and the other two people (both male) were sitting in the cockpit. The two males had great confidence in me. We all had parachutes. But the chest straps that held the arm straps were missing. I was nervous, but I seemed to have enough knowledge to fly a plane or skydive. I managed to get the plane off the ground, and all three of us jumped safely into the night. I don't remember landing after jumping out of the plane, but I do recall a sense of urgency about getting the plane in the air and over our jump spot. That's the end of the dream. I normally don't remember my dreams, unless they are visitations or prophetic in some way. Usually the prophetic ones are literal. This one has me stumped."

Jean-Marie is exactly right, prophetic dreams are literal, as are the vast majority of astral dreams. The dream she sent me is a wish dream. Please don't let it confuse you that she was flying in this dream without its being an astral experience. We definitely have the sensation of flying during astral trips, but we certainly have no use for a plane. And notice that she's at the controls of the plane, with two males looking on, completely confident in her. Even with flawed parachutes, they execute their jump safely, exactly over their target spot, without Jean-Marie ever handing over the controls to anyone else.

There are two men in Jean-Marie's life (and I can psychically add that one is older than Jean-Marie and one is approximately her age) who are doing their best to control her by making her feel inept and helpless. In her dream, she wasn't just in charge, she was in charge of a potentially dangerous situation, and it ended with the greatest success. In her waking life, she is getting ready to take charge, too, and dreams like this one are there to help build her confidence as that time approaches. In her dream, these two men are supportive of her. In real life, she'll get some resistance from the men in question. Their comfort level includes having some power over her, and they won't give up that power easily. But her comfort level demands that she "take the wheel" of her own life, and I guarantee, this dream is telling her that that's exactly what's in the process of happening, and that it will work out beautifully for her and, in the end, for the two men in her life as well.

The strangers in Jean-Marie's dream symbolized two very real men in her life. Strangers in dreams can also represent classic archetypes, as they did in two separate dreams from Esther: "I've had two dreams about a woman named 'Bee,' an elderly black woman who lived in an old white house. In the first, I was following her from room to room in her house while she dusted. She was talking to me, and I could feel she loved me, even knew me, and somehow I knew her. The rooms seemed to be very small and full of things she had collected over the years. There was an old man sitting in an old brownish-orange recliner in the living room, watching TV. That's all he did, ever. In the second 'Bee' dream, I was running into the woods on a foggy, moonlit night, trying to get away from an old white car I thought was chasing me, and there sat Bee's house in a clearing. As in the first dream, she said she was expecting me and welcomed me with a comforting, knowing smile. The old man was in the chair again. She seemed to talk to him with her eyes. I don't remember ever seeing his face. She was constantly moving, always taking care of things but still there to listen to me if I wanted to talk. I knew she loved me and wanted to help me, if only I'd ask. But I never did, and I have no idea what she wanted to help me with. I awoke feeling happier than I had been in a very long time. That day, like the first time I'd dreamed of 'Bee,' I received bad news. But 'Bee' had left me with the feeling that everything would be okay, and that feeling turned out to be right."

What I love most about these dreams is how classic the symbols in them really are, and how well they illustrate why we don't ever want to throw out the whole idea of traditional archetypes, no matter how much we might stress the importance of our own personal connections to the symbols we dream about. In both dreams, Esther finds her way to a house—classically, the archetype for *her*. Inside that house she finds a very busy elderly woman—classically, the archetype for the emotional side of our nature. She also finds a completely inactive, silent, disconnected, "faceless" elderly man—classically, the archetype for our intellect. When Esther receives bad news, it's Bee/the elderly woman/her emotional strength that sees her through and comforts her, while the elderly man/her intellect never enters the picture. Throughout her life, I'm willing to bet that Esther has found her greatest sense of skill and identity through her emotional depth, while feeling very little connection to her intellectual potential.

What I would love to see for Esther is an eventual dream where Bee and the elderly man, who doesn't even have a name in her dream, let alone a purpose, are equally busy, equally defined, and equally interested in connecting with her, to indicate that she has learned to rely on both gifts working together. And I promise that will happen if she simply starts putting some energy into all the learning she can get her hands on. I want her to make a list of three subjects that are of special interest to her, and then, one by one, start digging into them. Read. Take night classes or correspondence courses. Meet other people who share those interests. I can tell Esther, both psychically and logically, that because of the wonderful range of her emotional side and her ability to empathize with people without judging them, she'd be an especially talented psychologist, and that psychology would be a subject she'd be drawn to like a magnet once she started exploring it. Esther should watch how her dreams of the balance between her emotionalism and her intellect begin to change. Since the archetypes she uses in her dreams are so classic, it should become fairly easy for her to interpret them.

Believe it or not, there was a time in your life when there were no strangers in your dreams at all, and you astrally visited The Other Side in your sleep as often as possible, much more at Home there than here as you adjusted to the disquieting reality of finding yourself in a tiny, vulnerable, defenseless body again. And a lot of people, even some "experts," thought nothing of any particular interest was happening to you while you slept, because you didn't seem to have much to say about it the next morning. How much could you have had to say anyway, the logic goes, even if you had the vocabulary? After all, you were only a child.

Chapter Eleven

✳

WHEN CHILDREN DREAM

I can't begin to count the number of books, articles, and studies I've read in thirty years on the subject of children's dreams. Many of them are interesting, thorough, exhaustively researched, and earnest. Even more of them are boring, overwritten, and so clinical in their approach that you'd never guess they're dedicated to something as fascinating as what goes on in a child's mind and spirit during sleep. One thing that gets on my nerves about the majority of writing that's been done about the dreaming children do is that the children are always referred to as "they." I know it's a small point to get annoyed about, and I'll be using "they" myself in the course of this chapter. But there never seems to be a reminder that "they" aren't some strange, alien species with great research potential. Rarely would you guess that not only are "they" precious, complex, highly individual little human beings, but "they" are who "we" once were. To talk about children's dreams is to talk about our own earliest dreams as well, most long forgotten, many embellished over the years, but all of them as much a part of the fabric of our subconscious lives as our children's dreams are to them. And if you have trouble remembering that, I hope you'll turn back to Chapter 7, the chapter on astral visits, as often as you need to and notice how many of those "dreams" start with some version of the words "when I was a child."

Behind a Child's Dreams

Most researchers who specialize in children's dreams work from the premise that children are born brand-new, clean slates with their own unique genetic characteristics, starting from scratch and developing from there in fairly predictable ways. Which means those researchers and I are headed down two completely different roads before we've even started.

I work from the belief—actually, the *knowledge*—that we were all created an eternity ago, with an eternity left to live, in our real Home on The Other Side, and that from time to time we choose to incarnate here on earth, in circumstances of our own design, for the progress of our spiritual growth. Our spirits, carrying knowledge and memories from previous incarnations and from our lives on The Other Side as well, enter the embryo prior to birth, so that every newborn infant—every one of us, in other words—is born in possession of a vast wealth of wisdom, stored in the spirit mind of the subconscious. We come from perfection into imperfection, from complete freedom of movement and speech and thought into tiny, limited, limiting, preverbal bodies, to fully experience as much of each new lifetime as we feel we need to accomplish the goals we set for ourselves before leaving Home. To expect us to be thrilled about being on earth in these bodies again just because we chose to come here is like expecting soldiers to be giddy about every moment of boot camp just because they enlisted. Ultimately, we know why we're here, we've done it before, and we know we have the exquisite, sacred joy of The Other Side to look forward to when we've finished this particular leg of our souls' eternal journey. Blank slates when we're born, starting from scratch? Not even close.

When we're children and our spirit minds are turned loose while we sleep, there's a whole lot going on with us. Astral travel, our friends and loved ones back Home, and the spectacular beauty of The Other Side are part of our very recent past. We're surrounded by strangers, defenseless and vulnerable, and finding ourselves in a body again brings back a flood of cell memories from other lifetimes, some lovely, some terrifying. Who would blame us if we astrally escape for visits back Home on a regular basis for our first several years? Who would blame us if we sometimes wake up very frightened, wondering if some cruelty we went through in another time and place is going to happen to us again? Who would blame us if our still-developing conscious minds don't retain much of what our spirit minds are up to while we sleep, or if our almost nonexistent early vocabularies aren't adequate to try to describe it even if we do remember?

I've told this story before, but I happen to love it, and it also sweetly illustrates one child's recurring adventure during sleep. When my son Chris was three years old and I would ask him every morning if he'd had any dreams during the night, he frequently told me he was playing with his friends on the steps of a great big building. He wasn't any more impressed with the experience than when he told me about playing with his friends during the day, and there's no doubt about it, he kept his descriptions simple, brief, and to the point. I'd ask him a few questions about it here and there, trying to get more information without feeding him any of my own, but it was always just friends, steps, great big building, and a "no big deal" shrug.

This went on for a few weeks without my giving it much thought. But then one morning, after another quick report from Chris about the same "dream," my Spirit Guide Francine demanded a word with me. She wanted me to have a little talk with Chris about his nighttime activities. It seemed that he and any number of other children from earth were gathering with alarming frequency on the steps of the Hall of Wisdom, one of the most gorgeous and revered buildings on The Other Side, to run, play, giggle, and chase each other all over the place, decidedly disturbing the peace, and it would be greatly appreciated by the general population of Home if I would ask him to please either keep the silliness at a minimum or find another place to play with his friends.

For the record, I did gently scold Chris about it, he said he was sorry without once asking what in the world I was blathering about, and I never got another complaint from Francine or anyone else back Home.

Inside a Child's Dreams

I've worked with hundreds of children throughout my careers as a teacher and a psychic, and between my sons and grandchildren and several foster children, I've raised many of my own. As a master hypnotist, I've also had wonderful glimpses into the subconscious minds of children, that are so busily at work while they sleep. So I feel as qualified as any "formal" researcher to make a few observations of my own about children's dreams.

The younger the infant, the more frequent their astral trips to

The Other Side during sleep, as an escape to the Home and loved ones there, where they feel so much safer and more secure than they feel here for their first few years.

The younger the child, the more clearly they can remember their previous lifetimes, for better or worse, and the more likely they are to revisit those lifetimes while they sleep, as a cell memory/ "déjà vu" reaction to being in an earthly body again.

Researchers have found that very young children, i.e., before they're three or four years old, never include themselves in dreams. That's true. The reason for that is that infants and toddlers don't yet have a sense of their identities in this new lifetime. They have some memories of their personas on The Other Side, and they can remember much of who they were in past lifetimes. But for their first two or three years, they're strangers to themselves as surely as amnesia victims are strangers to themselves, taking in seemingly disjointed information from around them and trying to fit the pieces of the puzzle into some sort of order. I've worked with toddlers who knew their names on The Other Side better than they knew their names here, who remembered being their new mother's father in a past life and were still trying to piece together the odd new rules of their relationship, and who had clear memories of dying in a concentration camp, or in a terrible shipwreck that in later years they'd be able to describe in amazing detail as the *Titanic*. Any very young child who can tell you with greater certainty who they used to be than who they are now isn't likely to be attached enough to their current identity yet to find it useful in their dreams and astral travels while they sleep.

Researchers have also found that children don't tend to include strangers in their dreams until around the age of six. Again, I agree. Between their birth and the age of six, children's spirits while they sleep are very active and gravitate most often to what's familiar. At those young ages, familiarity can be found in past life-times, on The Other Side, and increasingly, in the people in their immediate vicinity. So yes, it's true that before they're six years old, strangers won't appear in children's dreams. But the fond and familiar faces they dream of and visit in their sleep aren't neces-sarily anyone we would recognize, and we might actually mistake them for "imaginary friends" if we're not tuned in to the amazing range of a child's spirit life.

And by the way, a little off the subject, but just as it's a mistake to underestimate the wisdom and eternity of memories children bring into this lifetime with them, it's also a mistake to underesti-mate their uncanny psychic abilities. Watch them from infancy on as they stare at, giggle about, talk to, and play with what might look like thin air to everyone else around them. In their young worlds—and *our* worlds at their age, don't forget—spirits are as real as we earthly people are. Sadly, many children lose their con-scious access to the spirit world by the age of ten or twelve, and a big part of the reason for that is that they're made to feel foolish and inappropriate, and they're even accused of lying, when they try to share a spirit experience with an adult. *Please* encourage your children to talk to you about their past lifetimes, their lives on The Other Side, the "invisible" people they talk to, and the journeys they take while they sleep. You might think it's not that important, but I promise you, it is. I once knew a child who, when he was four or five years old, loved to pull me aside and tell me all about the people from his past lives who were showing up in this life, and what a huge kick he got out of their not having a clue what he was talking about when he tried to remind them of it. He didn't discuss this kind of thing in front of his parents, though, because it seemed to upset them and, if I'm recalling his words correctly, "creep them out." The next time I saw him he was eleven years old, and he had no memory of any of our conversations or any of that knowledge.

As far as I'm concerned, without the open-minded, loving encouragement of the people around him, in those five or six years he lost his unquestioning acceptance of his own immortality, and I find that to be one of the most heartbreaking losses any of us can go through.

Nightmares and Night Terrors

"When I was a small child I had a recurring dream that had me and two other children walking down a dimly lit cobblestone street with the store shingles that sometimes moved with the wind and made sounds of metal against metal. We were unsure of ourselves and wanted to get inside, somewhere it was warmer. It felt like it was a street in England before the time of automobiles and such. We entered a door and there was no one there. Tiptoeing to some stairs, we began to move down toward what I think was a basement and one of the stairs squeaked. Peering around the corner, I saw a man with a large knife looking up at us with an angry and scowling face. We became terror-stricken and ran up the stairs, out the door, and down the street. Turning to look over my shoulder, I saw him chase us, waving the knife in his hand and shouting at us. I was holding the hand of each child that was with me and telling them to run as fast as they could, and then I awoke."—M.L.

"I still remember a dream when I was a child. I lived in a flat in San Francisco. Downstairs, below the different flats, was the basement, which had different locked storage areas. I was with my father and a few of my uncles. It was dark and we were searching the hallway. There was something behind me, something that so frightened me that I was too scared to call out for help. I opened my mouth, but my voice was paralyzed."—J.H.

"When I was a young child, I had a dream that a very short green alien came in through my window and I remember trying to scream but nothing came out. Do you know what it means?"—T.C.

"I remember having a dream that was so vivid in color and sound, when I was a child about eight to ten years old. What I remember of the dream is this: strange men came to our farmhouse, and I was afraid of them. I got on our only phone near the living room window trying to call for help (this was back in the era of telephones with short cords and no chance to wander about chatting). They saw me through the sheers hanging at the windows. I dropped the phone and ran. They shot at me through the window. They broke in (I think) and chased me up the stairs. I ran faster and headed down the other staircase and out the front door. They shot twice at me and I felt the bullets enter my upper arm (now I can't remember which arm or exactly when I was shot—in the house or in the yard). Shocked, I ran down toward the barn with plans to circle back and hide under our front porch, behind the concrete steps, until they left."—M.M.

I wanted you to read all four of those dreams without my interrupting to demonstrate something I've found to be true in the vast majority of children's nightmares: almost without exception, they involve being chased. I'm not completely sure why that is, but I have a strong feeling it's a combination of blended frightening moments from past lifetimes and the growing awareness of frightening elements in this new lifetime, along with some inadvertent revisions over the years that make the dreams more complicated than they probably were at the time. Researchers have found that children don't even start having nightmares until the age of three, which does give them plenty of time to be exposed to a sense of potential danger around them, whether it's from their parents' arguments (and don't *ever* kid yourselves that your children don't know you're fighting just because they're in another room at the time—even if they can't hear you, I'll stress again how unbelievably psychic they are) or from television or from some really hideous fairy tales and lullabies.

When my children and grandchildren were very young, I never let them anywhere near anything but the most child-oriented television shows, absolutely nothing violent or scary, no monsters or aliens, and nothing that would even *imply* that it's acceptable to be cruel or to hurt anyone. I also very deliberately refused to tell my kids any stories about witches in gingerbread houses who cooked children and ate them, or giants at the top of beanstalks who chased frightened little boys, or evil queens with poison apples, or bears chasing little girls who'd wandered into their house and fallen asleep. I never even hinted that there might be such a thing as a boogeyman, or a monster under their bed, or some horrible ogre of some kind hiding in their closet, and I certainly never sang them to sleep with songs in which babies and their cradles fell out of trees, or taught them prayers that included the possibility that they might die before they woke. And I swear to you, not one child that was raised in my house ever suffered from nightmares or night terrors. Not one.

There's another significant reason for that, too, though, that I've discussed in previous books, and it's important to discuss it here as well. I'll tell you right up front that this works and it makes a difference, so even if you don't buy a word of it and only do it to have a good laugh at my expense, I don't care, *just do it*. Every single night, from the moment you bring your new baby home from the hospital right on until they've started preschool or kindergarten, make a habit of standing beside their bed when you know they're asleep and very quietly, so you won't wake them up, giving them the following affirmation: "Precious child, tonight as you sleep, wherever your dreams and journeys take you, I want you to let all the fear and pain and illness and negativity you brought with you through cell memory from a past life be released and resolved forever into the cleansing white light of the Holy Spirit. And, with God's help, let all the joy and love and talents from those past lives infuse you through that same cell memory and bless this new lifetime you've chosen to share with me."

You might be wondering how an infant is supposed to understand a single word of that. If you are, just remember the beginning of this chapter: you're not trying to communicate with the conscious mind of this tiny baby, you're communicating with a spirit mind in the child's subconscious that is as old and wise and sophisticated as yours, and the spirit mind will appreciate and respond to everything you're saying, I guarantee it.

Still think I'm wrong, or maybe even crazy? That's okay. But look at it this way: if I am wrong, or crazy, that affirmation can't do any harm. And since it's such a small thing to ask of yourself, that takes less than a minute, and I know you want nothing but the best for your child's emotional and spiritual health, what have you got to lose by pretending to think I'm right?

The only real difference between nightmares and the night terrors of children is the fact that I've never met a child who can remember a thing about the cause of their night terrors. It's as if the conscious mind just refuses to deal with whatever was so frightening during sleep and simply blocks it out. Since children can't remember night terrors, they can't talk about them, which makes it very difficult for us to explore them.

I've wondered many times if a major percentage of night terrors might be caused by children's experiences with astral catalepsy. Two of the four dreams that began this section include a couple of the classic signs of astral catalepsy we discussed in Chapter 8: "I was too scared to call out for help. I opened my mouth, but my voice was paralyzed" and "I remember trying to scream but nothing came out." Astral catalepsy isn't that uncommon in chil-

dren, for the obvious reason that, while astral travel is as completely natural to them as it is to all of us, they're still trying to get
reacquainted with the process of their spirits having to leave and
return to a body in order to accomplish it, as opposed to the total
freedom of movement they were accustomed to on The Other
Side. It's no surprise that the spirit's reentry into the body that's
temporarily housing it is often awkward and uncomfortable, and
that, as a result, the child becomes aware of its spirit being half in
and half out of its body and experiences everything from paralysis,
to an inability to scream for help, to sensing an evil presence holding it down, to all the other sensations astral catalepsy can cause.
There's one account after another in Chapter 8 of this book of how
terrifying those sensations are in adults, who can research and
learn what's happening to them and why. Imagine how much more
terrifying they could be for children, who have no way of understanding why they woke up in literally mortal fear.

Again, since children seem to blank out whatever it is that
causes their night terrors, I can only offer this educated guess—
that astral catalepsy is a very likely candidate. I know that I suffered
from night terrors on a fairly regular basis when I was a child. I don't
remember a thing about what triggered them either. But considering that I'm not the most enthusiastic astral traveler in the world, I
have no trouble believing that waking up to find that my spirit was
just coming home from a night out might have upset me more than
enough to trigger a night terror. And I'm sure my mother, who believed that stories of boogeymen in the closet and monsters under
the bed were great ways to keep me from getting up and wandering around during the night, was a big comfort in helping me
through it.

Asking and Listening

I've urged you to be careful of the bedtime fairy tales and lullabies you use to put your children to sleep, and I've given you an affirmation that will effectively separate them from any past-life
negativity that's still plaguing them. I also want to urge you to let
your child know that their dreams are important, to them and to
you, listen patiently to the nighttime experiences they share with you,
and then help them as best you can to understand those experiences and put them in perspective. If the information in this book
makes that easier, nothing could please me more.

Several years ago a very earnest young father in the dream class
I was teaching at the time asked if I would talk to his four-year-old
daughter about a recurring dream she was having. The dream had
something to do with sailing away on a big boat. It didn't seem to
disturb her at all, but it was worrying him. Was his child expressing
a desire to get away from her home and a family who adored her?
Was this some past-life experience she needed help with, that I
could psychically uncover? He would appreciate my getting to the
bottom of whatever was causing his child to talk on so many mornings about being on a ship somewhere in the middle of the ocean.

It took less than five minutes, and it didn't take any of my psychic skills at all. If her father had asked the girl the same gentle
questions I did, he would have solved the mystery as easily as I did.
Yes, this little girl was having recurring dreams about sailing away
on a big boat. Had she ever seen a big boat in real life like the one
in her dream? Yes. On TV. Was anyone else with her on the boat?
Yes. Her mommy and daddy and two brothers and her dog. What
did they do while they were on the boat? They had fun. And how
did she feel when she was on the boat? Happy. In other words, this
recurring dream that her father was so afraid indicated her desire
to escape was really just a wish dream about having fun with her

family on a big boat like the one she saw on TV. And all he had to do to find that out himself was to ask.

A lot of really well-intentioned parents don't like to ask their children more than just a passing question or two about their dreams. Some of them are afraid to push, not wanting to make it sound as if they'll be disappointed if the child can't remember or if the dream wasn't all that complicated or interesting. Others are afraid that if the child's dreams are troubling, they won't have a clue what to say or do to help. Others prefer to downplay the importance of dreams in general, and let's face it, still others either don't have the time or don't take the time to have the conversation.

Tell me, would it have been helpful, or even just reassuring, if someone had encouraged the relationship between you and your dreams when you were a child? If they'd taught you the differences between wish dreams and release dreams and prophetic dreams, and talked to you about the wonderful people and places and times you can astrally visit without fear while you sleep? If they'd helped you understand that nightmares can really be useful, and that when something or someone is chasing you in a dream, all you have to do is stop running, turn around, and face them? If they'd taught you how to rewrite the endings of sad or scary dreams so that they'd turn out just fine after all? If they'd worked with you on what your dreams might mean, and planted the seeds of a worthwhile skill you could develop and explore as you grew older? If they'd shared the rich, timeless history of humankind's fascination with dreams and astral travel, and made you feel that while you sleep you become a part of blessings, magic, and mysteries as vast and eternal as God's creation itself?

If the answer to even one of those questions is yes, then you'll have some idea of what a difference you could make to a child thanks to regular conversations that start with a simple "Tell me about your dreams."

Chapter Twelve

✳

LUCID DREAMS AND DAYDREAMS: BETWEEN THE CONSCIOUS AND THE SUBCONSCIOUS

There are times when our conscious minds and our subconscious minds collaborate in some fairly common but fascinating ways. If we take these collaborations for granted and don't give them much thought, they can be just interesting little diversions. If we choose to take advantage of them, they can provide us with opportunities to give ourselves a regular supply of wonderful affirmations, and I happen to be a passionate believer in the power of affirmations.

Lucid Dreams

"Many years ago I had a dream that still intrigues me to this day. I was sitting in the window of my little office at home, writing correspondence on my type-writer. (I told you this was many years ago!) As I typed, something outside the window caught my eye, and I looked to see that maybe a hundred yards away, every word I was typing on the paper in my typewriter was also appearing on the high adobe wall surrounding my neighbor's house. I couldn't quite believe what I was seeing, so I typed the number '2' while keeping my eyes on the wall. Sure enough, at the sound of the typewriter key stroke, the number '2' appeared on the wall. I tried it again with the number '3' and it happened again. I made several more numbers appear on the wall with my typewriter before I suddenly realized that I was dreaming, since what was going on was so obviously physically impossible. I remember feeling relieved when I caught on that I was dreaming, because it explained this inexplicable ability to type on my neigh-bor's wall. And as soon as I figured out that it was a dream, I was never able to get another keystroke from my typewriter to appear on that wall."—Raymond

When you realize during a dream that you're actually dream-ing, you're having what's called a lucid dream. Nine times out of ten, what causes a dream to become lucid is the sudden conscious realization that something in it is too unlikely or downright impos-sible to really be happening, which makes the dream Raymond shared a classic example.

Lucid dreams have been part of the dream world for as long as dreams have existed, but the term "lucid dreams" came from a Dutch writer and doctor named Frederik van Eeden in the very late 1800s. "Lucid" simply means clear or rational, and van Eeden was so curious about the phenomenon and so adept at it that he recorded 352 of his own lucid dreams over a fourteen-year period and compiled them as part of a book called *A Study of Dreams*. Here is his description of the first lucid dream he remembered, in his own words: "I dreamt that I was floating through a landscape with bare trees, knowing that it was April, and I remarked that the perspective of the branches and twigs changed quite naturally. Then I made the reflection, during sleep, that my fancy would never be able to invent or to make an image as intricate as the perspective movement of little twigs seen in floating by."

Personally, I draw two conclusions from that account. The first is that Frederik van Eeden's writing isn't much fun to read. The second is that he was in the midst of an astral trip, not a dream, when it became a "lucid" experience. From what I've read, I don't have the impression that van Eeden was particularly sold on the idea of astral travel, or that the many researchers who are studying lucid dreaming today put much stock in astral travel either. That makes for a major difference between their dream philosophies and mine, but it certainly doesn't alter the fact that lucid dreams, these intriguing meetings of the conscious and subconscious minds during sleep, absolutely happen.

In the chapter on recurring release dreams we discussed how affirming it can be to rewrite or program new endings that turn upsetting dreams into happy ones. I want you to know right up front that I haven't had a vast amount of personal "hands-on" research experience with lucid dreams, but I've certainly explored the works of those who have. And their insistence that there are marvelous results to be found in performing those same rewrites on lucid dreams makes perfect logical sense to me. If, at the moment in a dream when it consciously occurs to us that we're dreaming, we can realize that in dreams we can do anything and everything we want with absolutely no consequences, the possibilities are endless.

For example, let's say that Raymond had been aware of lucid dreams and what they are before his first one occurred, so that it wouldn't have caught him so off guard. Instead of thinking, I can't possibly be typing on my neighbor's wall. Oh, I get it, I'm dreaming, so sure enough, this is impossible, he could have thought, Oh, I get it, I'm dreaming, which means nothing is impossible, so I can type the complete works of Shakespeare on my neighbor's wall if I want, and then have a huge blue elephant appear and hose the whole thing off with his trunk.

If we want to accomplish something a little more significant through lucid dreams than typing on and then hosing off a neighbor's wall, it stands to reason that we can use them as affirmation tools as well, for any number of real-life situations. If we find ourselves dreaming about an upcoming meeting we've been dreading, and the conscious mind intervenes to make that dream a lucid one, we could take that opportunity to watch ourselves bring that meeting to its best possible conclusion thanks to our own skill and brilliance, punctuated by a standing ovation from everyone else in the room if we feel like it. If a dream about being overworked becomes lucid, we could experience ourselves blasting through that work with hilarious ease and even finishing hours ahead of time, or marching in and quitting to a repentent boss who begs us to stay because the company can't possibly function without us. In a lucid dream we can win the lottery, score perfect 10s at the Olympics, have fifty people bidding on a house we're trying to sell, climb Mount Everest, win anyone's heart, travel the world, dance with Fred Astaire, out-sing Barbra Streisand, save a life, end world hunger, or be the world's greatest parent. Just as with release dreams, and every other kind of dream for that matter, lucid dreams are ours, to do with as we please without the waking world's judgment or consequences, and there's no reason on earth not to use them to affirm our potential, our power, the finest of who we are and then some, and above all our rightful place in this world as a divine and adored child of God.

Healing Through Dreams

Lucid-dream researchers insist that lucid dreams can be marvelously effective in promoting the healing and recovery of our general health. Again, I've had no firsthand research experience with the specific healing powers of lucid dreams, but I can say this without a single instant of hesitation: *I'd bet my life that those researchers are right.* Why? Because I have had thirty years of research experience with the healing powers of dreams in general, and I *know* that dreams are among our greatest allies when it comes to our physical well-being.

That's not just wishful thinking, that's a matter of logic and fact. Our bodies react in very clear, literal, undeniable ways to the information that comes from our subconscious minds. I've used this example from my years as a master hypnotist many times, but it's just plain true, so I'm using it again: if, while you're under hypnosis, I tell you that an ordinary pencil is a lit match, and I touch your arm with the tip of that pencil, a blister will form where the subconscious mind believes your arm has been burned. Multiply that truth by a thousand or so and you get some idea of how literally the body responds when the subconscious minds sends it a message that says, "You're sick," or far better, "You're getting healthier and healthier with every breath you take." It reminds me of one of my favorite quotes, which I'd love to take credit for, but actually Henry Ford came up with it before I could get around to it: "Believe you can, believe you can't; either way, you're right."

We know that while we dream, our subconscious minds are in charge, so it makes perfect sense that our dream time can be put to good use for the benefit of our overall health. In fact, we've all heard a gazillion times that we're supposed to get lots of extra sleep when we're sick. I swear that some of the recuperative properties of sleep can be found in those dreams in which we visualize ourselves as healthy and completely recovered. Programming our dreams and astral travel to accomplish healing while we sleep is the most powerful supplement to following our doctors' orders that we could possibly give ourselves.

Sleep researchers, with the help of electroencephalographs, have established that our brain waves are actually more active during the REM stage of sleep than they are when we're wide awake. That being true, why waste all that great brain activity, when we can use it to wake up stronger and healthier than we were when we fell asleep? In the worlds of dreams, lucid and otherwise, and astral trips, the word "impossible" has no meaning at all. We can get up from wheelchairs and hospital beds and run marathons through the countrysides of Greece or along the sands of the Maui shoreline. We can send a brilliant warm green light of healing through our veins and arteries to make them flow clean and free. We can astrally travel to the greatest healers on The Other Side and let them infuse our weak hearts, and our diseased organs, and our congested lungs, and our injured limbs, and our dislocated joints and spinal cords with the powerful energy of their sacred hands. You'll never, ever hear me downplay the importance of skilled, caring doctors. God bless every one of them. But you'll also never, ever hear me claim that we can't supplement their efforts with our own subconscious discipline during sleep.

For thirty consecutive days, I want you to say the following, in my words or your own, in the quiet moments before you fall asleep: "Dearest God, in these hours while my conscious mind and my body are at rest, please bless my dreams and my astral travels with affirmations of health, strength, and well-being, infuse every cell of this body I inhabit with a surge of Thy loving, compassionate healing, and help me wake with the certainty that as I slept, I was restored and renewed by Your divine grace."

It may take a day, it may take a week, it may take two weeks, but

I promise you that if you acquire the habit of offering this simple prayer, not only will your dreams and astral experiences become more health-related in the most positive ways, but you'll also feel your body gratefully responding, as surely as it responds to every other message the subconscious mind gives it. And just to punctuate these dreams and astral travels, every morning when you wake, no matter how you're feeling, thank God for your good health. It's a guarantee that your body will hear you, and so will He.

Daydreams

Daydreams are such common diversions that we rarely give them much thought. In fact, we often apologize for them. "Sorry, I was just daydreaming," we say when someone catches us with our minds "a million miles away." Even dream researchers tend to be dismissive of daydreams, ignoring how affirming, how informative, how stress-relieving, and how expansive daydreams can be.

Forgive me for stating the obvious, but for the record, daydreams are the spontaneous creation of images or scenarios, most often concerning either factual or fictionalized versions of past, present, or anticipated future events in our lives. We use them to relive treasured moments, to rehearse for upcoming situations, to play out a variety of options in our approach to a previous or upcoming circumstance, to identify with some outside circumstance that has captured our attention, or just to escape into remote viewing or pure fantasy. If you're one of those people who believe you're incapable of meditating, let me assure you that the only significant difference between daydreams and meditation is that we don't deliberately induce daydreams. In fact, we rarely if ever see them coming, and we're not even aware of them until we're already having them or, just as often, until they've ended.

Usually when we think of daydreams, we think of brief, pleasant little mental opportunities to wander off for several moments, an unplanned trick on everyone else in the room who'll swear we're every bit as present and accounted for as they are. And the last thing I want or intend to do is take the fun out of them by overanalyzing them, because I enjoy most of mine as much as I'm sure you enjoy yours. But just as there are ways to make our night dreams work more to our benefit, there are ways we can see to it that our daydreams can do the very same thing.

Daydream Areas

We can learn a lot about ourselves through our daydreams, and we can also program ourselves to rewrite them, exactly as we can with our night dreams, to keep them positive and affirming, rather than letting them reinforce our negativity, as they'll sometimes try to do.

I'll never stop emphasizing how critical it is to our mental, physical, and emotional health to take a "zero tolerance" stand on negativity. It's an indulgence we don't need and can't afford, because it's simply a fact that *what we think, we create*. If you doubt that, look around right this minute and try to point to something that would exist without someone having thought of it first. I predict you'll give up fairly quickly and accept that everything in existence began as a thought. Period. Thoughts are so powerful that they're our primary mode of transportation on The Other Side— wherever we want to be, we just think ourselves there. They're so powerful that here on earth we can be cured of all sorts of illnesses by a pill we find out later was just a placebo we *thought* would work. They're so powerful that, in collaboration with God's most basic laws, they make true the cliché that "what goes around comes around"—put out negativity, you'll get back negativity; put out deceit, you'll get back deceit; put out kindness, you'll get back kindness. And they're why we need to monitor our daydreams and make sure we don't take them so much for granted that we inadvertently let them undermine us.

There are six basic areas with which daydreams seem to concern themselves, many of which I'm sure we've all experienced at one time or another.

Success. From acing a test, to putting in an especially brilliant performance at work, to preparing the perfect Thanksgiving dinner without a hitch, to excelling at a sporting event, to meeting a job deadline, to gracefully and cleverly winning an argument or negotiating a deal, to effectively delivering a speech, to flawlessly performing a piece of music, to curing a patient's illness, to winning the lottery, to helping a child with a difficult problem, to cheering up a depressed friend, to navigating confidently through an awkward conversation—our success daydreams, whether they're memories or rehearsals, are wonderful affirmations, helpful reminders of our priorities, our goals, and our potential.

Love and romance. Replaying past cherished moments with loved ones, looking forward to new ones, reliving the exhilaration and security and sense of belonging love can provide, anticipating some wonderful surprise or vacation we're planning with a loved one, silently marveling over the enhanced kindness and thoughtfulness and self-confidence love can inspire—our love and romance daydreams are lovely, worthwhile ways of maintaining and flexing the most essential part of ourselves we have to offer.

Heroism. Whether we're pulling a stranger from a burning car, or uncovering the one piece of evidence that can save a defendant from being wrongly convicted of a crime, or scoring the winning field goal, or snatching victory from the jaws of defeat in a business meeting, or locating a missing child, or single-handedly subduing an unruly airplane passenger, or performing life-saving surgery, or being named Lifeguard of the Year, or handing a loved one the mortgage payment that will save their house from foreclosure, or performing any other act in which we and we alone save the day— heroism daydreams can be thrilling, there's no doubt about it. But if you find that your heroism daydreams are becoming too frequent, you might want to start asking yourself if there's something going on in your life, or *not* going on in your life, that you should take a look at or get help with. These daydreams can indicate that you're feeling unappreciated, underrated, or chronically disrespected, which can lead to anger and resentment if you don't tackle the problem head on. Heroism daydreams can also indicate that you're still clinging to guilt and regret from some past event where you feel you let someone down, when you could have made a difference but stood idly by instead. If that's the case, these daydreams are actually reminding you of some perceived failure. A far better solution is to forgive yourself, make any amends you might owe, and start making a difference from this day forward.

Fantasy. We're lying on the gleaming deck of a yacht off the shore of the French Riviera, surrounded by happy loved ones, being served lunch by our attentive staff. We're alone, driving, sharing our car with our favorite music and our most treasured possessions, heading to a whole new life in whatever town strikes our fancy, starting over with a new name, a clean slate, and no responsibilities to anyone but ourselves. We're the most popular ski instructor in the Swiss Alps, we're touring the exotic South Seas island we've just bought, we're in our own wild animal reserve in the heart of Africa with gentle lions and adoring tigers eating out of our hands.

Don't worry, I'm not about to take a stand against fantasy daydreams. I wouldn't give up mine any more than I would ask you to give up yours. Escaping through daydreams can be exciting, healthy, and a great way of learning where our fantasies take us when we're free to indulge them. As with so many other enjoyable things in life, the key is moderation. Having too many fantasy daydreams too frequently can be a red flag that we're feeling trapped, that we're in a rut we're feeling more and more oppressed by, and/or that our stress level is heading toward its breaking point.

Failure and crises. Your boss calls you into his office and says, "I've finally realized what an inept loser you really are. You're fired." A loved one is undergoing surgery, and you play out the scenario of being told they didn't make it. You're giving a solo ballet recital for thousands of people, come whirling out onstage, and tumble like a goose right into the orchestra pit. Your spouse or lover announces that they're leaving you for someone else and that, frankly, they never really loved you in the first place. A tornado hits your house and you're unable to get your family to safety in time. You stand up in front of your peers to give a highly anticipated speech and suddenly discover you left it at home and you can't think of a single thing to say.

Let's face it, we've all had failure and crisis daydreams. It's a natural defense against possibilities that frighten us, as if by imagining ourselves through the very worst case scenario we'll feel more prepared for whatever the outcome really is. We won't even discuss the failure daydreams I had before my first pay-per-view, which for some reason, even after four decades of more lectures and television appearances than I can count, absolutely terrified me, until I walked out onto the stage and realized how familiar everything felt. But this is another daydream area that we (and I definitely mean *we*) need to program ourselves to rewrite into happy, positive, affirming endings. As with release dreams during sleep, failure and crisis daydreams give us a chance to acknowledge and vent our fears, but allowing them to end in defeat time after time is to reinforce our self-doubts, our insecurities, and whatever negativity we're harboring. We can sadly create the very outcomes we fear the most by allowing our thoughts to give them energy and some semblance of realism, and self-fulfilling prophesies can be very hard to recover from.

Programming ourselves to write positive endings for our failure and crisis daydreams is exactly the same process as programming ourselves to write positive endings for our release dreams; we just offer the prayer about our daydreams shortly after waking up rather than shortly before we go to sleep. We can't anticipate daydreams any more than we can anticipate release dreams, but we certainly know that we *will* daydream, and we know the general nature of our own daydreams, so it's a safe bet that if we start every morning with this brief prayer, it will come in handy sooner or later: "God, as I make my way through this day with Thy constant presence guiding me, please help me experience any negativity my mind might create in my daydreams and then release it, transforming it into affirmations of my power, my courage, my capacity to give and receive love, and my awareness that, through You, there's nothing I can't endure in the course of the eternal life You've given me."

Spontaneous astral trips and remote viewing. Technically, astral trips are too real to qualify as daydreams, just as they're too real to qualify as night dreams. But since we do occasionally find ourselves taking astral breaks in what would normally be, for lack of a better term, our daydream breaks, they're certainly worth mentioning.

I've mentioned in previous books how adept my son Chris was at astral travel when he was very young, particularly during math class or when I was in the middle of giving him a good, well-deserved scolding. There's nothing like sitting down with your child and discovering in the middle of one of your more articulate lectures that the part of them you need to get through to has taken off on some lovely astral vacation, to the point where there might as well be a "vacancy" sign tacked to their head.

Not that most of us haven't done it ourselves from time to time. One minute we're suffering through the world's most boring meeting, movie, dinner party, conversation, chore, whatever, and the next minute, through no effort on our part at all, we're strolling through our childhood home, or chatting with a deceased loved one, or revisiting a past life, or hovering above the people we're with, looking for bald spots. Just as with astral travel at night, there will always be a logical sequence of events in an astral "daydream," no matter how brief, and getting that same feeling of flying isn't uncommon.

At least in my experience with clients over these many years, spontaneous remote viewing during the day is much less common, but it does happen, and as a letter from Anthony demonstrates, it can be upsetting if it catches us off guard.

"I have a job that isn't exactly a mental challenge, and I admit I daydream a lot, but this kind of daydream has never happened before. I had a huge pile of filing on my desk, and I remember starting to work on it. Then, suddenly, I was watching a scene on a two-lane highway near a small town in Utah. (I've never been to Utah, and I'd never heard of this town before. I didn't know it existed until I checked it out on the internet.) A blue fairly new Honda with a man and woman in it was going around a blind turn, and they were run off the road by a white pickup, with big primer paint spots on its driver's side, that was headed right for them in their lane. The blue Honda hit a tree, and I knew the people inside were hurt but I don't know how badly. The white pickup swerved and slowed down for a second, and then the driver took off without even checking to see if those people needed help. I saw his face so clearly, and I would easily recognize him again. Somehow I knew that he'd been up all night partying and caused this accident because he dozed off at the wheel. Then I was at my desk again, almost finished with my work, with no conscious memory of having done any of it. I didn't know any of those people, and I didn't have a feeling that this accident had anything to do with me at all. What in the world would make me have such an upsetting daydream like that about total strangers in a place I've never been?"

This was definitely a remote viewing experience, and especially interesting because it was so completely spontaneous and unexpected and clearly not routine in Anthony's life. If Anthony can find that town on the internet, he can find its newspaper archives and search to see if an accident like this one took place at around the time he "witnessed" it. He should check to see if the victims were okay and if the man who caused the accident was ever tracked down. If it turns out that what he "saw" really happened and that enough of his details were accurate, he should call either the local police or the reporter who wrote the newspaper article and politely offer to share his experience. Never pass up an opportunity to offer legitimate help, but be patient if it takes a few calls before you find someone who'll take you seriously. Sadly, we all pay a price for the crackpots and frauds in this world, but sitting quietly by doing nothing and letting them win is just out of the question.

I guess "never pass up an opportunity" is the most important message when it comes to lucid dreams and daydreams, come to think of it. Once we recognize them as opportunities, as opposed to just passing events we neither ask for nor control, we can use them as affirmations, as connections to magical gifts we've been given, and as reminders that our brilliant, tireless, limitless, eternal spirits, the sacred essence of who we are, never rest in their efforts to prove to us that at any given moment, we can soar.

Chapter Thirteen

✳

DREAMS THROUGH A PSYCHIC'S EYES

*A*s I said in the introduction, when this book was in its planning stages, I was determined not to just write about dreams in general, I wanted to write about *your* dreams. And that would obviously have been impossible without your help and generosity. The dreams I received from you have been invaluable as examples throughout this book, and I'm sure everyone who reads it will be as grateful to you as I am for sharing some very personal experiences with such unflinching honesty.

I read and appreciated every one of the hundreds and hundreds of dreams and astral trips you sent. I could fill a fascinating separate book with them. For the purpose of this book, though, I'll just fill a fascinating chapter instead, along with my interpretations. If you want to use what you've learned in the previous chapters to interpret them as well, for practice at interpreting your own, so much the better. These dreams and astral trips are deliberately arranged in random order so that I won't be planting category ideas in your heads before you've even had a chance to form your own opinions. It's worth repeating that dream interpretation is an art, not a science. There's no "right" or "wrong." The reward isn't in the accuracy, it's in the process of building a more affirming relationship between us and our dreams, to honor and learn from the hard work they do to teach us lessons from deep within ourselves, from loved ones both here and on The Other Side, and if we listen very closely, from God Himself.

"In this dream, I was in bed, waiting to fall asleep, thinking of a joke I was going to tell my mother the next day, when I heard a noise that I can only describe as the sound of a plastic bag crumbling. I thought it was my imagination and tried to ignore it. But then I felt someone bending over me, holding me down, and breathing in my ear. The pressure was very strong. I tried several times to open my eyes so that I could catch a glimpse of this man, but it felt as if my eyelids were sewn shut, and nothing I could do could seem to get me free from this man's grip. In my dream I finally woke up and crawled down the hallway to the kitchen where my mother was. I remember sitting on the kitchen floor hysterically telling her that there was a man in my room, or a spirit with the power of a large man. She brought me to the couch and asked if he had tried to strangle me. I told her no but suggested that maybe I should be taken to the hospital. That's when I lifted my shirt and saw wounds on my body that looked as if they'd been made by barbed wire. At that point, in real life, some distant noise finally woke me up. This isn't even close to the first time I've felt something evil coming after me. Please tell me what's going on so I can get rid of these nightmares once and for all." —M.P.

Don't let M.P.'s trip to the kitchen, conversation with her mother, and the appearance of wounds fool you. This is still a classic case of astral catalepsy, from the strange noise, to the feeling of something or someone holding her down on the bed, to the sense that the presence in the room was evil. The terror the semi-conscious mind can experience when it discovers that the spirit is half in and half out of the body triggers all sorts of dreamed efforts to find safe refuge, depending on how deep the fear is and how long it takes to fully wake up. Some manage to comfort themselves with a prayer that wakes them up fairly quickly without the sense of ever having left their bed. M.P., who's very close to her mother, sought her out for comfort instead, and the perceived wounds were just a manifestation of her sincere belief that she'd been attacked by something awful. According to most researchers, dreams last an average of anywhere from ten minutes to forty minutes. Since astral catalepsy is essentially a dream state, a result of the conscious mind's mistakenly equating the spirit's absence with death, those dreams can take any number of hysterical forms and go on for quite some time, but they're still just an aftermath of the astral catalepsy that caused them.

The simple awareness of what astral catalepsy is and what its common "symptoms" are can diminish its frequency and its impact a lot, and often put an end to it once and for all. But the added protections of surrounding ourselves with the white light of the Holy Spirit before we sleep, and praying that if our spirit travels during the night, it has a quick and easy exit and reentrance, can work wonders as well. In the meantime, astral catalepsy is a great example of the old adage "Knowledge is power." Know that, despite all feelings and appearances to the contrary, you're in no real danger, it's just the surprise of catching your spirit in the midst of coming home.

*   *   *

"I've been laid up recently with a back problem that refuses to go away. My doctors prescribed painkillers, which I've just stopped taking because even though I'm still in a lot of pain, they made me feel like a zombie. But while I was taking them, I had many dreams about losing people and things I love. In one recurring dream, I'm being forced to leave my home by plane. Before I leave, 'they' come to take away my cats, and I'm dragged toward the plane screaming for 'them' to let me and my cats stay together. I know these are just dreams, but I can't begin to describe how upset I am when I wake up from them and how long it takes me sometimes to recover from the sadness they leave me with." —B.B.

This is obviously a release dream, in which B.B. is addressing her fear of losing and/or being separated from something desperately important to her. What's fascinating is that release dreams like this one are very common under both of the circumstances she's been suffering from. When we're in physical pain, particularly when it's ongoing, we feel the loss and/or separation from our body's usual level of well-being, even if that pain is only adding to some other chronic conditions we might be accustomed to. Whatever level of health we're in a majority of the time, it's what we're used to and what we learn to define as "normal" for ourselves. Anything that disrupts and diminishes what we think of as normal is bound to be perceived by our subconscious minds as a loss or separation and acted out in our dreams.

The same goes for any kind of strong drugs, either prescribed or recreational. Now, don't ever let me override any orders your doctor has given you. I'm psychically very good with health issues, and I'm certainly experienced enough and well read enough to offer suggestions, but I'm not a licensed physician, I'll never pretend to be, and I'll never encourage you to throw away medications you've been prescribed without consulting your doctor.

It's just that the problem with drugs—let's face it, sometimes the *point* of drugs—is that they're mind-altering. It always amazes me how people who are on drugs, especially recreational ones, when we complain about the fact that they're not acting like themselves, swear that they're acting exactly like themselves, thank you. They enjoy drugs, they'll tell us, but it's not as if they can't handle them. In fact, for our information, drugs don't affect them at all. Duh. Of course drugs affect them. Why else would they go to the trouble and expense of taking them? And besides the fact that drugs are proven to interfere with our natural sleep and REM cycles, it's the mind-altering quality of drugs that creates such common release dreams about loss and separation from something or someone important to us. Just as we have a sense of what's "normal" for our bodies, we also have a sense of what's "normal" for our minds and their level of clarity. Strong drugs make us lose, or at the very least feel separated from, the minds and the clarity we're used to, and what could be more important than that? B.B. used her cats as the archetype for the "something important" she couldn't bear being separated from. Whatever archetype might show up in our own similar release dreams, the first question to ask when we wake up is "What significant part of my life seems to be in danger of slipping away from me, and what can I do about it?"

Fortunately for B.B., she's already given up the prescription painkillers she was taking, and her back pain will finally be cured with the help of a good neurologist she'll be referred to by her doctor, at her insistence.

"In a recurring dream, I'm going up a flight of stairs that never ends. As I look upward, all I can see are more stairs, and they seem to be coming to a point in the far, far distance. Although I keep climbing, I never get tired or short of breath. One time, I almost reached the top. I could see the last step ahead of me but could not see what was up there. I woke up before I could clarify what or who was waiting for me." —V.R.

This is a very interesting release dream, representing a lot of similar dreams I received that described climbing and climbing, or walking and walking, or running and running with no apparent progress, never getting any closer to your destination. And V.R.'s dream used the classic meaning of the "stairs" archetype, i.e., aspiring to a new level in his life.

Every person I've met or been in contact with who has some form of this recurring futility dream, in which they're unable to make progress toward a goal no matter how hard they try, has a perfection theme. To understand what that means, you need to know that every one of us, while we're on The Other Side preparing for another lifetime here, chooses a "life theme," which is our strongest motivator or driving force in this particular life, based on what it is we're here to learn this time around. There are forty-four life themes. I've listed them, and their meanings, in both *The Other Side and Back* and *Life on The Other Side*, so I won't repeat them here. But those with a perfection theme tend to set unrealistically high standards and goals for themselves and inevitably end up with a perpetual sense of disappointment, dissatisfaction, and failure, and since perfection isn't an earthly possibility, no amount of effort on the part of a perfectionist will get them any closer to what they're trying to accomplish. What better symbolism could dreams come up with for that feeling than an endless flight of stairs, or continually running toward something that never seems to be getting any closer?

V.R. is obviously in the process of conquering this downside of the perfectionist theme, though. Notice that in one dream he actually got a glimpse of that top step and something that was waiting there for him. What was waiting for him, what *is* waiting for him and for everyone who has this recurring theme running through their dreams, is the joy of setting challenging but realistic goals and then appreciating the whole process of accomplishing them—missteps, imperfections, and all. As soon as that reality takes hold and gets put into conscious practice, those frustrating futility dreams will stop, you can count on it.

"I recently had a dream that frightened me so much that it woke me up in the middle of the night. I don't remember seeing anything, but I clearly heard a loud male voice saying, 'You've been given a choice. Most people do not get that chance. You are in the way!' I can't imagine what this could mean. What am I in the way of?" —M.M.

Earlier in this book I discussed the fact that when we have a dream we don't understand, the first place to look for answers is ourselves and our own situation. The answer to so many questions when dreams are confusing is "You!" And this release dream is no exception. As happens to most of us more often than we care to admit, M.M. is getting in her own way. She's her own biggest obstacle, the most difficult hurdle between her and her goals. While she didn't include this in her letter, I know psychically that she's been given more than one opportunity that would lead her into the career she would love to pursue, and she finds excuses to sidestep those opportunities because ultimately she suffers from a fear a failure. It's not a fear she's consciously aware of, but her Spirit Guide, whose name is Frederic, is well aware of it. It's his voice she heard, pointing out that not everyone gets the same opportunities she's passed up, and that this is a great example of someone being in danger of letting their fear of something actually create the outcome they're most afraid of. Opportunities do stop showing up if we refuse them too often, after all. If M.M. will accept the fact that the most tragic failure is in not trying, and practice saying like a mantra, "Today and every day from now on, I'm staying out of my own way," she and Frederic will never have to deal with this particular issue again, and she'll follow that path into the right career where she knows she belongs.

"Here's a dream that happened at a time in my life when I was growing spiritually at a very rapid pace. I was in total darkness, standing face to face with what I believe was a very bad spirit. The feeling I received from this man was nothing but evil. He stepped close enough to me to be almost nose to nose, and although he was taller and towering over me, we were still face to face somehow. He screamed at me, 'I am God.' I calmly replied, 'No, you're not.' This happened three times, and although he was screaming and trying to intimidate me, I remained calm. It was really frightening after the dream was over, but during the dream I knew I was protected and he couldn't touch me, and that made him extremely angry. It was a very short dream but one I will never forget." —D.D.

This is another release dream, and absolutely not the visitation it obviously felt like. I've said this many times, and it bears repeating now: there's no one in the spirit world who's even a fraction as evil as the human beings we run across here on earth. Whenever any of you, including D.D., has a dream in which an evil spirit appears (without any of the other signs of astral catalepsy), it's a very safe bet that it's symbolic of a person in your life whom your subconscious has recognized as evil, whether your conscious mind is buying their act or not. Please, by all means, read a chapter in *The Other Side and Back* called "The Dark Side." It will help you spot the dark entities of the human persuasion among us, understand where they come from and what their purpose is, and realize why the more spiritual we become, the more difficult and aggressive they're likely to become. D.D. had exactly the right reaction in this dream, by knowing with absolute certainty that calm confidence in our glorious relationship with God will frustrate and ultimately repel dark entities every time.

"My husband died three years ago and left me with five children to raise on my own. I've seen him in three dreams since he passed away, and in all three dreams he told me he wasn't really dead. In one of the dreams my Spirit Guide took me to see him. He was working in a very unstable place with broken cement all around him. I'd really appreciate understanding what this means." —C.W.

Of course, these weren't dreams C.W. had, they were astral trips to visit her late husband, and she's absolutely right, her Spirit Guide did accompany her on one of those visits. I don't want this to overly upset C.W. or any others of you who might have similar experiences, but her late husband hasn't made it to The Other Side yet. He will in time. For now, though, to put it in the simplest of terms, he's a ghost. He's stayed behind out of his deep concern over the situation he left his wife in, as a kind of misguided self-punishment for abandoning his family.

There are two tip-offs in these astral visits that C.W.'s late husband hasn't been released, and they're worth keeping an eye out for in any astral experiences. One is that he told her during all three visits that he's not really dead. Ghosts, or earthbound spirits, truly have no idea that they're dead. It's a heartbreaking, confusing existence for them. Imagine feeling as alive as you're feeling right now, but suddenly everything around you seems to have changed, your friends and family and the world in general are ignoring you as if you're not even there, and you see your loved ones grieving and struggling but you can't do a thing to comfort and help them. You're lost, and nothing that used to make sense makes a bit of sense anymore. Eventually, all earthbounds are released, through the intervention of spirits from The Other Side and compassionate humans as well, who finally convince them that they're dead and all they have to do to put an end to their sad confusion and find peace is to go to the tunnel, toward the light, which is always accessible to them.

The second tip-off that C. W.'s late husband is earthbound is that C. W. found him working in "a very unstable place with broken cement all around him." The words "unstable" and "broken" do not and cannot apply to even one square inch on The Other Side. While we happily work at Home, in as wide a variety of professions as we have on earth, there is nothing unstable and broken in that very real place of universal perfection. Any time you see a deceased loved one working at a site that's flawed in any way, or they seem unhappy, either you're astrally visiting their earthbound spirit and need to help them find their way Home, or you're having a release dream trying to work through the grief, fear, and upheaval of losing them.

"In my dream I was driving my mom's car and flipped over somehow. Before I died I saw and heard the cops and my family talking about my tombstone and what it would look like. Then I died, and I saw my body lying in the casket at the funeral. As they buried me, I saw my tombstone, although I couldn't read it, and someone was putting flowers on my grave and saying, 'I'm sorry, Janet.' Who was that person, and why were they sorry?" —Janet

This is fascinating, and more complex than it might appear to be at first glance. Remember that anytime you can see yourself as Janet did, you're having an astral experience, not a dream. And even though the action is "fast-forwarded" from one scene to another, it's still in a logical sequence, which also helps define it as an astral experience. I feel completely safe in ruling it out as prophetic, because it's worth repeating—I have never known anyone, awake or asleep, to accurately predict their own death.

This was an astral visit to a past life, in which Janet's name happened to be Janice. No wonder she misheard it. If she'd been able to read the tombstone, she would have seen the dates "1902–1941," the years when that lifetime took place. Janet/Janice did indeed die in a car accident in that life in northern Virginia. The person at the grave site who said, "I'm sorry, *Janice*," was her very spoiled, self-involved mother, for whom Janice was trying to solve yet another manufactured crisis when the car hit a patch of ice, swerved out of control, and rolled over into a ditch. Her mother, by the way, felt so responsible for her daughter's death that she took her own life less than a year later.

There's an old wives' tale I hope this astral experience can help dispel. I've heard a hundred times, and you probably have, too, that if you actually die in a dream, you'll die at that same moment in your sleep in real life. That's not only untrue, it's downright silly. Look at it this way: if it were true, how would anyone know? In order to find that out, you'd have to ask people who died in their sleep what they were dreaming at the moment they passed away, and I'm guessing it would be a pretty one-sided conversation. Next time you hear someone trying to perpetuate that myth, please challenge them to name the source of their information. I'd love to hear the answer.

"I had a dream that has been haunting me for a long time. I dreamed that I was lying in bed, wide awake, and my deceased grandmother and my very-much-alive mother were floating above me having a conversation. My grandmother was telling my mother about having burned her arm on Mom's hot soup, or something equally trivial. Suddenly my deceased grandfather appeared, looked at me in terror, and said, 'You are next.' A few years after this dream my mother died of leukemia. I'm so afraid that I'm going to be the next person to die. Please help me understand this horrifying dream." —P.S.

It's not unusual for two different kinds of dreams to blend into each other, as with this experience from P.S. In what we'll call Part One, P.S., in an astral state, witnessed an astral chat between her mother and grandmother. She heard the conversation correctly—her mother and grandmother were recalling a burn that had left a small scar on her grandmother's arm, and her grandmother was showing off the fact that the scar had vanished from her "new" body on The Other Side, as all signs of earthly wounds, illnesses, and disabilities do the instant we return Home.

And then came Part Two, a release dream triggered by the appearance of P.S.'s deceased grandmother, in which P.S. used the image of her deceased grandfather to represent her own fear of death in general but her mother's death in particular. That's neither a psychic impression nor a guess, it's a matter of logically analyzing the clues within the dream. P.S. saw her grandmother, who was deceased, talking to her mother, which would have led her to an understandably upsetting question: if the two of them were talking in the same dimension, and one of them was deceased, did that mean her mother either had died or was dying? We know the answer to that question is no, since we "alive" people meet and visit with "dead" people on a regular basis while we sleep. But seeing that sight unexpectedly was unsettling, I'm sure, and set off P.S.'s fear-of-death alarm, which sent her into a release dream.

It's a guarantee that Part Two was a release dream and not a visitation. No spirit from The Other Side would ever look at a loved one "in terror" as P.S.'s grandfather did, or with anything other than pure, peaceful, unconditional love. As for his message, "You're next," let's take a close look at that. At the very least, he was wrong. We know P.S.'s mother was alive at the time the dream happened and then died a few years later, so obviously her mother was next, if "next" even means "next to die." And even assuming that's what it means, what's the time limit on "next," exactly?

I'm reminded of the five Exit Points I mentioned in Chapter 3, which we each write into our life charts before we come here. Those are the five opportunities we create for ourselves to exit this lifetime and head Home. Some of us might take advantage of the first Exit Point that comes along and bail out right away. Others of us might choose to wait until our second, or third, while others decide they've still got more to accomplish and stay around for number four or five. There's no obvious time pattern between Exit Points. You can have numbers one, two, and three in the first year of your life, your fourth when you're five years old and not have your fifth one come along until you're ninety. I experienced my third and fourth Exit Points when I was forty-five. I'm now sixty-six, and according to my Spirit Guide I'm still not going Home anytime soon.

Similarly, assuming we hadn't already figured out that the message in P.S.'s release dream was, to be polite, inaccurate, when might this "next" business happen if there were any truth to it? Let me put it this way: I can offer P.S. psychic assurance that she's going to be around for many, many, many more years and, by the way, has only had two of her Exit Points so far.

And I want to repeat, because it's important, that any kind of dream or astral experience can combine with any other kind of dream or astral experience from time to time, so keep an eye out for conspicuous clues like the ones that appeared in what felt like one very disturbing dream that continues to upset P.S. so needlessly.

"I have a beautiful seventeen-year-old daughter whom I dearly love. However, since she was a small child, I have had numerous dreams that she was demon-possessed. In these dreams, she had glowing red eyes and talked in a deep, awful voice, just like in *The Exorcist*. It's a really terrible and frightening feeling to have such evil dreams about my own child, and I don't understand where they came from."—F.R.

I do understand where they came from, and before I explain, I want to make a few things clear. As many of you know, I was raised Catholic, Jewish, Lutheran, and Episcopalian, and both attended and taught in Catholic schools. I've spent fifty years studying world religions out of sheer passion. I'm now a Christian Gnostic, with an eternal love and respect for all religions that cherish God by any name, and the dignity and sanctity of life.

So please understand that what I'm about to say is said with that same love and respect, and at the same time a very well-informed, exhaustively explored, and absolutely committed certainty: There is no demon. There is no devil. And there's nothing or no one who can possess anyone on this earth, ever, without their full knowledge and consent—which a child, by the way, isn't capable of giving. There's obviously such a thing as evil, rooted in those who've turned away from God. But I think there's too much emphasis put on this whole "devil/demon/Satan" concept by many religions, which causes its followers to be led by fear and guilt rather than by the boundless eternal love and compassion God has given all of us since time began.

Whether you agree with me philosophically or not, what I promise you can believe is that every time the devil/a demon/ Satan, or any other "embodiment of evil," appears in a dream, it's a symbol, in a release dream, of some fear you're harboring and need to address. Nothing more, nothing less. Often, if you had a strict religious upbringing, fear in demon form in a dream could revolve around a constant threat of being a sinner, unworthy and/or going to hell, and no, I don't happen to believe in any of those concepts either. In the case of F.R., and the image involving a demon possessing a child, it can easily be (and, in this case, *is*) the fear that sometimes overwhelms every parent, of feeling too inadequate to be completely responsible for shaping and guiding the morals, the character, the belief systems—all those huge essential foundations for the happy, successful lives we all want for our children. I once had a client whose dreams about her child being "evil" stemmed from the fact that the child was conceived out of wedlock, as if it were the child's fault or as if God disapproved of this innocent little life.

So remember, if the devil—or, for that matter, that hooded Death person with the scythe, come to think of it—shows up in your release dreams, don't take either one of them literally. The devil isn't cursing you with a lifetime of evil (there's also no such thing as curses, by the way), and Death isn't a sign that you're about to die. They're both your subconscious mind's way of drawing pictures of "fear" in a way you'll recognize and very probably remember. By looking deep inside, you can almost always get to the root of what your fear really is, and identifying a fear is guaranteed to be the first step toward overcoming it once and for all.

"As a child, I had a recurring dream about hiding in an attic while running away from something or someone. Then, when I was sixteen, I went to a friend's grandmother's home in another city, where I'd never been before. His grandmother asked us to get her Christmas decorations from the attic, and when we got up there to retrieve them, I found myself in the exact same attic I'd dreamed of so many times during my childhood." —J.I.

This letter obviously involves prophetic childhood dreams, but there's an interesting twist that all of you should keep an eye out for in your dreams, a variation on prophetic dreams that creates a sense of déjà vu. To understand these dreams, you need to understand what déjà vu really is.

I've talked a lot about the very detailed charts we write on The

Other Side before we come here for a new lifetime. The word "detailed" is an understatement. We fill in all sorts of very intricate details, partly to help ensure that we accomplish the goals we've set for ourselves and partly to give ourselves tiny, seemingly trivial signposts along the way to signal that we're right on track. From time to time we recognize one of those signposts from our charts and get that amazing, fleeting feeling that we're duplicating a moment we've experienced before. And it's rarely a moment that has any apparent importance. It's more like "I was in this same car, in this same light rain, with this same song on the radio, driving on this exact same street, reaching to retrieve something from the glove compartment just as I am now." What we call déjà vu is actually the arrival at one of those little signposts we wrote for ourselves back Home, the wonderful phenomenon, just for an instant or two, of remembering our chart and being reassured that we're in step with the game plan we so carefully designed.

What happened with J.I. occasionally happens to many of us, which is that while we sleep, our subconscious mind recalls those signposts, or some part of them, and enjoys replaying them, both out of Homesickness and as a way of reminding us of a small, affirming event to keep an eye out for. In J.I.'s case, one of the signposts included that attic that she repeatedly dreamed of as a child and then found herself in when she was sixteen. On one hand, we could say that this attic has no major significance in J.I.'s life—it's not as if she's going to end up living there, or get married there, or be kidnapped and held there against her will. On the other hand, I don't happen to think there's anything insignificant at all about a signal from our spirit minds, and from our lives on The Other Side, that we're in perfect synch with our charts.

"My mother died in March of 2001. There was a lot of guilt pertaining to her death, and I felt she was angry with me. I begged for her to come to me in a dream, or to give me a sign that she made it to The Other Side, but I received nothing that I was aware of. I finally talked with a psychic, who assured me that my mother was not upset but very pleased with how well she was taken care of, and that she'd been met by those she loved when she first arrived. After talking with the psychic, not only did I feel some peace of mind for the first time, but also my mother is now coming to me in dreams. Believe me, I'm grateful, but why did she wait to start showing up until I talked to a psychic?" —C.O.

First, let me say that I'm so glad you had a good experience with a psychic, and that they offered you honesty and compassion. Psychically, I can assure you that whoever it was gave you a completely accurate account of how your mother is doing, and I know without asking that your astral visits with her while you sleep are lovely and completely devoid of anger. Please be aware that no psychic, including me, has the power to make deceased loved ones appear to you or avoid you. What we can do, and what yours did, is help remove some of the understandable blocks, like fear and guilt and grief, that prevent the spirit world from being able to communicate with you and help open your mind to their visits and the signs to watch for that tell you they're around.

I have to add a strong word of caution on this subject, because so many people are being scammed out of hundreds or even thousands of dollars by supposed psychics who will callously take advantage of your fear, grief, and vulnerability and who should be tracked down and marched right off to prison. If any so-called psychic or medium or "spiritual counselor" ever tells you that your deceased loved one is earthbound, or trapped and suffering in hell or purgatory or some other awful place, and that only very expensive candles and/or very expensive prayers and/or very expensive ongoing sessions and/or very generous "donations" can secure your deceased loved one's peaceful ascent to The Other Side, hang up the phone or get up and leave their office *immediately* without giving them a dime, and don't hesitate to report them to the fraud division of your local police. It's heartbreaking but true that many intelligent people from all walks of life have fallen for this despicable scam, and that their fear that this "expert" might be right sometimes overrides the obvious fact that it's our very personal, singular relationship with God, not a credit card or cashier's check, that secures our passage Home, and He doesn't need a single dime of our money. A lucky thing, too, since every dime will stay right in the pocket of the low-life you're handing it to. So please, *please* be careful, especially when you're grieving and in pain and at your most vulnerable.

"In this recurring dream, I'm looking at older, Victorian style homes. I find a three-story home with all the features I love—a square tower, a wraparound porch, and big bay windows. My husband and I are talking to the Realtor who's showing us around. My husband is really into it, and he and the Realtor walk into another room together, talking eagerly. I can still hear their voices as I turn to find an old woman there. She's short and small and looks right through me, and every time I reach this point in the dream, I feel the same fear, an evil feeling that stays with me in brief flashes throughout the next day. There are parts of this home in which it's hard to even stay in the room, as if some force is trying to push us out. But I can never get this woman to talk to me or find out who she is." —F. J.

This is another combination dream, a few different experiences blended into one. To start with, the original house F. J. has in her head was her family home in the north of England in the late 1600s. She's still attracted to that style of house, with those specific features, because of her past-life memories of a happy lifetime there. With those memories in mind, she's having a recurring prophetic dream of a house she and her husband will indeed look at someday, a house that seems perfect but that she's being warned away from.

It might go without saying, but in case it doesn't, our ability to see spirits and ghosts is heightened dramatically during astral travel, for the simple reason that our spirits travel on the same higher vibrational level that ghosts and the spirit world live on. F.J. hasn't explored her potential for seeing ghosts and spirits during her waking hours, and without these prophetic dreams she would undoubtedly feel uneasy in some parts of this house she'll be tempted to fall in love with, to the point where she might dismiss her uneasiness as her "imagination." (One of the most overused words in the English language, by the way.)

So F.J. isn't just taking a prophetic astral trip to a house she'll find herself looking at someday, and be tempted by because of its similarity to a past-life house in which she was very happy, she's actually meeting the ghost who lives there. In this case, it's the ghost of an old woman named Alice who was born, lived, and died in that house, more because it was once the grandest house in the area than because she loved it. In her own mind, it made her superior to everyone else, and she spent her life feeling entitled to being spoiled and catered to even though she'd done nothing to deserve it. Late in her life she married a man she wrongly believed to be her social and financial equal, only to discover that he was a fraud who was systematically robbing her of her comfortable inheritance. She killed him and buried him on the property, and legally speaking, she got away with it. But she died afraid that she was going to be caught, and she's stayed behind to make sure no one, especially the police, ever finds her husband's body. As a ghost, she's harmless, but she's also as confused as any other ghost in her belief that she's still alive, and more fiercely protective than most, because in her mind, any intruder might stumble across her secret and take away her freedom. To that extent, she is evil, and she'll relentlessly torment anyone who moves into that house. F.J. should point out to Alice that she's quite dead and in no danger of being arrested, but beyond that she should stay away from her and from that house. And all of us, when we get an uneasy feeling about a person or place, awake or especially asleep, need to honor those psychic instincts and stop waving them away as "imagination."

"My best friend passed away a year ago, and she's been coming to me in dreams. Since these dreams about her began, other dreams have been happening that I feel I'm supposed to be using in some way I don't understand. For example, in one of the dreams about my best friend, she told me she would be with our mutual friend's unborn child. That's all she said, and I couldn't imagine what she meant. Then the baby was born with serious health problems. I dreamed the baby would die, and two days later, she did pass away. Next came a dream about my husband's twenty-year-old brother. The dream was that he was very far away and very confused and that some girl was pregnant by him. The day after that dream my husband got a call saying that the brother I dreamed about was in trouble, hanging out with a very bad crowd and involved in a lot of illegal activities, and no one could find him. (Nothing was said about a girl being pregnant by him, though.) Is it a coincidence that I never had dreams like this in my life until my best friend died? And am I supposed to be warning people when I have dreams like this about them? Or do I just miss my best friend so much that I've gone crazy?" —B.D.

Now all you people who've asked if prophetic and psychic abilities mean they're crazy know how *I've* felt for most of my life. And let's all make a pact to throw the word "coincidence" into the same wastebasket as the word "imagination," okay?

What I love about the prophetic "dreams" B.D. is having is

where they're coming from, and this will help a lot of you who are having similar experiences.

You need to know that not only do our spirits have access to all the life charts in the Hall of Records on The Other Side, which allows us to gather prophetic information during astral trips, but each and every resident on The Other Side also has access to them, and believe me, the Hall of Records is one of the busiest, most popular sites back Home. While the majority of us get our prophetic information by our own astral visits to those charts, B.D. is getting hers from her deceased best friend, who's reading the charts herself and passing upcoming events and insights along. The two of them started having wonderful astral communication almost immediately after the best friend died, and you'll notice it was the best friend who first started dropping hints that there would be problems with their mutual friend's baby. The fact that B.D. is getting more adept at remembering the information she's given than she is at remembering exactly where she got it is appropriate and much more productive than if it were the other way around—how helpful would it be if she woke with lovely memories of the time she spent with her best friend during the night but couldn't recall a word of what they talked about?

I know that B.D. isn't the only one of you receiving prophetic information from deceased loved ones once they've "researched" the charts in the Hall of Records, although it isn't all that common, either. Just to clarify, this doesn't mean that your deceased loved one has now become your Spirit Guide, or one of your Angels. Spirit Guides aren't anyone we've known on earth. They're someone we know on The Other Side who commits before we come here to be our constant companion, observer, agent, confessor, and most intimate friend throughout our upcoming lifetime. We arrive on earth with our Spirit Guide already in place, and we don't add new ones as we go along, even though deceased loved ones can obviously help us along the way as well. And Angels, our most gorgeous and divine protectors, are a species all their own, and they never, ever incarnate or spend a single lifetime in human form.

As I said in Chapter 3, on prophetic dreams, however you receive the information, it's extremely important to pray that you not be made aware of anything that's so vague, so inaccurate, or so incomplete that it won't be of help, and it's equally important that you be scrupulously responsible with whatever you're told. Again, I'm relieved to say that my prophetic gifts are limited to my waking hours, so that I'm not hit with a nonstop barrage I can't escape from. But you'll never hear me predict more than someone wants to know, you'll never hear me warn someone of something without offering some suggestion of what they can do about it, you'll never hear me be dishonest with anyone, and you'll never hear me be so vague that I actually leave someone more confused than they were before they met me. Predictions offered irresponsibly, without compassion and sensitivity, aren't just counterproductive, they're cruel, and an abuse of a potentially invaluable humanitarian tool.

As for B.D.'s brother-in-law, she can ask every night before she goes to sleep to be told where he is, and share any answer she gets with her husband, since in this case the family genuinely wants to find him and help him. It's a guarantee that he doesn't want to be found right now, but that's only because he's humiliated and very confused and can't see his way out of the trouble he's in. All of you should do the same if you're given only part of a story you feel is important—ask questions, ask for answers, ask for more, and keep right on asking until you get responses. They'll come sooner or later. If God has given you the gift and the burden of prophetic dreams, you most definitely owe it to Him not to waste them, after all He's done for you.

* * *

"I had a dream about my beloved dog, whom I had to have put to sleep over five years ago. She was in heaven and eating out of my hand. There were other animals around her but none that I could identify. That same night while I was sleeping, my cat, whom I had for almost five years, disappeared. I've searched for ten days and can't find him anywhere. Was the dream my dog's spirit telling my cat to come join her, that she would take care of him, or is that just wishful thinking on my part?" —S.H.

Never doubt for one moment that animals are among the most cherished spirits on The Other Side. Their transition from earth to Home happens in the blink of an eye, no exceptions, and when we go Home ourselves, we'll be greeted by every pet we've ever had in every one of our lifetimes here. In fact, my Spirit Guide Francine has told me many times that on our arrival on The Other Side, the people waiting to greet us can barely get to us because of all the animals gathered around for the reunion.

Animals are also more psychic than any of us will ever be, and watching over us from Home as vigilantly as our Spirit Guides, and with that same pure, uncompromising love they give us while they're here. So there's no question that S.H.'s dog was with her on The Other Side the night her cat disappeared, knowing the cat was coming Home and wanting to offer comfort and reassurance to S.H. that they'll all be joyfully together again, because animals' lives are every bit as eternal as ours. This was most definitely not a dream but a very real astral visit, as is every happy "dream" that we ever have about our cherished departed pets.

Parenthetically, in case you're wondering, yes, by all means, most animals do dream. If you've ever watched a dog or cat "run" in their sleep, you've probably already figured that out. But researchers have actually hooked up a variety of animals to electroencephalographs while they slept and discovered that REM sleep does occur in mammals and birds (but not in reptiles, for some reason), even more frequently than it does in us humans. I'm becoming more and more convinced every day that we humans who consider ourselves superior to animals really are just kidding ourselves.

"This is a dream that has haunted me since the night I had it. I am in a car, at night, driving. I see a motel and pull in to stay the night. Straight across the street are three older houses, and across the street and to the left is a fairly large Conoco station, its lights on, with the white shelters over the pumps, like most truck stops in Colorado. I go into the motel and check in, and then I decide to walk across the street to the Conoco station to get a soda, since I've been in the car all day and need some fresh air. I'm crossing the street when I realize that the station's lights have been turned off. Suddenly I notice a tall lanky man circling me. He is referred to as 'the shadow,' but I don't know why I know this. He is over six feet tall and very skinny, but he's also very strong. He circles me several times, then attacks me by punching me in the chest. I can't tell if he has a knife or if it's just his fist, but he sends me flying into the air as if I'd been hit by a car. I seem to spin up into the air for miles before I start to fall, and I think to myself as I'm falling that this landing is really going to hurt and maybe even kill me. When I do land, it's not hard at all but amazingly gentle and painless. The man now begins sexually molesting me and punching me in the chest. Then I woke up." —R.P.

This is a fairly uncommon phenomenon, and a bit complicated to explain, so please be patient.

First of all, it's an astral experience, not a dream. The clarity of the details and the meticulously logical sequence of events are unmistakable.

And I can tell you psychically that this is not something that ever happened or ever will happen to R.P. It happened to someone else, someone R.P. doesn't even know. Don't misunderstand. R.P.

was not occupying this person's body, but she was viewing a horrible assault through the eyes of the victim.

When we're in the Hall of Records, researching the countless charts that are meticulously filed and preserved there, we actually have a few choices of how we want to review those charts. We can watch a person's chart play out in front of us, which only takes a few moments and resembles a movie, but in three-dimensional clarity, like a hologram. We can listen to a chart, as if a book-on-tape existed in virtual reality form, complete with surround-sound, eliciting our total and complete involvement. Or we can do what R.P. did, which is to essentially enter that chart and let our spirit "merge" with the spirit of the person whose chart we're studying.

"Merging" in the spirit world is the ultimate form of empathy. We never lose our identity or take over the identity of the spirit we're merging with. We do, however, become temporarily able to assimilate their spirit's total reality into ours, so that while we don't literally experience events in their lives, we do experience every emotional and sensory detail they went through during those events—but none of the physical pain, which is why R.P. wasn't hurt when she landed from her long fall and never mentions pain once throughout the entirety of this brutal attack.

Again, R.P.'s experience of merging her spirit with this particular victim's spirit and chart is fairly uncommon but absolutely real. I would love for her to check local archives, particularly in Colorado Springs, to verify this event and, even more important, to make sure an arrest was made and that the right man was arrested. R.P. could certainly identify this man and, incredible as it sounds, may be the only "eyewitness."

"My dad passed away from a massive stroke on a Saturday morning in July of 1999. The next night I saw him, clear as day, in a dream. He was sitting on a chair, and he had his right arm raised upward. In his very strong voice, he said, 'So, explain this death business to me!' He seemed almost jovial about it, as if he would be okay as soon as he figured out what was going on. Dad was very smart, highly educated, and a leader. No one could make him do anything he didn't want to do. Did I really see him asking for an explanation? Was he really doing the same thing in death that he did in life? Did he need an explanation before he could go on?" —K.R.

There's no question that K.R.'s father had a very quick and easy passage to The Other Side for his spirit to be able to astrally visit so soon after his death, and those of you who have had similar experiences can rest assured that your deceased loved one made it Home in a heartbeat and happily adjusted to it just as quickly. I envy you. It took my father eight months to visit me, because he had to go through Orientation first, as so many other spirits do when they return to The Other Side.

And yes, K.R.'s father was doing the same thing in death that he did in life, as we all do. Our spirits were created an eternity ago with certain basic, very distinct, and individual qualities, just as we're born into each lifetime with basic, distinct, and individual qualities. While we weave those qualities into a variety of personalities, one with every new incarnation, the same basics are always there in some degree or other. Some of us have senses of humor, others of us don't. Some of us are stubborn, other of us are passive. Some of us are leaders, others of us are followers. Some of us are outgoing, others of us are more reserved. Our God-given qualities shine at their glorious best when we're at Home. But never, ever, no matter how many lifetimes we live on earth, are we anyone else but *us*, just as, with countless variations, we're the same person we were the day we started kindergarten, we're just older and wiser and taller and have better table manners (some of us more than others).

And so, with the same basic qualities he had on earth, K.R.'s father visited from The Other Side the very next night and said, "So, explain this death business to me." A timid person who never makes a move without getting approval first might have meant by that, "Please tell me what's happened to me so that I can go on." But K.R.'s father, a highly intelligent man with the strong, self-assured confidence of a natural leader, was saying to his daughter, almost in the form of a pop quiz, "Okay, I'm now an experienced expert on what goes on when we die. Let's hear what you think goes on, so that I can enlighten you about it."

When any deceased loved one comes from Home to visit, there's no question that you'll find them to be kind, loving, at peace, and devoid of anger and guilt and blame and all other earthly negativity, but you'll also be pleasantly surprised to find yourself smiling to yourself and thinking, That sounds exactly like something they'd say.

"I've been having dreams that my husband is cheating on me. Most of the time in these dreams, I walk into a room and he's there with this twenty-year-old girl he's been talking to on the internet. But last night I had a dream that I walked into a store and found them together and somehow knew that he was sending her money and gifts. I was so upset that I ran out of the store and got hit by a car. Do all these dreams mean he really is cheating?" —S.

I must have received two dozen letters on this very same subject. In some cases, they're release dreams about insecurity acted out in the form of a spouse or lover who's not really cheating at all. In S.'s case, I'm sorry, but I can psychically assure you that yes, your husband is cheating. Your release dreams are only telling you something you already know to be true, and demonstrating that running away from the truth instead of facing it head on will only hurt you—in this case, cause you to be hit by a car, but as with most release dream symbols, that's not to be taken literally.

I'm including this painful dream not to go out of my way to hurt S.'s feelings but to address a common fear and use it as a reminder of the importance of programming ourselves to rewrite the endings of any release dreams in which we're made to feel small, disrespected, and powerless. We have release dreams to get rid of our fears, not to reinforce them. S. might choose to rewrite the ending of her dream about finding her husband in the store with another woman to involve his looking over to see his wife walk in and then turning to the other woman and saying, "For the last time, I'm a happily married man, my wife is everything I've ever wanted and more, and I'm not about to do anything to jeopardize my commitment to her."

What I would choose for her, though, and for many others of you who are struggling as she is, goes like this instead: you walk into the store, find your spouse with another person (not all of these letters came from women, after all), you don't even think of running out the door into traffic as if you're the one who's done something wrong, but instead you stand your ground and say to your spouse, "I deserve nothing but the best. I thought that was you. My mistake. Let me know when you want to stop by and pick up your belongings."

And by the way, as tempting as it might be, please don't rewrite the ending to include attacking the person with whom you suspect your spouse of cheating. Whoever they are, they're not the one who is betraying a commitment they made to you, they're not the one you've been building a life with in good faith, and when you get right down to it, they're completely beside the point. I have a friend whose husband, the love of her life, left her for another woman. For more than a year, her release dreams about it were all variations on the idea of running the other woman down with her car. Like I said, understandable, but not until I convinced her to rewrite those dreams and replace the other woman with her hus-

band was she finally able to start moving on. Spending a year rein-
forcing while she slept the illusion that somehow he had nothing to
do with it only postponed her facing and starting to deal with the
fact that he, not the other woman, was the appropriate target of
her anger. (P.S. She's now happily remarried to a man who adores
her, and her husband and the other woman are divorced after an
utterly miserable two years of marriage—what do you know, he
cheated on her. Duh.)

Again, any release dreams in which you appear helpless, powerless, and inferior aren't telling you that that's what you are, they're
demonstrating that there are no happy endings to be found in *believing* that's what you are. Rewrite those endings into happy ones
in your dreams and I swear to you your waking life will follow suit.

"In this dream, I'm in a room, and on the wall are shelves, and
on the shelves are packages of his and hers watches, two watches
per package. I then look down to see a box, and in the box are two
baby dolls. Suddenly I'm in a country western bar, where there are
lots of people dressed as if they're at a prom, and they're all doing
the two-step. After dancing, I go over to a table where a group of
girls are playing dominoes. Every domino has two dots on it. A
friend of mine then gets up to speak and says that she has been
working double duty. That's the end of the dream. What on earth
was that about?" —M.P.

Isn't it nice when an occasional dream comes along that's just
kind of light and silly, sending a message but not a particularly life-
altering one? I hope M.P. enjoyed the image of a room full of people in formal prom wear doing the two-step in a country western
bar, because I've been chuckling about it ever since I read it.

This dream demonstrates that not all release dreams are deep,
tortured, and upsetting. Some of them are just there to remind us
of a bit of information, usually trivial, that our subconscious minds

are storing. That's invariably the case with dreams like this one in which a certain number is going so far out of its way to get our attention. In M.P.'s case the number two did everything but tattoo itself on her forehead, and I know many of you have had similar "number dreams" and wondered what in the world those dreams were trying to tell you.

The answer is frustratingly simple: numbers in a release dream are reminding you that that particular number has significance in your life. Nothing more, nothing less. And the ways a number can have significance are so varied that, with thought, you'll be able to figure it out more easily than I can.

Take M.P., for example. I refuse to go off on a tangent it would take a whole book to explain, but her primary numerological number might be 2, which according to those who study numerology would mean she's probably practical, supportive, gentle, patient, loving, trustworthy, and willing to compromise for the sake of unity in a dispute. The number 2 might mean that significant events tend to happen for her on the second of the month, the second month of the year, or the eleventh day or month (11 can be translated as 1+1, which equals 2). It might mean that she's been a twin in one or more of her past lives. It might indicate a street address that will be important to her whose numerals add up to a number that can be broken down to a 2. (641 Maple Drive, for example, can be translated as 6+4+1, which equals 11, which we know can equal 2.) It might mean that she's charted herself to have two children, or two husbands, or two careers, or that she tends to excel at things on her second try at them rather than her first. In her case, it's safe to assume that whatever significance the number 2 plays in her life, it's pleasant rather than unpleasant, since nothing negative happens to her in the course of the dream and the symbols are all harmless, from watches to dolls to people dancing to playing dominoes to a friend.

If a certain number starts appearing with obvious regularity in your dreams, start watching for it to show up during your waking hours, and make a note of it whenever it does. Whether or not you're able to get to a specific definition of what it means to you, you'll certainly get an idea of whether you associate it with something positive or something negative, and that in itself can be all the answer you need.

"I had a student named Ricky for one semester ten years ago. I wasn't close to him. In fact, I'm sad to say I really didn't get to know him at all. At the beginning of December this year, he started popping up in my dreams and in my thoughts. I found it odd, because I live far from that community, and he's not someone I've kept up with or even asked about over the years. He continued to pop up in my dreams and thoughts. I became very anxious and depressed as the month progressed. Near the end of the month, I was saddened to read that Ricky had been killed with his father in a car accident the Thursday before Christmas. My anxiety and depression lightened after that." —N.L.

At first glance, you might dismiss this as typical holiday depression that N.L. simply attached after the fact to the news about her former student. But that doesn't explain the dreams and thoughts about him that started weeks earlier, and I think we miss a lot of marvelous little details about our lives by being so quick to leap to some "rational explanation" that's often more of a stretch to come up with than the truth turns out to be.

It's a common and understandable assumption that if we've known someone in a past life, or they're someone we've been friends with in our lives on The Other Side, they're bound to be very significant to us in this lifetime. And of course that's often the case. I'm willing to bet that you can scan everyone you know and give an immediate yes or no answer to the question, "Have you known this person before?"

But then there are those people who are only passing acquaintances at best, who don't necessarily pique much of our interest or curiosity, let alone take on any particular importance, with whom we find we have some sort of sporadic telepathic connection, whose lives we seem to kind of subconsciously keep track of whether we're consciously aware of it or not. It's not always reciprocal. They might never give us so much as a passing subconscious thought. That doesn't invalidate the connection, it just means that they're not as telepathically sensitive as we are, and/or that we have a better memory than they do.

It's impossible to calculate how many people we know from Home and from our previous incarnations here on earth. I'll tell you what—estimate the number of people you know in this life, counting family, friends, coworkers, neighbors, acquaintances, etc. Being conservative, let's say you came up with an estimate of fifty. Now multiply that by the number of past lives you've had. If you're not sure, you're welcome to use mine, which is fifty-four. That's 2,700 people, not counting your many other friends and acquaintances from The Other Side. Do you have the time, let alone the energy or desire, to maintain close spiritual connections with 2,700 people in this lifetime? Me neither. It makes me tired just thinking about it.

But that's how we end up with telepathic connections to people we don't feel especially close to—we've known them in other times and places, we may have even had very intimate relationships with them, but by mutual agreement before we came here this time, we've taken separate paths to accomplish our goals for this life. It's no different than going to a large business party with a group of friends. You all have agendas to address, contacts to make, people to meet, and things to do. You'd make little or no progress if your group traveled around in a tight clump all evening to the exclusion of everyone else, so you split up and take care of business, peripherally aware of each other but maybe saying no more than five words in passing, and simply looking forward to reconnecting later to compare notes and share stories.

So if and when you become aware that you're somehow tuned in to some virtual stranger to the point where they're showing up repeatedly in your dreams, don't feel obligated to do something about it. Just smile to yourself and make a note to mention it to them when you see each other again back Home.

"I used to have a recurring dream when I was around six years old. I would wake up terrified, only able to remember fragments of the dream. But it had something to do with a baby being unable to be born. I was floating over a hospital gurney, horrified, and then there was darkness and something about bushes. I also remember something awful about the color red in this dream, and in real life I hated the color red throughout my childhood. According to my mother, I would wake up from this recurring dream, run into her room, stand at the foot of her bed, and talk to her in what sounded like a foreign language. I do recall trying to tell her about the dream very quickly before I forgot and getting extremely frustrated that she couldn't understand me." —F.C.

I'm sure you all recognize this as an astral trip to a past life, and psychically I know exactly what happened. F.C. was in India, in the early 1900s, still in the womb and waiting to be born to a young girl who'd been impregnated by her wealthy, powerful, unrepentant father. To avoid embarrassment and inconvenience, the newborn was taken, as planned ahead of time by the young girl's father and slavishly obedient mother, directly from the hospital to a mass of heavy foliage beside a river, covered with a red blanket, and left to die.

There are a couple of aspects of F.C.'s recurring past-life visits that are very much worth pointing out. First of all, notice F.C.'s awareness that there was a baby "unable to be born." In truth, before she was born into that lifetime, she heard many loud, angry conversations among the family, in which it was repeated over and over that this pregnancy was unwanted, this baby should never be born, the tragically young mother could not be allowed to keep the child and might be unable to deliver it alive anyway because her body and hips were so small, and on and on, endlessly, dominated by the wrath of a cruel, arrogant man who felt entitled to rape his daughter and then claim to be victimized by the consequences. From those jumbled arguments the thought "unable to be born" was pieced together.

Now, I've seen many people scoff at what I'm about to say, even though I'm far from being alone in my absolute conviction that it's true: from the moment a spirit enters a womb, it can hear and understand everything that's being said in its presence. Dismiss the idea if you want, but humor me and pretend I'm right just in case—whatever it takes to make you very careful about what words and tones of voice any unborn child in your world is exposed to. That poor, helpless child in India that F.C. once was, for example, had already heard its fate before it left its mother's body. No wonder F.C. remembers being "horrified" as her spirit hovered above the hospital gurney that took her mother into a room to deliver a doomed baby. Any infant coming into this world already aware that it's unwanted, unsafe, resented, a burden, disrespected, and unloved is a tragedy, and all it takes to avoid it is simple discretion when an unborn child is in the room. Isn't the emotional welfare of a helpless infant worth at least that much effort?

I also want you to stop and think about F.C.'s past-life experience from another point of view. Your six-year-old child suddenly comes dashing hysterically into your bedroom in the middle of the night, wakes you out of a sound sleep, and begins speaking to you a mile a minute in frantic Bengali. I hope that after reading F.C.'s account of her astral trip to a heartbreaking past, and reading the rest of this book as well, for that matter, you'll take the time to talk to your child while you comfort them and calmly ask them to tell you everything they remember about the dream that upset them so much. The more you assure them that their dreams matter to you, and the more you encourage them to talk about their dreams and help them understand what their dreams mean, the more of their dreams they'll remember and, take my word for it, the more you'll learn. And this should help to reinforce my hope that starting when your child is an infant, you'll surround them with the white light of the Holy Spirit while they sleep and quietly tell them to release any negativity they've brought with them from their past lives and let it be resolved into that white light. This lifetime they're just beginning is bound to be challenging enough all by itself without added painful baggage for them to have to lug around and trip over every step of the way.

And if you want to have a really interesting experience with your child, every once in a while, starting when they're around three years old or so, first thing in the morning or after a nap, while the astral trips they took while they slept are still fresh in their subconscious minds, casually say to them, "Who were you before this?" Don't grab them by the lapels and demand an answer. You don't want them to feel as if they'll be disappointing you if they don't come up with something, and if their response is a simple "I don't know," let it go and ask again some other day. Sooner or later, they'll very probably tell you all about it, and you'll hear some of the mesmerizing stories I've heard from my own children and the hundreds of children I've worked with, everything from a cowboy with a horse named Cinnamon, to a detailed account of going down with the *Titanic*, to surviving a concentration camp, to tanning animal hides by a river, to being a railroad conductor, to anything you can possibly name, that very often your child is too young to be making up out of thin air.

One day my grandchildren and their mother and I were sitting around casually chatting when, in one of those odd group amnesia moments, neither Gina nor I nor my granddaughter Angelia, who was seven at the time, could come up with the name of the most famous tourist attraction in Paris. We stammered and struggled with it, drawing pictures of it in the air, marveling at what total blanks we were, when my grandson Willy, who hadn't yet turned four years old, looked up at me from the floor where he was playing nearby and said, with only thinly disguised impatience, "The Eiffel Tower, Bagdah." I have no trouble imagining a three-year-old coming up with that, if he happened to be Parisian. But from a preschool three-year-old from San Jose who'd barely been out of his yard at that point (and doesn't have a psychic bone in his body, by the way), I found it more than a little remarkable.

The point is, there's a sparkling, amazing, infinite world behind the eyes of every child that is easiest for them to reunite with and explore while they sleep. Encourage them to explore it, teach them how, help them leave the pain in that world behind them, and make sure they know how eager and open you are to hear all about that world. You'll be giving them a precious gift that will last them all their lives and beyond.

And speaking of children, I can't resist sharing a letter from the youngest contributor to this book, a girl named Nina who recently had to give up her dog and is hoping to get a ferret. This "dream" made me smile. I think it will make you smile, too:

"I recently had a dream. In my dream I feel happy. I feel expectant, like I'm going to meet an important person. All of my mother's living family and my deceased aunt (who I lived closely with) were there. I knew them all and they were happy. My cousins and siblings from my mom's side of the family were there, too. Everyone acted happy. However, they were all in one room. It seemed a happy, familiar room. There was a door at one side of the room. It seemed like a rite of passage to go through the door. People went into the room but none came out. When my turn came, I started to go to the door. However, when I did, everyone said, 'Wait.' I did wait. What seemed like a couple of minutes later everyone turned toward the door and made me the closest to it. I was a little scared. When the door opened, a woman came out. She had two 'aides' helping her stand, but she didn't look weak. She was about four-foot-eleven or five feet. She was somewhat obese. She had black hair about shoulder length. She was smiling really big. I had never seen her before, but I knew she was my grandmother Ruby. She seemed to see me as one of God's finest creations. Next thing I knew we were hugging and crying and laughing. I felt that all things after this would be fine."

You are one of God's finest creations, Nina, and your whole family, living and deceased, proved it by arranging such a beautiful astral reunion on The Other Side so that they could officially present you to your very special grandmother Ruby, who'll be watching over you and adoring you all your life. And to answer a question you asked in your letter, yes, you will absolutely get your high school diploma. Your grandmother Ruby and I are counting on you.

"I recently had a dream that I was back in Paris, where I vacationed six years ago with my niece who was killed in the World Trade Center tragedy on 9/11. I can't remember her in the dream, but the reality of being in Paris was irrefutable." —I.B.

This, of course, is a full-fledged astral visit that I.B. took to Paris, a place where she and her loved one spent such cherished time together. So many of us astrally revisit treasured sites like that while we sleep, our spirits' way of comforting us and helping to remind us that we were happy once and we'll be happy again. Don't ever doubt that those astral visits are as real as the trips we take when we're awake, and I can't encourage all of you enough to ask both God and your Spirit Guide to arrange for your loved ones to meet you at those places that, I promise, they continue to cherish just as much as you do.

And to I.B. and all the rest of you who've had dreams and astral experiences about loved ones you lost in the horrendous events of 9/11, and those of you who still have those visits to look forward to, I can't express often enough or sincerely enough that, now more than ever, you're part of a worldwide family that is grieving with you and praying for you, and that your deceased loved ones are among the legions of Angels who are always, always with you in the infinite embrace of God's sacred, loving arms.

Epilogue

*W*hat a joy it's been to write this book. I started out eager to share my unique body of knowledge and my unique perspective with you, wanting to deepen your love, understanding, and appreciation of your own intimate relationship with the dream world. I wanted to offer logical information and reflections on dreams you wouldn't just read, you'd actually understand. I wanted to affirm the power of the spirit mind, alive and well in our subconscious, proof of our eternity, our genetic gift from God. But then, as so often happens when I'm excited about teaching something, by the time I'd finished, I realized how much I'd learned, and that, thanks to your dreams and to seeing this material through your eyes as I wrote, I'd fallen in love with the dream world myself all over again.

I thought of Grandma Ada, my first dream teacher, a million times throughout these pages—of how she'd sit on my bed first thing in the morning and ask me about my dreams and listen as if she'd never heard anything so fascinating in her life; of how she taught me about making friends with my nightmares, and about why I so often felt as if I'd actually left my bed and traveled while I slept when clearly I'd been right there the whole time; and of how, as I stood up to teach my first dream class a few years after she died, I wondered if all those eager students knew how much luckier they would have been if Grandma Ada had been standing there instead of me. I hope I've been as helpful and interested and understanding of my grandchildren's dreams as she was of mine. And I smile, realizing that instead of thinking, Grandma Ada would have loved this book, I'm thinking, Grandma Ada *will* love this book. In case you don't know this, she's back on earth again. Her name is Angelia Dufresne, she's eight years old, and she's my granddaughter. Don't ever say in my presence that God isn't generous.

Thanks to you and the experience of this book, I find myself wanting to teach dream classes again. It's just a thought at the moment. I'm not sure where the extra time would come from. But as I said many, many pages ago, everything that exists started with a thought, so if there's any way for us to keep exploring dreams together, you can bet I'll figure it out.

Thanks to you and the experience of this book, I also have a confession to make. I carried on at some length about the value of keeping a dream journal and pen within easy reach of your bed, and writing down everything you can remember about a dream or astral trip the instant you wake up. And I meant every word of it. I can personally attest to how fascinating it is to read back through a well-documented dream journal every few weeks and discover the patterns and recurring archetypes and frequency of astral travel and all the other hints about what's really going on in your conscious and subconscious mind and what you might want to start addressing during your waking hours. I've cherished every dream book I've kept. To be honest, though, I haven't kept one in years. I got too busy, I was focused on a thousand other things, I was traveling all over the world like a madwoman, and somewhere in the midst of all that, I broke my dream journal habit. Writing this book has reminded me that I miss it and that it's time to acquire the habit again.

Please don't ever take your dreams for granted, or dismiss them as just trivial replays of your day, told through a parade of goofy, incomprehensible images you've picked up along the way.

If that were the case, how would newborn babies dream? And they do.

If that were the case, how would the blind dream? And they do.

Dreams connect us all to each other, because there's not a person on this earth who doesn't dream. They connect us to our ancestors, because dreams are as old as humankind. They connect us to biblical times, when dreams foretold everything from the weather to the coming of Christ. They connect us to a tiny civilization in Australia called the Aborigines, who so honor their dreams that the creation itself is called Dreamtime. They're one of the things we have in common with people in countries whose names we can't even pronounce, and with loved ones who have their own dreams to tell if we'll just take the time to listen.

During the writing of this book, I was telling a good friend about it. She's a very busy, very down-to-earth wife and mother, and not someone I expected to be all that interested, but don't ever ask me what's new if you don't really want an answer. I said something about lucid dreams. "What are those?" she asked. I told her. She replied, "Oh, I love those. I've only had ten or twelve of them that I remember, but every time I have one, if I don't like the way it's going, I just manipulate it to come out however I want it to." From there she went on to tell me about living on a big hill as a child, and how she loved running down that hill while she was asleep, opening her arms when she got to the bottom and taking off to fly around the neighborhood. I've known her for many years, and I was fascinated, because this was all news to me. Finally, after several great lucid and prophetic dream and astral travel stories, I said, "Why am I just now hearing all this?" She answered, "You never asked."

Ask. Share this book with friends and family you're sure you know everything about. I guarantee you'll know them better and feel even more connected to them when you use this book to guide you into that world they explore when they're sleeping. Talk about the archetypes they've come up with, and what kinds of dreams and astral trips they have, and practice interpreting them together, like little mysteries you're determined to solve. It's just a fact that the more practice you get at interpreting dreams, the better you'll get at understanding your own and putting them to good use while you're awake.

Remember, there are five categories of dreams.

Prophetic dreams are always in color, and their action always takes place in a logical sequence. Because you're "dreaming" about events that haven't happened yet, which you'd have no other way of knowing about, you can count on it that your prophetic dreams are really the result of an astral trip to the Hall of Records on The Other Side, where all of our life charts are housed and where, then, by definition, the future is written and just waiting to unfold. Never assume you can't have prophetic dreams because you're not psychic during the day. I *am* psychic, and I've never had a prophetic dream in my life. And don't ever forget that if prophetic dreams are among your gifts, they were given you to use kindly, compassionately, and responsibly, or not at all.

Release dreams are our way of "emotionally exhaling" and working out some of our fears and frustrations and stress and anger during the night so that we won't have to carry the whole burden of them during the day. Nightmares fall under the heading of release dreams, and thank God for them, because without them we'd all be certifiably insane and/or homicidal. They're usually jumbles of chaotic images, as turbulent as the negativity they're helping us get rid of. The minute you spot something in the dream that makes no logical sense, appreciate knowing that it's not a prophetic dream, and that you can program yourself to rewrite it to a happy ending, where you face whatever's chasing you or defeat whoever or whatever is tormenting you.

Wish dreams are exactly what they sound like, but often deeper than we give them credit for. Occasionally they're meant to be taken at face value, and dreaming of buying a sports car or taking a trip to Disneyland means nothing more than that you want a new car or a trip to Disneyland. But the real value of wish dreams is in looking beneath the surface to the emotional and spiritual results you'd get from that sports car ("I want to boost my self-image" or "I'm feeling ignored and want to be noticed") or from that trip to Disneyland ("I need to escape" or "I wish my family could have a happy day together").

Information and problem-solving dreams lead us to wake up with solutions we didn't have when we went to sleep, a guarantee that our spirits have been very busy while we slept, either receiving the information or solutions telepathically or astrally traveling to wherever they can be found, whether it's on earth or at Home. It's pure logic: if something doesn't come from inside us, it has to have come from somewhere else, and our spirits know how to get there even when our conscious minds don't. Like prophetic dreams and astral experiences, information and problem-solving "dreams" unfold in a logical, sequential order.

Astral visits are as real a connection to loved ones, both here and on The Other Side, as they invariably seem to be. We can astrally travel to anyone we want to see, and with our busy, skeptical conscious minds out of the way, we can have wonderful reunions with anyone who comes to visit us. Anytime you see yourself flying in a dream without the benefit of a plane, you're on an astral trip, and when you wake up feeling as if you've spent time with a loved one while you slept, you'll do yourself a great disservice if you dismiss the feeling as nothing but your imagination. Don't ever doubt the power, joy, and comfort the spirit world has to offer, and it's a world your spirit knows like the back of its hand because, when it's not occupying a human body for an incarnation it's decided it needs, your spirit is alive and thriving in that world back Home.

There are also some terms you'll want to keep in mind as you work on making sense of and friends with your dreams.

Archetypes are the symbols we use in our dreams to represent the people, fears, frustrations, and other emotional issues we're processing while we sleep. While there are countless classic, traditional definitions of what those symbols mean in the context of dreams, no definitions are more important or more accurate than your own unique emotional and spiritual connection to whatever archetypes you're using. Before you ever turn to a "dream dictionary" or the list of archetypes and their traditional definitions in this book, always ask yourself first, "What does this symbol really mean to *me?*"

Astral catalepsy is a scary but harmless phenomenon that happens when the conscious mind becomes vaguely aware that the spirit has been out of the body and is in the process of reentering, which causes the conscious mind to panic. And panic is an understatement. Classic symbols of astral catalepsy are a feeling of physical and vocal paralysis, the sense that there's an evil presence holding you down and/or lying on top of you and/or molesting you, and loud inexplicable noises that sound like anything from crackling to explosions to every radio in the world playing a different station at full blast. Astral catalepsy is fairly common and again, despite all sensations to the contrary, completely harmless. A simple nightly prayer for your spirit's quick and easy reentry into the body can cure astral catalepsy once and for all.

Daydreams are, in a way, spontaneous meditations, blessings that hit us when we're not expecting them and that we only know are happening when they're already in progress. They're usually positive, happy experiences, but when we're using them inadvertently to reinforce worries and fears, we can program ourselves to refuse to indulge in negativity and see to it that all of our daydreams become affirmations.

Lucid dreams can fall into any of the five dream categories, with the difference that in a lucid dream, you actually realize during the dream that you're dreaming. The instant that realization hits, the dream is yours to do with as you please, and lucid dreams are a great opportunity to "show off" for yourself and practice being everything you've ever wanted to be and more.

Remote viewing is a skill that lets us perceive details about an item or a location that we're separated from by physical, geographical, or time barriers. It's a great talent for the conscious mind to develop, since it helps develop that mental "muscle" that opens us to the realization that we can see anything we want, whenever we want, without ever leaving the house. The better we get at remote viewing during our waking hours, the more easily we'll be able to remember the details of our astral travels at night.

Telepathy is the direct, silent communication of information, knowledge, or feelings from one person's mind or spirit to another without either the "sender" or the "receiver" using any of the five senses in the process. Telepathy can be accomplished while we're awake or asleep, but it's especially convenient during prophetic and information-and-problem-solving dreams, when our spirit minds are wide open to sending and receiving instantaneous knowledge.

Totems are the animals we handpick on The Other Side to watch over us and protect us for the lifetime we're about to undertake. They frequently appear in our dreams and are mistaken for a threatening animal who's chasing us to hurt us, when the truth is they're only running because we are, so that they can do their job and never leave our side.

Throughout this book, you'll find prayers that will help you in every aspect of connecting to and embracing your dreams. I hope you'll use them and offer them generously, in my words or, better yet, your own. God hears my voice so often that I wonder from time to time if He gets tired of it, although I know He never would. But He loves hearing your voice, too, and no matter what you have to say or how you put it, He always understands.

For the record, the prayers are there as much for my benefit as for yours, because the day I stop acknowledging that everything comes from God is a day that no one, including God, will ever see.

And so, in closing, "Dear God, we thank You for all the dreams we've had and all the dreams that are still to come, knowing that You give them to us for the growth and nourishment of our spirits, which You created in Your perfect, unconditional, eternal love. In return, we offer the wisdom that comes in our dreams to Thy finest, most compassionate service. Amen."

God bless you and your dreams.

Sleep well.

                                                              Sylvia

About the Author

Sylvia Browne is the #1 *New York Times* best-selling author of *The Other Side and Back*; *Life on The Other Side*; *Past Lives, Future Healing*; and *Adventures of a Psychic*. She has been working as a psychic for nearly fifty years, and appears regularly on *Montel*. She has also appeared on *Larry King Live*, *Good Morning America*, CNN, and *Entertainment Tonight*.

Visit Sylvia's Web site at www.sylvia.org

Piatkus Books

If you have enjoyed reading this book, you may be interested in other titles published by Piatkus. These include: